THE STRIPPER GODDESS OF JAPAN

The Life and Afterlives of Ame no Uzume

THE STRIPPER GODDESS OF JAPAN

The Life and Afterlives of Ame no Uzume

by Shunsuke Tsurumi

Translated and with an Introduction by
Tomoko Aoyama and Penny Bailey

TRANS
PACIFIC
PRESS

The Stripper Goddess of Japan: The Life and Afterlives of Ame no Uzume
Translated from the Japanese *Ame no Uzume den: Shinwa kara nobite kuru michi*
Copyright © 1991 TSURUMI Shunsuke
English Translation, Notes and Introduction © 2023 Tomoko Aoyama and Penny Bailey

Trans Pacific Press Co., Ltd.
2nd Floor, Hamamatsu-cho Daiya Building
2-2-15 Hamamatsu-cho, Minato-ku,
Tokyo 105-0013, Japan
Telephone: +81-(0)50-5371-9475
Email: info@transpacificpress.com
Web: http://www.transpacificpress.com

Copyedited by Miriam Riley, Armidale, Australia
Designed and set by Ryo Kuroda, Tsukuba-city, Ibaraki, Japan

Distributors

USA, Canada and India
Independent Publishers Group (IPG)
814 N. Franklin Street,
Chicago, IL 60610, USA
Email: frontdesk@ipgbook.com
Web: http://www.ipgbook.com

Europe, Oceania, Middle East and Africa
EUROSPAN
1 Bedford Row,
London, WC1R 4BU
United Kingdom
Email: info@eurospan.co.uk
Web: https://www.eurospangroup.com

Japan
MHM Limited
3-2-3F, Kanda-Ogawamachi, Chiyoda-ku,
Tokyo 101-0052
Email: sales@mhmlimited.co.jp
Web: http://www.mhmlimited.co.jp

China
China Publishers Services Ltd.
718, 7/F., Fortune Commercial Building,
362 Sha Tsui Road, Tsuen Wan, N.T.
Hong Kong
Email: edwin@cps-hk.com

Southeast Asia
Alkem Company Pte Ltd.
1, Sunview Road #01-27, Eco-Tech@Sunview
Singapore 627615
Email: enquiry@alkem.com.sg

All rights reserved. No reproduction of any part of this book may take place without the written permission of Trans Pacific Press.
ISBN 978-1-920850-15-9 (hardback)
ISBN 978-1-920850-13-5 (paperback)
ISBN 978-1-920850-14-2 (eBook)

Contents

List of Figures vi

Contributors vii

Note on Japanese Names viii

Acknowledgements ix

Preface: Voice of the Voiceless *by Yoshio Sugimoto* x

Translators' Introduction *by Tomoko Aoyama and Penny Bailey* 1

Glossary of Deities 12

The Stripper Goddess of Japan 17

    1 The Power to Open a Closed Cave 17

    2 A Genealogy of Likening 29

    3 A Light in the Dark Night 41

    4 Laughter and Politics 55

    5 The Naked Body as Metaphor 67

    6 Burlesque and Striptease 79

    7 Various Forms of Appeasing Violence 93

    8 The Day Japan Became Naked 103

    9 Painting the Body in Two Colours 117

    10 Ame no Uzume in the Home 133

    11 Japan and Abroad 147

    12 Past and Present 161

Afterword 177

Bibliography 178

Index 183

List of Figures

1.1: Kosugi Hōan's *Ame no Uzume no Mikoto* (1951) 21

3.1: Okame mask 42

3.2: Hyottoko mask 42

3.3: Kawasaki Hiroko 43

3.4: Ichikawa Utaemon 43

3.5: *Hannya* mask 45

3.6: Utagawa Kuniyoshi's *Adachigahara hitotsuya no zu* (The Lonely House on Adachi Moor, 1856) 46

3.7: Shunbaisai Hokuei's image of O-Iwa emerging from the lantern (1832) 46

3.8: *Dame Oyaji* 46

3.9: *Obatarian* 46

3.10: Ame no Uzume and sea slug in Kōno Fumiyo's *Bōrupen Kojiki* 50

4.1: Izanami by Kosugi Hōan (part of his *Kojiki hachidai* [The Legendary Stories of Old Japan, 1941]) 56

5.1: Posada's *Calavera oaxaqueña* (1903) 72

6.1: Poster for *The Hot Mikado* (1939) 83

8.1: Kitamura Sayo 105

8.2: Self-effacing dance 112

9.1: Setouchi stands in support of Fuji's family as they announce her verdict of innocence 119

11.1: Kūya 152

11.2: Nenbutsu odori in *Illustrated Biography of the Itinerant Monk Ippen* 153

11.3: O-Kuni and Sanza 154

11.4: *Kiri-kami* hairstyle 155

12.1: Scene from *Utau tanuki goten* 164

Contributors

Author

TSURUMI Shunsuke (1922–2015) was a philosopher, cultural and intellectual historian, sociologist, critic, editor and social activist. He was born and raised in Tokyo. In 1942, after obtaining a bachelor's degree with honours in philosophy from Harvard University, he was repatriated to Japan. Then in 1943, he was posted to Java, where he worked as a navy intelligence officer. After the war, in collaboration with Maruyama Masao and others, Tsurumi established the journal *Shisō no kagaku* (Science of thought, 1946–1996). He was also one of the key figures in the pacifist movement Beheiren (The Citizen's League for Peace in Vietnam, 1965–1974). Between the late 1940s and 1970, Tsurumi taught at Kyoto University, Tokyo Institute of Technology and Dōshisha University. He authored *An Intellectual History of Wartime Japan* (1986) and *A Cultural History of Postwar Japan 1945–1980* (1987), both of which were based on lectures given at McGill University, Montreal, as well as numerous publications in Japanese, some of which are collected in *Tsurumi Shunsuke shū* (1991–1992, 12 volumes) and *Tsurumi Shunsuke shū zoku* (second series, 2000–2001, 5 volumes).

Translators

Tomoko Aoyama is an Honorary Associate Professor of Japanese at The University of Queensland, Australia. She is the author of *Reading Food in Modern Japanese Literature* (2008) and co-editor of *Girl Reading Girl in Japan* (with Barbara Hartley, 2010) and *Configurations of Family in Contemporary Japan* (with Laura Dales and Romit Dasgupta, 2015). Her recent publications include: 'Ame no Uzume crosses boundaries' (2018) and 'Youthful first impressions: Tsurumi Kazuko and Shunsuke in Australia, 1937' (2020). She has also co-translated two novels by Kanai Mieko, *Indian Summer* and *Oh, Tama!*, as well as short stories and essays by Itō Hiromi, Mishima Yukio, Honda Masuko and others.

Penny Bailey is a researcher in Japanese studies and art history at The University of Queensland. Her research focuses on Japanese and Korean art history and design, particularly in the modern period. Her doctoral thesis examines the ways in which the founder of Japan's Mingei Undō (Folk Craft Movement), Yanagi Sōetsu, theorised Korean visual cultures during Korea's colonial period (1910–1945) in order to protest the Japanese occupation. She has published articles and translations in various journals including *Monumenta Nipponica*, *Review of Japanese Culture and Society*, *Japan Focus: The Asia-Pacific Journal*, *International Review of Korean Studies* and *TAASA Review* (The Asian Arts Society of Australia).

Notes and Glossary

Mariko Kishi-Debski is a NAATI-certified translator who holds a Master of Arts in Japanese Interpreting and Translation and a Bachelor of International Studies (majoring in Japanese and International Relations) from The University of Queensland. Her published translations include four essays on food from Itō Hiromi's *Delicious!*, co-translated with Tomoko Aoyama.

Note on Japanese Names

This book follows the standard conventions for Japanese names used in scholarly English-language publications on Japan: that is, family names are rendered before personal names (e.g. TSURUMI Shunsuke), except in cases where an author's work is published originally in English with the anglicised name order (e.g. Yoshio SUGIMOTO). For the convenience of librarians and booksellers, Tsurumi's name is shown in anglicised order on the cover and title page. When authors are known by a *gagō* (literary or artistic pseudonym), we follow the convention of referring to them by those names rather than their surnames (e.g. Hakuchō rather than Masamune).

Acknowledgements

We wish to express our sincere gratitude to a number of colleagues and mentors.

Firstly, we extend our thanks to the Tsurumi family for giving us permission to translate *Ame no Uzume den*. Dr Kawasaki Kenko generously assisted us in obtaining this permission and answered numerous queries in the translation process. We are also grateful to Professor Emeritus Yoshio Sugimoto and Director Yuko Uematsu at Trans Pacific Press for their constant support and advice in seeing this work to fruition.

In addition, a number of other scholars in various fields kindly offered their expertise, including Dr Sachi Schmidt-Hori (Dartmouth College), Professor Emerita Janine Beichman (Daitō Bunka University), Professor Saitō Hideki (Bukkyō University, Kyoto), Professor Shimamura Teru (Ferris University), and Professor Emeritus Roger Pulvers (Tokyo Institute of Technology).

As the Translators' Introduction notes, Tsurumi's trip to Australia in 1937 played an important role in the development of his interest in Ame no Uzume. A Japan Research Grant from the National Library of Australia awarded to Aoyama in 2016 provided innumerable benefits, not only regarding Tsurumi's trip but also in obtaining a wide range of information essential to understanding the socio-historical and biographical background of *Ame no Uzume den* and its author.

We are grateful to the Idemitsu Museum of Arts for their permission to reproduce Kosugi Hōan's picture of Ame no Uzume in this book, both for the book cover and in the first chapter.

We also extend our thanks to the School of Languages and Cultures at The University of Queensland for financial support from the 2022 School Research Fund. We are most grateful to Dr Akiko Uchiyama for her help in facilitating this process.

Finally, we express our heartfelt appreciation to Ms Mariko Kishi-Debski for her careful preparation of the footnotes and glossary, and for the myriad other tasks that she helped with in bringing this project together.

Preface: Voice of the Voiceless

Yoshio Sugimoto[1]

Tsurumi Shunsuke (1922–2015) was one of the most influential thinkers in Japan from the post-war era through to the early twenty-first century, with his writings and activities affecting many public debates and political movements throughout this period. Written from innovative, unconventional and often unexpected perspectives, his work reverberates as an enduringly relevant voice of Japanese society today. His pursuit of common people's thinking traversed a wide range of areas—from the nation's war responsibilities to its popular culture, from the Japanese Constitution to the education system, and beyond. I was greatly privileged to be acquainted with him for more than half a century from my university student days in Kyoto.

Tsurumi was an incredibly prolific writer, authoring and editing a few hundred books. His publications were assembled in a seventeen-volume collection of his lifetime work (Tsurumi 2000–2001 and 1991–1992). In addition, he published many verbal discussions with novelists, academics, film makers, artists and numerous other intellectuals as the nation's foremost philosophical conversationalist. These talks were collated and published in a ten-volume series in 2001. The two small English-language books (Tsurumi 2010 and 1987) do not remotely reflect the immensity of his work and influence on the reading public and the reformist community in Japan. One would hope that this new title in English is another step, albeit small, toward spreading his philosophy further across the world map.

Tsurumi was born into a wealthy and distinguished family in Tokyo. His father, Tsurumi Yūsuke, was a powerful politician who held the post of Minister of Health and Welfare after World War II; his mother, Aiko, was the daughter of a mayor of Tokyo. Tsurumi's exceptionally privileged background provided him with both a highly intellectual environment and a source of rebellion. He often referred to his mother as a domineering disciplinarian who tried to educate

---

[1] Professor Emeritus, La Trobe University, Melbourne, Australia. This contribution is based on Sugimoto (2007).

Preface

him with extreme rigidity. He rebelled against his situation, became a delinquent, and even attempted suicide several times.

Unable to control the boy, the family decided to send Shunsuke to Adelaide, Australia, for a short time. After returning to Japan, he went to Massachusetts in the United States. Away from home and free from family pressure, he studied at a preparatory school and secured admission to Harvard University to major in philosophy. Influenced by pragmatism, he wrote a thesis on William James's philosophy and became the first scholar to introduce this thinking to Japan's academic community in the early post-war years.

After the Pacific War broke out, Tsurumi was arrested while at Harvard and imprisoned as a dangerous alien. He never felt that he was treated unfairly within the prison, however, and he thought he glimpsed the bedrock of American democracy there.

Tsurumi chose to go back to Japan by repatriation ship in 1942 and was then conscripted into the Imperial Japanese Navy. During the war years, he worked as an intelligence officer stationed in Indonesia, mainly listening to Radio Australia and translating its English news broadcasts into Japanese.

Immediately after the war, in 1946, Tsurumi and other left-liberal scholars published a journal, *Shisō no kagaku* (Science of thought), providing a forum and platform for writers interested in the analysis of the lifestyles, aesthetics, conceptions, beliefs and philosophies of common people. His debut article titled 'On the talismanic use of words' attributes enthusiastic mass support for Japan's war mobilisation to the government's effective agitation by the propagation of such grandiose and ambiguous words as *kokutai* (national polity), *Nihonteki* (Japanese-like) and *kōdō* (imperial way). The exact meanings of these words were neither explained nor substantiated but were employed somehow as a linguistic safeguard for their users, in the same way as amulets give their holders baseless, vague feelings of protection.

Depressed by his inability to resist Japan's wartime activities, Tsurumi also organised a research group in *Shisō no kagaku* to study the way in which Japanese intellectuals converted to nationalist, colonialist and imperialist ideologies under the military regime. The project resulted in a three-volume collaborative study titled *Tenkō* (Conversion) (Shisō no kagaku kenkyū-kai, 1959, 1960 and 1962). Tsurumi led this undertaking, as he found it necessary to examine how and why liberal-minded politicians and writers, including his father Yūsuke, altered their views and proselytised to pro-war campaigns.

Tsurumi was an anti-intellectual intellectual. He maintained a deep-rooted suspicion of intellectuals and academics for much of his adult life. He was much more optimistic about the potential of the masses, arguing that intellectuals must follow the lead of the populace rather than assuming leadership over them. After resigning from his professorial post in 1970 in protest against the introduction of police forces onto campus to remove activist students, he relinquished his university career, working to his final days as an independent philosopher, writer and columnist.

Tsurumi was an anti-left leftist. Despite being a staunch critic of the hierarchical structure and self-complacent ideology of the Japan Communist Party, he has consistently supported them in post-war elections on the basis that only the JCP consistently opposed Japanese militarism before, during and after the war. Yet, he never embraced Marxism as such.

Tsurumi was an internationalist nationalist. He supported the development of Japan's endogenous culture and critiqued the one-way importation of Western ideas and practices into the country. In his view, humanities and social science disciplines of Japanese universities have tended to introduce and interpret Western intellectual trends without fostering Japan-based ideas and methodologies. Accordingly, he highly appraised, for example, Yanagita Kunio, a founding father of Japanese folklore studies, Yanagi Muneyoshi, an art theorist who advanced the art of common people, and Miyazawa Kenji, a writer whose poems and children's stories drew influence from Buddhist philosophy and Japanese agrarian culture.

Tsurumi also focussed on popular culture, reading and studying *manga* (Japanese comics) and analysing films, novels and songs as the expressions of the philosophy of the masses. In his ground-breaking text titled *Genkai geijutsu-ron* (On marginal art, Tsurumi 1967), Tsurumi classifies art forms into three analytical categories: pure, popular and marginal. In pure art, the producers are professional artists and those who appreciate their art are equipped with a degree of expert knowledge. Pictorial arts, symphonies, operas, *noh* and formal tea ceremonies executed or performed by professionals all fall into this category. Popular art is produced by professional artists in collaboration with mass media organisations but is consumed by the non-specialist public and is therefore often regarded as vulgar art or pseudo-art. Examples include television programs, popular songs, posters, detective stories, animations and comic strips.

The third category, marginal art, differs from both pure and popular art in that both producers and consumers lack professional expertise. Marginal art emerges in the domain where everyday life and artistic expression intersect and includes graffiti, house decoration, children's toys, everyday gestures, song variations, festivals, funerals, family videos and albums, political demonstrations, nicknaming, tongue twisters and even gravesite decorations.[2] The various ways in which people and objects are named represent a verbal domain of marginal art, as do riddles, anecdotes, short humorous tales and proverbs that have survived for centuries among the masses. In the non-verbal sphere, the ways in which one smiles, cries, eats and drinks often manifest themselves as marginal art.

Tsurumi includes in his discussion a wider range of human activities than are conventionally considered artistic, and questions the narrow dichotomy between pure and popular art forms. He suggests that marginal art, as the most primordial form of art, has existed since ancient times and thus precedes the other two forms. He contends that the development of the mass media and of modern economic and political institutions has removed marginal art from the sphere of legitimately recognised art.

By temperament, Tsurumi tried to avoid engaging in political activities. He was, however, involved in anti-government, anti-war and anti-US movements in the 1960s and 70s. When waves of political demonstrations against the ratification of the Security Treaty between the United States and Japan swept the nation in 1960, Tsurumi was associated with a dissenting citizens' group called Koenaki Koe no Kai (Voiceless Voice Group). The group was initiated by Kobayashi Tomi, a member of Shisō no Kagaku, who objected to the ruling Liberal Democratic Party's successful attempt to force the ratification bill at the National Diet and instigated a one-person demonstration in the streets of Tokyo in protest. She invited anybody who disagreed and was dissatisfied with the bill to participate; a unique attempt at a time when political demonstrations were almost exclusively organised by such established associations as labour unions, student organi-

---

2 For a more extensive list of examples, see Sugimoto (2021: 296).

sations and political groups. Her demonstration gathered momentum and mushroomed, attracting unaffiliated citizens, including Tsurumi. The spontaneity, namelessness and non-affiliation of these participants inspired Tsurumi who remained a populist, non-Marxist, liberal anarchist.

Tsurumi became a more visible political figure when the anti-Vietnam war movement gathered pace. Deeply remorseful about his inability to act against Japan's war two decades previously, and seriously concerned about the United States' military invasion of Vietnam, he formed an anti-war group known as Beheiren whose branches sprang up across the country. It was loosely and horizontally coordinated—like Koenaki Koe no Kai—and forged links with the anti-war movements in the United States, inviting American activists to Japan for lecture tours.

The key members of Beheiren later formed the Japan Technical Committee to Aid Anti-War GIs which helped American military deserters hiding in Japan escape to third countries. Bi-lingual and bi-cultural, Tsurumi played a key role in this underground operation which enabled relatively uneducated, inarticulate Americans from disadvantaged backgrounds to run away from the theatre of war. Tsurumi often recalls his participation in these operations as the highlight of his life.

The so-called 'Hidaka affair' brought Tsurumi back to Australia in 1982, some half a century after he first came to Adelaide as a hopeless teenager. This time, he attended a conference on alternative models of Japanese society held in Noosa Heads, Queensland, on behalf of Professor Hidaka Rokurō, a former professor of sociology at the University of Tokyo, who was refused an entry visa to Australia. I initially invited him in 1980 to La Trobe and Monash universities as a visiting professor supported by the Japan Foundation, the cultural arm of the Japanese Ministry of Foreign Affairs. For reasons that remain mysterious and opaque even today, the Australian Immigration Department claimed that he was a persona non grata on the false suspicion that he had been associated with the Japanese Red Army. In 1983, the Australian Government admitted that the allegation was groundless and gave Hidaka permission to enter the country. For some three years, top intellectuals and Japanese studies specialists in Australia fought against the Immigration Department

Preface

to remove the baseless allegations against Hidaka.[3] Tsurumi was one of the Japanese public figures who regarded the unfounded claim as a serious matter that would not only affect the autonomy of cultural exchange between the two countries but also violate the basic human rights of individuals who have been incorrectly accused of wrongdoing by a foreign government with no recourse to legal and other challenges. During his stay in Australia, he worked hard with academics and journalists to clear Hidaka's name.

As a dedicated pacifist, Tsurumi consistently defended the present Constitution of Japan, in particular Article 9 which contains the so-called peace clause and, in 2004, played an important role in the establishment of the Article 9 Society in Japan as its founding member, which has numerous local branches across the nation today.

The *Ame no Uzume* book now available in English brings back many fond memories, including a couple of instances that occurred many years ago. In the 1960s, a small group of us put on an amateur theatrical play at Honmokutei, a storytellers' performance house in Tokyo. The play was about the grassroots movements at the time of the Meiji Restoration, and I was honoured to be given the role of Sakamoto Ryōma, a radical activist. Tsurumi played the role of a female whose details I cannot remember, though I was impressed very much at the time with the way he performed with his acquired Kansai accent, because he normally spoke in uptown Tokyo Japanese. He was a marginal artist himself.

I also recall a small episode that took place in the 1970s when I was back in Kyoto for a short stint. Tsurumi took the time to ring me, extremely pleased with a present I had given him the previous day, a picture book about Australian Aboriginal mythologies dealing with the creation of the cosmos. On the phone, he was greatly excited to see common people's powerful imagination in the mythological world— be it Japanese or Australian—a sphere surpassing geographical and temporal boundaries. He was always a committed consumer of marginal art.

Tsurumi passed away in 2015 at the age of ninety-three. True to his convictions, no funeral was held.

---

3 On the Hidaka affair, see Gavan McCormack's postscript to Hidaka (1984).

Translators' Introduction

Tomoko Aoyama and Penny Bailey

Tsurumi the Polyhedron

TSURUMI Shunsuke (1922–2015) is internationally recognised as an 'author, philosopher and editor, and one of the most influential intellectuals in post-war Japan' (Pulvers 1982). What makes his work and personality so fascinating is his ambivalence and complexity: he has been variously described as 'The Top Scholar Who Failed at School' (Pulvers 1982),[1] 'an anti-intellectual intellectual', 'an anti-Left Leftist' and 'an internationalist nationalist' (Sugimoto 2007: 58–59, see also Preface). Or to use French literature scholar Ebizaka Takeshi's words, Tsurumi was 'a polyhedral person' (*tamentai no hito*):

> He was a writer and a talker as well as a person of action. As a writer, his personae include Tsurumi the expert on *tenkō*,[2] Tsurumi the scholar of mass (*taishū*) culture,[3] Tsurumi the semiotician,[4] Tsurumi the philosopher of everyday living,[5] and Tsurumi the author of monographs.[6] In terms of talking, he gave lectures and

---

[1] This is the title of Roger Pulvers's article in reference to Tsurumi being a 'wayward schoolboy' who was 'thrown out of three Japanese schools'.

[2] *Tenkō* (literally, 'changing direction') specifically refers to the coerced conversion of leftist intellectuals and activists from the mid-1920s until the end of World War II. Tsurumi published a series of essays and studies on this topic, which are reproduced in volume 4 of his collected works (Tsurumi 1991–1992). In English, see Tsurumi (2010), which is a re-issue of his 1986 publication, *An Intellectual History of Wartime Japan 1931–1945*, based on his lectures given in English in 1979–1980 at McGill University, Montreal, and then published in Japanese in 1982.

[3] Among his numerous publications on this topic, in English see Tsurumi (1987), and in Japanese volumes 5–7 of Tsurumi (1991–1992). As Sugimoto (2007: 59, Preface) explains, 'Tsurumi classifies art forms into three categories: pure, popular and marginal', the last of which, *genkai geijutsu*, emerges in the domain of everyday life without any professional expertise. For a more detailed discussion on 'marginal art', see Sugimoto (2021).

[4] See volume 3 of Tsurumi (1991–1992).

[5] See volume 10 of Tsurumi (1991–1992).

[6] For example, *Amerika tetsugaku* (American philosophy, 1950, included in Tsurumi 1991–1992, vol. 1), *Takano Chōei* (1975, Tsurumi 2000–2001, vol. 3), *Yumeno Kyūsaku* (1989, Tsurumi 2000–2001, vol. 3), *Yanagi Muneyoshi* (1976, Tsurumi 2000–2001, vol. 4), *Takeuchi Yoshimi* (1995, Tsurumi 2000–2001, vol. 4) and *Ame no Uzume den* (1991, Tsurumi 2000–2001, vol. 5).

interviews, and participated in dialogues and roundtables.[7] As an activist he not only participated in demonstrations but also supported US deserters, took part in hunger strikes and sit-ins, and resigned from academic positions in protest at crucial historical moments.[8] Importantly, each of these polyhedral faces is linked to Tsurumi's wartime experience. (*Gendai shisō*, 2015: 9)

Even this substantive list has inevitable omissions. Critic Katō Norihiro (2007: 20), for example, commented that Tsurumi's editorship of the journal *Shisō no kagaku* (Science of thought, 1946–1996), spanning half a century, would qualify for entry into the Guinness World Records. Tsurumi's activities and characteristics outlined here, including the significance of his wartime experience, are highly relevant to his remarkable work *Ame no Uzume den* (The Legend of Ame no Uzume, 1991). The present book, *The Stripper Goddess of Japan: The Life and Afterlives of Ame no Uzume*, is the first complete English translation of the work.

Why Ame no Uzume?

Tsurumi repeatedly mentioned the special place of this book within his vast and varied corpus. In his 'Afterword' to the book, also translated here, he writes that in the early 1970s he had three book topics in mind: the art critic and thinker Yanagi Muneyoshi (1889–1961), the comic performing art of *manzai* (see Chapter 4, footnote 21) and Ame no Uzume, who is one of the milliard deities who appear in the *Kojiki* (Records of Ancient Matters, 712) and other ancient texts.

Although not as important as some other deities such as the Sun Goddess Amaterasu (see the appended Glossary of Deities), Ame no Uzume plays a crucial role in saving the world, both Heaven and Earth, with a comic shamanistic performance outside the Heavenly Cave (Ama no Iwato). Her performance, which involves a half-naked

---

7 See Tsurumi (1996, 10 vols.), Tsurumi (1997, 2 vols.), Tsurumi (2002), Tsurumi (2015) and Tsurumi, Ueno and Oguma (2004).
8 For example, in 1960, Tsurumi resigned from the Tokyo Institute of Technology in protest against the US-Japan Security Treaty (Anpo). Then in 1970, he resigned from his professorial position at Dōshisha University, Kyoto, in protest against the introduction of police forces onto the campus.

dance, comic bawdy gestures and false words (to trick Amaterasu), is regarded as the origin of comedy in Japan.[9]

In an interview conducted several years after its publication, Tsurumi remarked that of all his books, only *Ame no Uzume den* had managed to achieve his ideal of an open-ended book that was liberated from narrow, rigid or cliquish interpretations:

> It's great that no one has told me that the true Ame no Uzume should be like this, or that I got it all wrong. Of all my writings, I like this book the best. It's given me such a sense of achievement and relief. I'd be happy to be known as the author of just this one book; all the others could be forgotten. (Tsurumi 1997, vol. 2: 44–45)

The special value Tsurumi attaches to *Ame no Uzume den* is also evident in a 2003 interview which was published the following year under the title *Sensō ga nokoshita mono: Tsurumi Shunsuke ni sengo sedai ga kiku* (What the War Has Left Behind: Tsurumi Shunsuke Interviewed by the Post-war Generation; Tsurumi, Ueno and Oguma 2004: 190–193). One of the interviewers, sociologist Oguma Eiji, asked Tsurumi to elaborate on the phrase 'state versus sex' that he used in an earlier (1954) essay about his wartime experience in Java. Tsurumi was posted there as a Navy intelligence officer in 1943, after he was repatriated to Japan from the US. Before leaving the US, he completed his graduation thesis in philosophy at Harvard University while incarcerated in an immigration facility for three months.[10]

> **Tsurumi:** What my sexual desire tells me has nothing to do with the state, or rather, it is opposed to the state. I wanted to oppose the "comfort" organisation prepared by the state by means of my own sexual desire. That's what I meant by the formula of "state versus

---

9 Cohn (1998: 12–13) and Aoyama (2018).
10 On numerous occasions Tsurumi has written and talked about his experiences in the US and Asia. *Watashi ga gaijin datta koro* (When I Was a Foreigner; Tsurumi and Sasaki 1995) is an autobiographical story for young readers featuring Sasaki Maki's illustrations. For information in English about Tsurumi's pre-war and wartime experiences, see Olson (1992: 115–124), Sugimoto (2007) and Aoyama (2020).

sex". It was the only place where I could revolt against the state. (Tsurumi, Ueno and Oguma 2004: 189)

When the other interviewer, feminist sociologist Ueno Chizuko, asked Tsurumi why he did not elaborate on this theme in his later works, he gently but firmly retorted that even though he had to wait for his writing to mature, *Ame no Uzume den* directly deals with the theme.

Although earlier, before going to the US in 1938, he was a sexually precocious 'delinquent', in Java—unlike many of his compatriots—he refused not only to visit military 'comfort' stations but also to exploit women. This was because he did not want his sex and his being to be 'dictated by the state'. Instead, he decided 'to be acutely conscious of [his] own sexual desire and divert it to something else' (Tsurumi, Ueno and Oguma 2004: 190). One important source of inspiration was Havelock Ellis's *Studies in the Psychology of Sex*, which he found in the Batavian Library (present-day National Library of Indonesia). He read all six volumes cover to cover. As mentioned in Chapter 11 of this book, Tsurumi first read Ellis's *The New Spirit* on his voyage from Kobe to Java.

Interestingly, while acknowledging Ellis's influence, Tsurumi also declares that *Ame no Uzume den* is, in a sense, his biography of the stripper Ichijō Sayuri (1928–1997):

> **Tsurumi**: Ichijō fought against authority right up until her death. I never met her, but I happened to hear about her from her lawyer Ono Nobuyuki, who told me about her upbringing and background. She was known for fabricating the details of her life. But according to Mr Ono, it is true that Ichijō's birth mother was arrested and executed for killing her birth father, and that Ichijō was then sent to an institution where she was raised. Afterwards she joined a theatre company, where she was gang-raped, and she ended up becoming a stripper. Therefore, my focus was "*how could she live otherwise?*"[11] Had she been dealt better circumstances, I believe she would have achieved something truly great, and that made me want to write about her. So I traced my own memories and wrote a biography, using the *Kojiki* as a reference point, and the method of *frottage*. (Tsurumi, Ueno and Oguma 2004: 191–192)

---

11 Tsurumi uses English for this italicised question in the otherwise completely Japanese interview.

Introduction

Frottage is, according to Webster's dictionary, 'the technique of creating a design by rubbing (as with a pencil) over an object placed underneath the paper', but interestingly it also means 'the act of obtaining sexual stimulation by rubbing against a person or object'.[12] In the published interview, the term is given in katakana, *furottāju*, with the gloss *harimaze* (literally, 'pasting and mixing') in parentheses, which sounds more like another technique that the Surrealists and Cubists explored in the early twentieth century—namely, *collage*. Tsurumi explains that what he calls *frottage* here was already practised by sociologist Robert Merton in his *On the Shoulders of Giants*, which playfully yet eruditely traces the origins of Isaac Newton's aphorism 'If I have seen farther, it is by standing on the shoulders of giants'. As Merton's subtitle 'A Shandean Postscript' indicates, its witty pedantry and digression are akin to Sterne's *Tristram Shandy*.

In Tsurumi's *Ame no Uzume den*, Ichijō is in fact mentioned only in Chapter 6, 'Burlesque and Striptease', and even then she is featured merely as one of several key figures on the topic. Notable also in this particular chapter is that Tsurumi explains: 'My own method of writing like this, stringing together various materials, is rather like burlesque'. Therefore, although Ichijō was a motivating force in writing the book, his claim that it is her biography should not be taken at face value. What can be established with certainty, however, is that the 'giant's shoulders' crucial to this work belonged to Ame no Uzume, and that his *frottage* involves a massive array of historical, literary and scholarly texts as well as performing arts, artefacts, festivals, folksongs and other cultural products and practices, which are embedded, or rubbed over, to create a complex portrait of the eponymous stripper goddess.

At the same time, Tsurumi states that '*Ame no Uzume den* is not a history book; it's a story of my wandering spirit, cultivated over many years' (Tsurumi, Ueno and Oguma 2004: 193). Or to refer to the 1997 interview, the book is a journey of 'regression' into a delinquent youth characterised by a strong sexual consciousness—a position Tsurumi later reversed and turned into an ideal (Tsurumi 1997, vol. 2: 55). The reader will find his style as digressive as Merton or Sterne and yet there is also a clear trajectory of the wandering soul of a

---

12 https://www.merriam-webster.com/dictionary/frottage

'failed schoolboy' over several decades—before, during and after the war—in search of non-violent ways to break open the cave door.

Another point to note is Tsurumi's emphasis on the 'democratic' nature of the cave scene. Notwithstanding Ame no Uzume's state of possession, and her seemingly free and uninhibited movements, the performance is part of a careful plan prepared by a group of other deities in order to lure the Sun Goddess out of the cave and bring light and warmth back to the world. At the beginning of the introductory chapter, Tsurumi details his 1937 encounter in Adelaide, South Australia, with a booklet in English outlining a 'democratic' meeting of deities.[13] Ame no Uzume's performance is staged with the assistance and participation of the other deities, both as actors and audience. Their uproarious laughter, audible even from inside the cave, raises Amaterasu's curiosity. This may provide a hint to the question Tsurumi posed about Ichijō Sayuri: 'how could she live otherwise?' Just as the 'democratic' congregation of deities successfully resolved the disaster surrounding the disappearance of the Sun, which was caused by a series of violations by Amaterasu's brother Susano'o, there must also be non-violent and democratic solutions to all sorts of problems and crises.

Who Was/Is/Are Ame no Uzume?

The title of this translated work, *The Stripper Goddess of Japan: The Life and Afterlives of Ame no Uzume*, indicates that this *frottage* or burlesque not only focuses on the depiction and representations of the goddess in Japanese mythology and classical texts (i.e. the 'life' of Ame no Uzume), but also her 'afterlives' in a series of ancient through to modern texts, performances and 'marginal' arts such as rituals, festivals and penis and vagina stones. Furthermore, what makes the book uniquely 'polyhedral' are the discussions of this goddess both as a prototype and a metaphor. Even in the first couple of chapters where Tsurumi outlines the key points about the goddess, he refers to various seemingly unrelated people, events and objects wherein he has detected some similarities to or traces of Uzume's characteristics. As suggested by his subtitle, *Shinwa kara nobite kuru michi* (Roads that Unfold Beyond the Mythology), Ame no Uzume

---

[13] See Aoyama (2020) about this trip to Australia in 1937.

is thus not confined to myths and the ancient Japanese world; her 'afterlives' can be found across various forms, genres, spaces, times, genders and cultures.

In Chapter 2, Tsurumi lists the characteristics of Ame no Uzume and people who may have affinities with her:

1. First of all, they are not beautiful, but are charming.

2. They do not care about their appearance. They move without inhibition and are not concerned about respectability.

3. They invite and encourage people to enjoy the party/company.

4. They are full of vitality, which brings out the life force in others.

5. They make people laugh and relieve anxiety. They will even tell a lie to reassure others.

6. They do not shy away from obscenity. They play a role that goes beyond sexual repression.

7. They do not mind if an outsider joins the company; they are open-minded and do not find it necessary to guard themselves closely. They would never call someone a spy, for example, and incite others to punch that person.

Importantly, these characteristics already indicate a considerable departure from various conventional stereotypes about Japanese women and Japanese culture. As if to deliver a finishing blow, Tsurumi adds an eighth characteristic of the trickster goddess: 'the act of exposing her private parts' (Chapter 2). While Tsurumi does discuss Ichijō Sayuri and the history of modern burlesque and striptease dancing in Chapter 6, the discussions of nudity and exposing one's genitals extend far and wide to other aesthetic, philosophical and political contexts. Referring to Susanne K. Langer and others, Tsurumi argues that 'The combined expression of [Uzume's] face and her private parts form a creative power, which accompanies an illusion that makes it seem as though she has two faces' (Chapter 2).

The Stripper Goddess of Japan

This powerful illusion is effectively used to coax Amaterasu out of the cave.

Revealing one's body is also linked to anarchist and pacifist thoughts and movements, ranging from Ishikawa Sanshirō's utopian fantasy of international anarchists, both men and women, meeting in a hot spring in Hakone (Chapter 5) to Mahatma Gandhi's practice of non-violent resistance (Chapter 7). 'Naked Body as Metaphor', which is the title of Chapter 5, is also closely connected to Ame no Uzume's brave and unprejudiced attitude in a later episode of the *Kojiki* in which she confronts a stranger giant as she descends to Earth to ensure that it is safe for Amaterasu's grandson Ninigi to come down and reign. Instead of using weapons, she reveals her body and puts on a funny face. Tsurumi admits that such a strategy to avoid violent confrontation does not always work; much depends on the opponent who may not be as welcoming as the giant, Sarutahiko, who later becomes Uzume's partner.

One special significance of this book is its recognition of women's humour and its subversive power. As mentioned above, Ame no Uzume's dance is regarded as the origin of Japanese comedy. Studies of humour, however, have long neglected women's contributions to the field. Throughout this book Tsurumi cites a number of women writers, such as Nagase Kiyoko (Chapter 2), Okkotsu Yoshiko (Chapter 3), Ochiai Keiko (Chapter 7), Setouchi Harumi/Jakuchō (Chapter 9), Tanabe Seiko (Chapter 10) and Ariyoshi Sawako (Chapter 12). He also discusses the founder of the 'dancing religion', Kitamura Sayo (Chapters 1 and 8). While not all of these women and their works may strike the reader as humorous as Ame no Uzume, each certainly exerts the same kind of subversive power as her, expressed through a variety of characteristics, including irony, boldness and cheekiness. Their cases may elicit laughter from the reader, or at least raise a smile.

Even if not directly connected to humour, women's contributions to religion, culture, scholarship and politics are also recognised throughout the book. The founder of the kabuki theatre, Izumo no O-Kuni, for example, is discussed in Chapters 11 and 12, with references to the scholarly work of Ogasawara Kyōko as well as Ariyoshi's novel and its adaptations for theatre and television. Despite such pro-feminist treatment of women's powers and contributions, some readers may find slight limitations in this book, written more than thirty years ago, in regard to Tsurumi's choice of texts and his comments about them. One example is the character Tomoe in Tanabe Seiko's short story (Chapter 10). She is certainly a trickster and matches most of Ame no Uzume's characteristics. Even so, readers may feel a certain sense of reservation about this selection.

Ame no Uzume Is Alive

The characteristics associated with Ame no Uzume outlined above can be found in a multitude of other legendary, fictional and historical figures and events, as well as in some religious sects, political activities, philosophical thoughts and culture, including what Tsurumi called the 'marginal' arts. In each chapter of this work, Tsurumi, the 'polyhedral' thinker and writer, freely and frequently crosses and subverts all sorts of boundaries—just as his subject, Ame no Uzume, did.[14] His template can be applied to endless more cases across time, space and culture, in a wide variety of texts, performances and activities—especially, though not exclusively, to those enacted by women.[15] Additionally, these cases are not limited to theoretical investigations, but extend much further to practical applications of the Ame no Uzume philosophy as well. For example, the writer, editor and activist Mori Mayumi, who cites *Ame no Uzume den* as one of her favourite books by Tsurumi, quotes two lines from the first chapter of Tsurumi's book in order to express her wish to follow Uzume's example in daily life:

> "She has laughter within herself and she elicits laughter from others." "When others are plagued by oppressive anxieties, she has the power to raise morale simply by conjuring a gust of wind." In civic activism I wish to be like Ame no Uzume. When facing bureaucrats who talk down to citizens, I would like to break the tense atmosphere with laughter, and perhaps even singing and dancing. (*Gendai shisō*, 2015: 40)

---

14 See Aoyama (2018) about Ame no Uzume's border-crossing.
15 For example, Aoyama (2012) uses this template to discuss 'Gender and Humor in Sano Yōko's Writing', and Aoyama (2018: 48) cites the contemporary 'vagina artist' Rokudenashiko's humorous and subversive arts and performances as an example of Ame no Uzume 'continu[ing] to grow and multiply'.

Sociologist Satō Kenji, who wrote a review of *Ame no Uzume den* for the *Mainichi shinbun* newspaper when it was first published in 1991, revisits the book in the same *Gendai shisō* special issue commemorating Tsurumi. Satō recognises the importance of Ame no Uzume's communicative practice in many situations in the contemporary world as her method 'opens avenues of exchange not through verbal persuasion based on an ideology of righteousness or through oppression by brute force on the pretext of a conflict, but with the sharing of laughter as a key' (*Gendai shisō*, 2015: 178). Furthermore, Satō highlights how this communication can apply not only vis-à-vis others but with/against the self—that is, not only in social situations but within oneself. If this book is, as the author remarked, 'a story of [his] wandering spirit', it does help other wandering spirits to find a way out.[16]

As we have seen, among his prolific publications, Tsurumi expressed his own high regard for this book. While some critics such as those mentioned above have recognised its significance in various ways, overall, it is still underestimated within Japan, and hardly known outside Japan. It is our hope that this translation will help to change this situation and let infinite variations of Ame no Uzume flourish all over the world. Amidst continuing serious global issues including human rights and climate change, as well as escalations in political conflicts and nuclear armament, her creative, egalitarian and refreshing approach to problem-solving seems more timely than ever. An anonymous postcard Tsurumi received in May 1945 (Chapter 4) inscribed with the following line is indeed just as valid and relevant now as it was then:

> *ima zo ima, Ame no Uzume no mune hadake*
> (And now is the time Ame no Uzume bares her breasts.)

---

16 Tsurumi suffered from depression three times in his life, at age 12 (1934), 29 (1951) and 38 (1960). Feminist writer Tomioka Taeko calls him a 'depression friend' (*utsuyū*) (*Gendai shisō*, 2015: 13).

Notes to the Reader

A number of conventions have been adopted in this English edition that were not included in Tsurumi's original book. Firstly, each chapter starts with a summary of its contents, prepared by the translators. Secondly, the translation team chose to use footnotes rather than endnotes to facilitate the reader's ease of access to sources and further information. Thirdly, the work contains a Glossary of Deities as a handy reference guide to the many Japanese mythological figures who make an appearance in the book.

The bibliography contains not only the sources mentioned by Tsurumi but also many additional titles. The in-text citations generally follow the customary format used in Japanese publications—namely, page numbers are omitted even for direct quotations. However, in instances where the translation team was able to locate and consult original sources (or their English translations), page numbers have been added. In the case of sources published as e-books, page numbers can change depending on the type of device used to read them. To avoid confusion, we have added the page number(s) followed by the total page count.

Glossary of Deities

Ama no Hohi no Mikoto (1)[1]
The second son of Amaterasu, and the first god sent by the other deities to rule over Earth. The *Nihon shoki* records that Ama no Hohi no Mikoto was born from the spray emanating from Susano'o no Mikoto's mouth after he washed Amaterasu's necklace in a well and then bit down on it.

Ame no Koyane no Mikoto (4)
A male deity who, together with Futodama no Mikoto, performed a ritual prayer to call Amaterasu out from the cave. For further details, see Chapter 4, footnote 11.

Ame no Sagume (1)
An obscure trickster goddess, possibly the origin of malicious, troublemaking spirits known as Amanojaku.

Ame no Tajikarao no Mikoto (1, 3)
A male deity with great physical strength whose name literally means 'heaven hand power'.

Ame no Uzume no Mikoto
A female deity known for her good humour and striptease. Following her union with Sarutahiko no Ōkami, she became known as Sarume no Kimi.

Ame no Wakahiko (1)
A male deity whose name means 'young lad of heaven'. The gods of the Heavenly Plains sent him as a third envoy to Earth, after both Ama no Hohi no Mikoto and Ōsobi no Mikuma no Ushi failed to send correspondence.

---

[1] The number in parentheses indicates the chapter in which the deity is discussed or mentioned.

Amaterasu Ōmikami (1–5, 7, 8)
The sun goddess, from whom the Japanese imperial line is said to descend. Amaterasu hides in a cave because of Susano'o no Mikoto's destructive behaviour, plunging the world into darkness. She is lured out by a display of hanging jewels and a mirror, and the dancing of Ame no Uzume no Mikoto. Amaterasu is also known as Ōhirume no Muchi (see Chapter 4).

Futodama no Mikoto (4)
A male deity who, together with Ame no Koyane no Mikoto, performed a ritual prayer to call Amaterasu out from the cave. For further details, see Chapter 4, footnote 11.

Izanagi and Izanami (2, 4)
Izanagi ('the male who invites') and Izanami ('the female who invites') were brother and sister *kami*, and the eighth pair of deities to appear after the creation of Heaven and Earth. Out of their union were born the Eight Great Islands of Japan, as well as other great *kami*, including Amaterasu Ōmikami.

Konohanasakuya-hime (2)
The goddess of Mt. Fuji, all volcanoes, blossoms and a symbol of delicate earthly life, whose name literally means 'lady blooming tree blossoms'. Konohanasakuya-hime was particularly beautiful, and Ninigi no Mikoto elected to marry her over her older sister, Iwanaga-hime ('lady lasting rock').

Kotoamatsukami (11)
A collective name (literally meaning 'separate heavenly *kami*') for the first five gods that came into existence, without procreation, in Takamagahara when the universe was created.

Nanashi Kigishi (1)
A green pheasant that is both human and bird, Nanashi Kigishi ('nameless pheasant') was dispatched from the Heavenly Plains after Ama no Hohi no Mikoto, Ōsobi no Mikuma no Ushi and Ame no Wakahito all failed to send word home.

Ninigi no Mikoto (1, 2, 4)
In the traditional narrative detailing the founding of Japan's imperial line, he is Amaterasu's grandson and the grandfather of Emperor Jinmu, Japan's first emperor.

Ōkuninushi no Mikoto (aka Ōanamuchi, 1, 11)
The original ruler of the terrestrial realm Ashihara no Nakatsukuni, located between the heavenly Takamagahara and Yomi (the underworld).

Omoikane no Kami (1)
A tactician god and advisor to the spirits of heaven, whose name means 'thought over'.

Ōsobi no Mikuma no Ushi (aka Takemikuma no Ushi, 1)
Ama no Hohi's child, sent to Earth after Ama no Hohi no Mikoto failed to send correspondence back to the Heavenly Plains.

Ototachibana-hime (2, 12)
The wife of a semi-mythical Japanese prince (Yamato-takeru) who sacrificed herself to soothe the anger of the sea god and defend her husband. Her name means 'lady younger sister orange tree'.

Sarutahiko no Ōkami (1–3, 5, 7, 12)
The leader of the earthly *kami*, depicted as a towering, bearded figure, who meets Ninigi no Mikoto when he descends from the Heavenly Plains.

Shitaderu-hime (1)
A daughter of Ōkuninushi no Mikoto and wife of Ame no Wakahiko, also commonly referred to as Shitateru-hime.

Susano'o no Mikoto (1, 2, 4)
The storm god and Amaterasu's mischievous younger brother, whose destructive behaviour drives Amaterasu to hide in a cave, thereby plunging the world into darkness.

Takamimusubi no Kami (1)
The Governor of Heavenly Politics and a god of agriculture, who was the second god to appear in the Heavenly Plains.

Toyohirume (4)
A goddess of agriculture and industry, also known as Toyo-uke-bime ('lady bountiful fare').

Umashi Ashikabi Hikoji no Kami (11)
One of the Kotoamatsukami, and a deity thought to symbolise energy and vitality.

Yamatotakeru (12)
A semi-legendary Japanese prince noted for his courage and ingenuity, who may have lived in the second century CE. The husband of Ototachibana-hime, his name means 'Yamato brave'.

Chapter 1
The Power to Open a Closed Cave

In this chapter Tsurumi introduces the subject of the book, Ame no Uzume no Mikoto (Ame no Uzume for short), by outlining two important scenes from the ancient texts *Kojiki* and *Nihon shoki* in which she appears: the celebrated dance scene outside the Heavenly Cave which lures Amaterasu back into the world, and her encounter with the stranger god Sarutahiko no Ōkami at a fork in the road. Tsurumi contrasts the nationalistic use of the mythology in his school days before the war with the free and democratic interpretation that he found in 1937 Australia. He also highlights how the depiction of Ame no Uzume by artist Kosugi Hōan skilfully captures her great sense of warmth and mirth. Tsurumi closes the chapter with his observations on how Ame no Uzume is able to raise morale, offer friendship and confront authority through her animated and open personality.

I first encountered the mythological Japanese text *Kojiki* (Records of Ancient Matters, 712) at primary school.[1] It materialised in various places, ranging from textbooks on Japanese history and language to lessons in music and morality. In those days, the state employed the *Kojiki*'s mythological narratives to align with its own purposes, and in that sense, it paralleled the usage of the original text.

Several years later, I encountered a very different approach to the *Kojiki*, when I was handed a rough and very liberal English translation of an abridged version in Adelaide, Australia. At that time (that is, the

---

1 *Kojiki* (古事記) is an ancient Japanese text consisting of myths, legends and anecdotal histories that detail the origins of Japanese gods and goddesses and their links to Japan's imperial family.

Chapter 1

summer of 1937)[2] there were no Japanese living there, but there was an association of sorts that grew from the members' shared interest in learning about Japan and the Japanese language. As their study was limited to English-language sources, they were very keen to invite me—as a native Japanese speaker—to one of their meetings, which were held in a place that looked somewhat like a museum basement.

The pamphlet given to me when I arrived described a gathering of eight million gods.[3] It was a democratic gathering, which included such deities as the Typewriter God and the Striptease Goddess. Even today I am baffled by the Typewriter God, so I assume it must have been some sort of misinterpretation. The Striptease Goddess, however, must surely be a reference to Ame no Uzume no Mikoto.

I began to see a different interpretation of Japanese mythology to the one that I had encountered at primary school. The Adelaide meeting sparked in me a much freer and liberal view of the *Kojiki*, which has continued to grow inside me now for more than fifty years. It made me realise that a number of lesser figures appear in Japanese mythology. It would be good if there were ways to communicate with them directly.

§

One day, when the Sun Goddess known as Amaterasu Ōmikami was weaving, her mischievous brother Susano'o no Mikoto climbed atop the roof of the weaving house and threw the flayed corpse of a piebald horse into a maiden's loom. The maiden was so startled that she impaled her vagina on the loom and died. Amaterasu became very upset and retreated to a cave, refusing to see anyone. An ominous mood enveloped the entire world.

---

2 Tsurumi was fifteen when he visited Australia. This experience was partly responsible for inspiring Tsurumi to write *Ame no Uzume den*. For further details, see Aoyama (2020: 25–43).

3 Tsurumi uses the Japanese word *kami* (神), which does not specify gender and can be understood to mean god, goddess, deity, spirit, or any other sacred power venerated in the Shinto religion. To date, the pamphlet that Tsurumi mentions has not been found.

And so it was that the eight million gods gathered at the Heavenly River to carry out their elaborate plan to coax Amaterasu out of the cave, agreeing that the brawny Ame no Tajikarao no Mikoto would hide by the cave's entrance while Ame no Uzume no Mikoto would perform a shamanistic dance.

With a heavenly cord made from ground pine slung across her chest, and a wreath of evergreen *masaki* vines adorning her head,[4] Ame no Uzume gathered up a bundle of dwarf bamboo leaves in one hand and mounted an inverted pail. As she became possessed and her trance deepened, she exposed her breasts and pushed her skirt-band down to her genitals, all the while dancing and stomping with reckless abandon. The echo of her stomping feet reverberated across the Heavenly Plains (Takamagahara).[5] All around her, the gods were greatly amused, and they laughed with glee.

From inside the cave, Amaterasu wondered what in heavens was going on outside. Opening the door just a fraction, she asked:

> 'I assumed that with the darkness that enveloped the world after I retreated to this cave everyone would be depressed. Why do they sound so merry? Why is Ame no Uzume singing and dancing, and why are the other gods laughing with her?'

Ame no Uzume replied:

> 'We are all happy and laughing because we have found a goddess more wonderful than you.'

During this conversation, two other gods took out a mirror and set it in front of Amaterasu so that she could see her own image. Curious, she poked her head out of the cave's entrance. Tajikarao, who was still hiding close by, grabbed her by the hand and pulled her out from

---

4 Ground pine (*Dendrolycopodium obscurum*) is a clubmoss with a subterranean main stem and short aerial shoots that can be woven into garlands or wreaths. *Masaki* vine, or Asiatic jasmine (*Trachelospermum asiaticum*), is an evergreen plant that produces white flowers that turn yellow over time.

5 In Japanese mythology, the heavenly gods reside in the Takamagahara (Heavenly Plains) located in the sky which is connected to Earth via the Ame no Ukihashi (Floating Bridge of Heaven).

the cave. The two gods quickly draped a sacred straw rope across the entrance, preventing Amaterasu from retreating inside again.

At the moment Amaterasu ventured back into the world, darkness gave way to light all around.

In the *Nihon shoki* (Chronicles of Japan, 720) version, the setting of the narrative is much grander. The planning is carried out by the tactician god Omoikane no Kami, who gathers together a flock of roosters to announce the dawn with a protracted chorus of crowing. He transplants a sacred *sakaki* tree[6] from Heaven's Fragrant Hill in Nara, decorating its upper branches with jewelled necklaces and bracelets, its middle branches with a large mirror,[7] and its lower branches with ribbons made of pale blue hemp and pure white cotton.

Ame no Uzume appears in the centre of the prepared stage carrying an enormous phallus-shaped pike in hand. Her head is decorated with a wreath of *sakaki* leaves, and her chest is slung with a cord made from *sagarigoke* (ground pine). She stands atop an inverted pail; once in a trance, she begins to shout all manner of words as she dances by the flickering light of a bonfire. Her audience begins to stir. Listening from inside the cave, Amaterasu is surprised and wonders why Ame no Uzume is so full of mirth. As she opens the door, Tajikarao catches her hand and pulls her out from the cave.

Ame no Uzume's bare-breasted, exposed-genitalia, pike-carrying dance simulates sexual intercourse. Two thousand years later, such an act now manifests in striptease shows. According to the *Nihon shoki*, court ladies called *sarume* specialised in dancing, based on their remote lineage to Ame no Uzume. Although Nara period (710–794) court dancing may have retained a similar sort of primitive wildness, it is doubtful that it would have been the same type of unregulated sex-simulating dance of mythological times.

Since my time at primary school, I have seen many images of Amaterasu Ōmikami. Ame no Uzume no Mikoto, however, is rarely

---

6 The evergreen *sakaki* (榊) tree (*Cleyera japonica*) is especially sacred to Shinto and appears frequently in Japanese mythology and literature.

7 Tsurumi's text indicates that the mirror is 8 *sun* (寸), or roughly 16cm, which accords with the Chinese measurement of approximately 2cm per unit. Like the larger *shaku* (尺) unit, the measurement varies in different locations and times; in Japan, the length of 1 *sun* is approximately 3cm. This mirror came to be known as the Heavenly Mirror (see footnote 15 for more detail).

The Power to Open a Closed Cave

Figure 1.1: Kosugi Hōan's Ame no Uzume no Mikoto (1951)
Source: Idemitsu Museum of Arts.

depicted clearly. Often she seems to appear featured just from the rear, in order to enhance Amaterasu's primary role.

However, a number of exceptions come to mind. A master plasterer working at the end of the Edo period (1603–1868), Chōhachi of Izu (1815–1889), is said to have drawn pictures of Ame no Uzume with his trowel, presenting them as gifts.[8] Another direct descendant of Ame no Uzume is the comic female Okame, who is featured in the *okagura* dances at Shinto shrines.[9]

A more recent and impressive example was included in an exhibition of the work of Kosugi Hōan (1881–1964), which represented Ame no Uzume in a semi-frontal view.[10] She is depicted to the right of an enormous golden sun, dancing with outstretched arms and exposed breasts. Her dance is not the kind of salon dance that we see today taught by the traditional Japanese dance schools such as Hanayagi or Inoue.

Rather, it looks like a dance that predates the Edo period—that is, earlier than Japan's closure to the outside world. It also seems somewhat similar to dances of the South Sea islands, such as the Hawaiian hula. In Japan, too, similar forms of free movement must

---

8 Izu Chōhachi (aka Irie Chōhachi) carved and painted frescos and reliefs on plastered walls. One famous work featuring Ame no Uzume, Amaterasu and Sarutahiko decorates Yoriki Shrine in Shinagawa, Tokyo.

9 *Okagura*, or *kagura* 神楽 (literally, 'god-entertainment'), dances are ceremonial Shinto dances. Originally performed by supposed descendants of Ame no Uzume, they have since evolved into different forms that are still enacted today.

10 Kosugi Hōan (aka Kosugi Misei) was a Japanese painter and son of a Shinto priest.

have existed, for example, in the Buddhist incantation performances for Amitābha initiated by the Venerable Ippen (1239–1289) in the Kamakura period (1185–1333). In more recent times—early in the summer of 1944 to be exact, at the height of Japan's wartime isolation from the outside world—Kitamura Sayo (1900–1967) devised a new 'dancing religion' called Tenshō Kōtai Jingūkyō after kicking her husband's pillow.[11] As the nation-state crumbled following Japan's defeat in the war, the religion gained a strong following in Japan before attaining cult status overseas as well.

The clothing worn by Hōan's Ame no Uzume is not the type of sophisticated attire worn by the court ladies of the Nara period (even those specialising in dance), but is more akin to the simple western clothing (called *appappa*) that was common in the Shōwa period (1926–1989). Immediately following the war, especially, it was perfectly respectable for women to wear this sort of unglamorous outfit to go shopping on the black market. In other words, what was ordinary clothing for women in ancient Japan looks nothing like contemporary Japanese kimono (which is now worn primarily at graduations and hotel wedding ceremonies). It has, rather, a sort of 'international' feel.

Because Ame no Uzume is a dancer, she is not fat, but Hōan has depicted her as fleshy. Her plump cheeks are welcoming. The entire image emanates a warmth, perhaps due to the sunshine. There is no hint of the chilling air brought about by the eternal darkness.

The work's representation of the sun is not evocative of the nation (and metaphorically the current Japanese government) so much as an abstract form that can be appreciated by any viewer. That is to say, the image is more of a depiction of the joy of life with the sun shining upon us, rather than one proselytising the greatness of the nation.

Like Amaterasu, the image prompts us to enquire of its subject '*Ika ni zo* Ame no Uzume no Mikoto *kaku eraku ya*' (Why is Ame no Uzume laughing like this?). According to a note in the *Nihon koten*

---

11 Kitamura was a farmer's wife. Tenshō Kōtai Jingūkyō (天照皇大神宮教), known colloquially as Odoru shūkyō ('dancing religion'), articulated her uncompromising vision for a new society that would release her followers from the 'maggot world' of post-war Japan. For a detailed study, see Dorman (2012: 168–203). Kitamura is discussed in more detail in Chapter 8.

bungaku taikei (Japanese Classical Literature) series (Iwanami Shoten, 1967), '*eraku*' as it appears in the first volume of *Nihon shoki* means 'to rejoice and laugh happily'.

What did the ancient people think of Ame no Uzume no Mikoto? Of course, there is no way to know. From our reading of the *Kojiki* and *Nihon shoki*, we can surmise, however, that she was one of the eight million deities surrounding Amaterasu, well before Amaterasu's progeny became the ruler of Japan. Ame no Uzume did not remain with the other gods, but descended to Japan along with Amaterasu's grandson, Ninigi no Mikoto.

The deities of the Heavenly Plains (wherever that might have been) attempted to start a colony in the remote land, but each of the envoys dispatched to investigate failed in promptly completing their assigned task. The first envoy, Ama no Hohi no Mikoto, appeared as a result of a negotiation between Amaterasu and her younger brother, Susano'o. When Ama no Hohi became friendly with the king of a remote land, Ōanamuchi (aka Ōkuninushi no Mikoto), he began cohabiting with a local woman and neglected to send reports back to the Heavenly Plains. According to the *Nihon shoki*, he became an ancestor of Haji no Muraji[12] of Izumo province. Following three years of no correspondence, the Heavenly Plains headquarters decided to send Ama no Hohi's child, Ōsobi no Mikuma no Ushi (aka Takemikuma no Ushi). But just like his father, he neglected to send correspondence home. The gods got together to discuss who the next envoy should be, and decided to appoint Ame no Wakahiko, whom they considered strong enough to complete the task. However, he also married a daughter of Ōkuninushi no Mikoto, Shitaderu-hime (Princess Shitaderu), and enjoyed his new life surrounded by nubile young women. Eight years went by, and he too sent no word back home.

Next, Nanashi Kigishi (Nameless Pheasant) was dispatched from the Heavenly Plains to investigate. Nanashi Kigishi is the name of a green pheasant that is both human and bird.[13] When he was perched

---

12 Haji no Muraji was in charge of funerals for the imperial family.
13 In Japanese mythology, pheasants are regarded as messengers from heaven. The *kiji* (雉, 雉子), or green pheasant (*Phasianus versicolor*), is the national bird of Japan.

Chapter 1

atop a *katsura* tree[14] outside the house of Ame no Wakahiko, the gossipy Ame no Sagume felt compelled to report the presence of an unusual bird to her master. Wakahiko responded by shooting Kigishi with a bow and arrow. The arrow that pierced the pheasant was sent to the Heavenly Plains. When the governor of heavenly politics, Takamimusubi no Kami, saw the bloodied arrow, he exclaimed, 'I gave this arrow to Ame no Wakahiko long ago. Is it stained with the blood of Wakahiko, shed in a battle with a god of the remote land?' As he threw the arrow from Heaven to Earth, it pierced the chest of Ame no Wakahiko, killing him. The screams of Ame no Wakahiko's wife, Princess Shitaderu, could be heard even as far away as the Heavenly Plains.

After this series of failures by each of the appointed envoys, the Heavenly Plains headquarters discussed the matter again, and this time prudently sent two gods with reputations for bravery to negotiate firmly with the local god Ōkuninushi no Kami. The envoys pressed him to allow Amaterasu's grandson Ninigi no Mikoto to govern the remote land. After consulting his son, Ōkuninushi agreed to their request. The date was formally set for the descent of the heavenly grandson. However, given the history of bloody conflicts, it was decided at the Heavenly Plains that to ensure his safety, Ninigi no Mikoto would be accompanied by a retinue of protectors. As a skilled negotiator, Ame no Uzume was included in the entourage.

On the day of the departure, a scout returned with the ominous news that at the fork in the road was a god who stood more than seven feet tall, the corners of his mouth blazing red. His nose was seven inches long, and his eyes, which bore a striking resemblance to the Heavenly Mirror,[15] glowered with the red incandescence of the fruit of the Japanese lantern plant. A number of the protection retinue were dispatched to investigate, but none was able to look him in the eye, let alone exchange any words. Based on the compelling power of

---

14 The *katsura* (桂) tree (*Cercidiphyllum japonicum*) is also known as the Japanese Cinnamon or Japanese Judas tree.
15 *Yata no kagami* (八咫鏡, Heavenly Mirror) is the mirror that was hung on the tree to lure Amaterasu out of the cave. It is one of the *sanshu no jingi* (三種の神器, Three Sacred Treasures) bestowed by Amaterasu on her grandson Ninigi no Mikoto. The other two treasures are the *Kusanagi no tsurugi* (草薙劍, Kusanagi Sword) and the *Yasakani no Magatama* (八尺瓊勾玉, Grand Jewel).

The Power to Open a Closed Cave

her eyes and her persuasive ways, it was decided that Ame no Uzume should be the one to approach the giant.

Again, Ame no Uzume bared her breasts and lowered her skirtband below her navel. With a smile on her face, she stood boldly in front of the giant, who knew her name. 'Ame no Uzume, why do you bare yourself so?' he asked.

Ignoring his question, she responded 'Who is this giant who blocks the way of the grandson of Amaterasu Ōmikami?'

'I am only here because I heard that Amaterasu's grandson is coming this way', he responded. 'I am waiting to welcome him. My name, since you would like to know, is Sarutahiko no Ōkami'.

And so it was that Ame no Uzume asked Sarutahiko to guide the entourage, and advised Ninigi no Mikoto of the new plan. The heavenly grandson was to descend upon Kujifuru no Take at Himuka Takachiho in Tsukushi province.[16] Having put these arrangements in place, Ame no Uzume agreed to Sarutahiko's request to accompany him to the upper stream of Sanada's Isuzu River in Ise Province.[17] In those times, one did not tell a stranger where one lived without good reason. Because Sarutahiko had revealed such intimate information, he requested that Ame no Uzume travel with him. As they were about to depart, Ninigi no Mikoto made a divine announcement that Ame no Uzume should adopt Sarutahiko's name, thus bestowing upon her the new moniker Sarume no Kimi. From then on, the court dancers belonging to Ame no Uzume's lineage were called 'Kimi' regardless of their gender, and enjoyed a certain guaranteed standing. As for Ame no Uzume, she left her lord, hand in hand with Sarutahiko, and disappeared altogether from the *Kojiki*.

§

Ame no Uzume appears in two main scenes in the *Kojiki* and *Nihon shoki*. In one, she restores the mood of the leader who is upset and has hidden herself away. In the other, she calmly initiates dealings with a different ethnic group when her fellow deities are hesitant to

---

16 Kujifuru no Take is one of the peaks of Mt. Takachiho, located in Tsukushi province, an ancient Japanese location thought to correspond to either present-day Fukuoka prefecture or Miyazaki prefecture.
17 The Isuzu River is located in the city of Ise in Mie prefecture. It flows through Ise Grand Shrine, one of Shinto's holiest sites, which is dedicated to Amaterasu.

Chapter 1

do so. In each case, her method is to open her clothing to expose her breasts and genitals in order to invite laughter and thereby ease the other party's tension.

Whether in her own country or a foreign land, Ame no Uzume does not fear the authorities. Neither does she assume that foreigners are enemies.

She has laughter within herself, and she elicits laughter from others. She is always in an animated mood. When others are plagued by oppressive anxieties, she has the power to raise morale simply by conjuring a gust of wind. This power has earned her the trust of her compatriots.

Very little research has been undertaken examining the ideological roles of dance. This must be because, by its very nature, dance is fluid rather than static.

Several years ago, I visited Mano Sayo (b. 1913), who wrote the novel *Kōkonki* (A Twilight Record, 1981) based on the latter years of her mother's life.[18] Ms Mano explained to me the differing nature of conversations with her mother and daughter to those with her ex-husband and son:

> If, for example, something annoys me, I explain what happened, who said what, what the response was, and then what happened, and so on and so forth. My son would always become increasingly bored before finally stopping me and asking, "What is it that you really want to say?" And I would respond by saying "Everything! All of it!" Everything from beginning to end. It's like a novel.
>
> My daughter is also process-focused, so she would listen to my story. But not my son. So here's the big difference: mother and daughter get on very well, and quarrel very well! (Mano et al. 1982: 20)

Husbands and sons (once they are independent and working) are so accustomed to the logic of production efficiency that they cannot accept stories without concluding propositions. They believe that novels—and much less dance—have no ideological significance.

---

18 *Kōkonki* was originally published by Minerva Shobō in 1981. It is also included in Iwanami Shoten's Dōjidai Library series (1990).

However, if that were the case, what would be the meaning of holding elections? The other day, there was an election for the Mayor of Kyoto. Forty percent of voters supported the Liberal Democratic Party, Democratic Socialist Party and Kōmeitō; 39% the Communist Party; 20% the Socialist Party; and 1% other independents.[19] The historian Kawano Kenji published a commentary on the election results in *Kyoto shinbun* newspaper pointing out that when tallied by individual votes, there is one clear winner, but if viewed by parties, it is possible to interpret the data in various different ways.[20] This allows us to see that political outcomes are primarily determined by the election process rather than just by results. If that were not the case, the winning vote alone would be recognised as determining the outcome, whatever form the election took. The responsibility for adjusting the winning platform would fall to the incumbent.

Ame no Uzume's performances are dance moves and may therefore be regarded as incoherent. To bring an end to a domestic argument, a husband may tell his wife that her words are incoherent. But what if the wife responded by saying that incoherence was exactly what she wanted to convey? I think it is important to recognise ideological existence outside the realm of linear reasoning.

Authorities like to summarise their ideologies (at various junctures) in a single hermetic system. Those people who wish to soften this approach by drawing on experience create laughter to throw the system off balance and turn it into an incoherent form before directing it to another phase. To me, Ame no Uzume seems to be a deity who created an opportunity to change Amaterasu's authority by means of an election.

---

19 In the 1989 election for Mayor of Kyoto, the conservative candidate Tanabe Tomoyuki (1924–2002) defeated the runner up Communist party candidate Kimura Manpei (1924–2014) by just 321 votes.

20 Kawano Kenji (1916–1996) was a professor of history at Kyoto University, specialising in French economic history.

Chapter 2
A Genealogy of Likening

In this chapter, Tsurumi examines instances where Ame no Uzume's name has been used to liken the traits of people in contemporary culture to those of the ancient goddess. He recalls episodes from his school days to explore the power of nicknames, pondering who gets to create them and why they stick. Drawing from the work of scholars in disparate fields, Tsurumi then delves into various theories about the practice of 'naming', concluding that Ame no Uzume is brought to life again every time her name is invoked as a nickname. Finally, he enumerates seven fascinating qualities he thinks should be considered in likening someone to Ame no Uzume, before adding an eighth: the exposure of the body to form a creative, illusive power.

In autumn 1950, when the writer Masamune Hakuchō (1879–1962) received the Order of Culture, there was a party to celebrate the occasion in his hometown, Okayama.[1] The poet Nagase Kiyoko (1906–1995), a resident of the city, made a speech.[2]

Nagase praised Hakuchō's contributions to literature. Although she also praised his modesty in not attending the hometown celebration—as he felt he had never done anything for the place—she stated that she wanted to make the event such a great success that he would regret not attending it. That's why she'd agreed, she said,

---

1 Masamune Hachukō (born Masamune Tadao) was a critic and leading master of Japanese naturalist literature.
2 Nagase was a pioneering poet, activist and essayist. Her 12 books of poetry include *Shokoku no tennyo* (諸国の天女, Heavenly Maidens on Earth, 1940) and *Akegata ni kuru hito yo* (あけがたにくる人よ, O You Who Come to Me at Dawn, 1987).

Chapter 2

to play an Ame no Uzume-like role and stand up in front of everyone (Nagase 1981).

Nagase's way of using the name Ame no Uzume fascinated me. It was the poet's wish that like Ame no Uzume's act of luring Amaterasu out of the cave, she could bring this famous writer out of his surly seclusion in Tokyo where he continued to write literature embodying chronic dyspepsia. The reference may also be a sign of Nagase's own humility, appearing on stage under a spotlight to make a speech when she herself was nearing seventy at the time.

Here we see a resurrection of Ame no Uzume, the character in the *Kojiki*.

Long before this incident, sociologist Nakano Takashi (1920–2014) went on a two-day walking tour of some villages in northern Kyoto with his friends in the Second Kyoto Middle School History Society, accompanied by their teacher, the folklorist Inoue Yoritoshi (1900–1979). During their trip, Inoue told the students that the mountains in the area look like those in the Hida (i.e. north Gifu) region. Nakano recalls:

> He [Inoue] told us: "The most impressive thing I found during my travels in Hida and Shinshū [i.e. Nagano] was the women there. They reminded me of ancient goddesses such as Ototachibanahime and Ame no Uzume no Mikoto, and later figures such as Lady Tomoe and Lady Shizuka.[3] It was so great." (Nakano 1989)

The above was dated 2 October 1937; up until around that time the name Ame no Uzume no Mikoto had the power to evoke a clear image of a character in daily conversation.

In the same period, I went to three different schools, one after the other, and noticed that some school environments are more conducive to the creation of nicknames than others. At academically-oriented schools, students don't bother wasting brain space thinking up nicknames, resorting instead to the ordinary types of nicknames found everywhere. At the Tokyo Metropolitan Fifth Middle School,

---

3 Tomoe Gozen and Shizuka Gozen were quasi-mythological Japanese figures based upon women who lived in the 12th century. The former was an *onna-musha* (女武者), or female martial practitioner, while the latter was a *shirabyōshi* (白拍子), a female court dancer who dressed in men's attire.

which was the third one I went to, one of the teachers of Japanese was nicknamed 'Damenanpū', which impressed me.

Let me explain why. The teacher was allied with the then mainstream school of imperialist Japanese history, represented by the Tokyo University professor Hiraizumi Kiyoshi (1895–1984). In his class, when the teacher was reading aloud from the travel diary of Yoshinoyama (which was in the school textbook in those days), he recited with deep lamentation the phrase *nanpū kisowazu* (literally, 'declining southerly wind', i.e. the decline in power of the Southern Court during the mid- to late-fourteenth century).[4] One student (who, like me, was in the second year) went to see him later for a permission or something concerning an extracurricular activity. Puffing out his fat cheeks, the teacher uttered, 'That sort of thing just won't do [*dame nan*...]...', then, failing to end the sentence properly, he inhaled and breathed out, making the sound '*pū*'. This episode spread from student to student, and before long the nickname Damenanpū had caught on. Based on the student's canny observation, the nickname also lightly mocked the era's rising ultranationalist ideology.

Even though I stayed at this school only for two terms, I still cherish some fond memories of my time there, thanks partly to these sorts of nicknaming episodes.

In terms of naming, the writer Nakano Shigeharu (1902–1979) makes an interesting observation in connection with the term 'vision', which has come into vogue recently.[5]

> People seem to like the word 'vision' these days. I have no objection to it, but why not think about it this way: when they talk about vision, what they really mean is naming things. (Nakano [1967] 1978)

Abstraction is necessary, but it is impossible to transform the content of a work of literature into abstract words and still cover all its nuanced appeal. Consider this, for example: a high school student,

---

4 The Nanboku-chō period (1336–1392) was one of conflict between the Northern Imperial Court and the Southern Imperial Court. Though the North eventually triumphed, the Southern Imperial Court was later deemed the legitimate court during the Meiji era.

5 Nakano was also a poet and social critic, and a member of the Japanese Communist Party (JCP).

Chapter 2

who is dumped by his girlfriend because she was 'blinded' by a diamond, becomes so angry that he leaves school and becomes a moneylender. Such an outline alone would not entice people to plant a pine tree in the spot where the climactic scene takes place in the story. It is only when the spot at Atami beach is recognised as where the couple with the names O-Miya and Kan'ichi meet in the novel *Konjiki yasha* (The Golden Demon, 1897–1902) by Ozaki Kōyō (1868–1903), that the idea of planting a pine tree to commemorate the scene arises.[6]

Naming, according to Ichimura Hiromasa (1987), 'signifies an act of creating or generating things, as well as cognition of what has been created':

> Human beings cut and divide the world on a continuum through names, and by separating things from one another, and generating new things. Moreover, through the systematisation of those names, they understand phenomena.

Name-giving plays a significant role in mythology. In the world of children's play as well, the act of naming performs an important role. Children often depart from the names adults have taught them, assigning different monikers to things.

For example, they might rename a whirligig beetle a 'lettering bug', or apply the name 'sumo-wrestler plant' both to Chinese plantain and to violets, which adults of course distinguish as two different plants.

> At the very least, here we can see the child's observant eyes that register an insect's movement as letter writing on the water, and also the child's sense of thinking that two different kinds of plants are the same as long as their stalks can be used for playing sumo wrestling. (Ichimura 1987)

---

[6] Ozaki Kōyō (born Ozaki Tokutarō) was an immensely popular Japanese author and poet who played a leading role in the development of modern Japanese literature. In his incomplete serial novel *Konjiki yasha* (金色夜叉), which was serialised in *Yomiuri Shinbun* from 1897 to 1902, Ozaki tells the story of a penniless youth (Kan'ichi) who becomes absorbed by money after losing his fiancée (O-Miya) to a wealthy man. The work has been made into a number of film and television adaptations.

What is important is that once a new name is given, other children find it interesting, and then its use keeps spreading. The same applies to nicknames that are amusing to fellow students—they spread quickly, and remain unchanged, at least while those students are at the school.

It is not that the teacher, Dr, Ms or Mr Such and Such, suddenly loses their original name; instead, the new name makes everyone see the teacher in a different light.

> Nicknames, which may incorporate insults, affection or praise, involve an effect where the named transforms into someone or something else. This clearly shows why naming should not be carried out without careful consideration. The act requires meticulous observation and accurate expression—in other words, critical thinking. [...]
>
> The critical ability in nicknaming must be reflected not only in praise but even more so in badmouthing and censure. Unless the criticism strikes at the opponent's core, derision and ridicule are ineffective; hence, in order to achieve maximum effect, it is necessary to maintain maximum interest in one's opponent as well as concentrated attention on details. The decline in nicknaming ability, therefore, undoubtedly signifies the weakening of mutual concerns in society and the decay of cultural standards, including the critical senses. (Ichimura 1987)

§

No one can tell how long the age of the Takamagahara (Heavenly Plains) lasted. Ame no Uzume, who revealed her breasts in a dance while Amaterasu hid in the cave, now accompanied Amaterasu's grandson, Ninigi no Mikoto, as he descended as a grown-up god onto the Japanese archipelago. When she faced a mysterious figure standing at the crossroads as if to block their way, she again bared her breasts, grinning broadly. No matter how long the career of a Japanese striptease dancer might be today, there is no comparison. In the history of the Takamagahara, the name Ame no Uzume had already turned into a nickname used for all those bearing her name. In other words, we can regard her as an entity who was born and reborn, again and again. If this is the case, it is ontologically similar to the present-day Ame no Uzume, who is brought back to life every time her name is used as a nickname. At least when Nagase Kiyoko called herself by that name in Okayama in 1950, Nagase as Ame no Uzume materialised in front of other people around her age who were gathered at the reception (and who would have thus had the same knowledge of pre-war primary school textbooks).

According to Kuratsuka Akiko (1935–1984), leaves and flowers used as head decorations at festivals were called *uzu*, while *uzume* meant a woman, perhaps a *miko*, who used such decorations in her hair.[7] Uzume stood on a pail set upside down in front of the cave, stomped loudly in a possessed state, and continued to dance exposing her genitals until she successfully drew Amaterasu out of the rock cave. Kuratsuka (1986) writes:

> This frenzy was that of a shaman. Against the sound of jarring musical instruments, shamans go into a trance, sending their spirits into the psychic sphere, and, using the spiritual power they gain there, they try to heal the ailing body and soul. The myth of the Heavenly Cave reflects the court ritual for the repose of the dead, but it was also a festival to activate both the power of the sun around the time of the winter solstice, and the soul of the monarch. Ame no Uzume's role in the myth was to restore the depleted power of the Sun Goddess.

One theory suggests that Sarutahiko and Ame no Uzume were originally siblings. If this is true, why would Ame no Uzume, who came down from the Heavenly Plains, bare her breasts to face her brother? Were they brought up in separate places and hence unable to recognise each other? However, in another theory they are husband and wife. In mythological times, Amaterasu and her younger brother Susano'o can have children together, so it is not impossible that Sarutahiko could be the older brother of Ame no Uzume, and at the

---

7 *Miko* (巫女, shrine maidens) are young women who work as priestesses at Shinto shrines. Once thought to have shamanistic powers, their role has become largely ritualistic in modern times.

same time be her husband.[8] In any case, they meet at the crossroads, and leaving the central stage of politics, go to the countryside to live together.

In one episode of the *Kojiki*, Sarutahiko's hand is caught by a *hirabugai* shellfish, and he drowns while fishing on a beach in Ise.[9] Since he is said to have preached to all the fishes and shellfishes that they must be loyal to Amaterasu's grandson, perhaps they weren't too pleased and played a little trick on him. Perhaps it was not his hand, but his nose (phallus) that was nipped. This interpretation would certainly suit his comic role.

Returning to our main topic, when we feel that someone in front of us is like another person, a sort of illusion is at work, for it is impossible that one person is completely identical to another. It is for this reason that I hesitate to answer immediately when someone wants me to agree that this person resembles that person. The person who thinks that A looks like B is viewing them from an angle unique to herself or himself. Since I cannot share that particular angle and viewpoint, A is not like B to me. Only, to be polite, I may agree and say, 'Yes, indeed'. With nicknames too, it is usually through the user's agreement with the original name-givers that they enter common usage. Before long, those who give nicknames are recognised as having the ability to do so.

Since no one has ever seen the goddess Ame no Uzume, the grounds for agreeing or disagreeing as to whether or not someone looks like her are weak.

This reminds me of my experience with the dentist Dr Ogita Seinosuke in Mexico.[10] He abruptly started talking about Oaxaca, which is about ten hours by train from the capital city:

---

8 In chapter 15 of the *Kojiki*, eight children are born to Amaterasu and Susano'o. The first three are females whom Amaterasu 'births' by chewing and spitting out pieces of Susano'o's sword, while the last five are males who are born when Susano'o chews and spits out various decorative beads worn by Amaterasu. Indeed, both Amaterasu and Susano'o, in addition to other deities and the Eight Great Islands of Japan, are themselves offspring of the brother and sister *kami* Izanagi ('the male who invites') and Izanami ('the female who invites').

9 *Hirabugai* is a type of shellfish, sometimes thought to be *tairagi* (*Atrina pectinata*). *Tairagi* belong to the family *Pinnidae*, which consists of large saltwater clams that are commonly known as 'pen shells'.

10 Tsurumi spent a year in Mexico from September 1972 as a visiting professor at El Colegio de México, A.C.

Chapter 2

"I met her in a forest at Oaxaca. She immigrated in the age of *Man'yō* [*Man'yōshū*, the eighth century poetry collection]. Ms XXXX is a descendent of Konohanasakuya-hime and about eight hundred years old, but she's so beautiful."

He kept on talking like this, but then after a while, he changed the topic to his present-day dentistry work, all of which was based on verifiable facts. As he was a practising dentist, it would have been a problem if he had been divorced from reality at work.

Mr Idaka Hiroaki, who introduced me to the Ogita family, had known Dr Ogita for a decade. According to Mr Idaka, the dentist starts playing this fantasia whenever he meets someone for the first time. If people argue against him, saying that there couldn't possibly be anyone living for many hundreds of years, he closes his heart to them, and they end up missing an opportunity to access the rich Mexican experiences that Dr Ogita has accumulated.

During his life of almost fifty years in Mexico, he lost his wife. In order to support his solitary life, he must have built a bridge of dreams in his imagination that connected Japan and Mexico. I really enjoyed that conversation.

Reviving Ame no Uzume as a moniker today probably arises from a similar way of thinking. We hardly ever hear Amaterasu or Ninigi used as nicknames today, probably out of a subconscious fear of showing irreverence towards the imperial family, though this may change in the future. In fact, perhaps Susano'o, Tajikarao, Ame no Uzume, Sarutahiko and other figures who are distanced from orthodox rulers are likely to appear as monikers in the future.

During the 120 years from the Meiji (1868–1912) through to Taishō (1912–1926) and then Shōwa (1926–1989) periods, municipal officers in charge of birth registrations in Japan advised everyone to avoid the names of emperors, empresses, and crown princes and princesses for their newborn babies. I have never met any parent who dared persist in their will to flout this request.

If we were to nickname some people Ame no Uzume, not in comparison with the goddess herself but according to the narratives about her, what characteristics would we consider as Ame no Uzume-like?

A Genealogy of Likening

1. First of all, they are not beautiful, but are charming.[11]

2. They do not care about their appearance. They move without inhibition and are not concerned about respectability.

3. They invite and encourage people to enjoy the party/company.

4. They are full of vitality, which brings out the life force in others.

5. They make people laugh and relieve anxiety. They will even tell a lie to reassure others.

6. They do not shy away from obscenity. They play a role that goes beyond sexual repression.

7. They do not mind if an outsider joins the company; they are open-minded and do not find it necessary to guard themselves closely. They would never call someone a spy, for example, and incite others to punch that person.

People with these abilities are qualified to be called Ame no Uzume.

Regarding the characteristic of not being beautiful, we need to consider the definition of 'beauty', which of course changes over time. For a long time in Japan, beauty has been a referent to facial features. Each period has had its own orthodox physiognomic standards, and those who fit those standards are regarded as beautiful. Such beauties therefore do not hold the power to change their features dramatically at a whim. That is, frequently changing features is not considered suitable in the maintenance of beauty. Moreover, those whose facial expressions change in accordance with their body movements are not beauties, and such changes and movements are indeed characteristic of Ame no Uzume.

I once saw a photograph in a weekly magazine of the winner of a Gurning contest, which are apparently held annually in the UK. The photograph showed the first prize winner, a pub owner, with his face all squashed up, his false teeth removed, and his eyes wide open.

---

11 The plural 'they' is used here to indicate the existence of numerous Uzume-like people.

Chapter 2

Surely Amaterasu could never have performed the art of squashing up her own face like this. But Ame no Uzume could; in fact, we can define her as someone who is capable of contorting her own face in all manner of ways. One moment she may squash herself flat against the wall like a rubber ball, and the next she bounces back to her round self. This instantaneous art form creates many illusions.

There is an eighth characteristic of Ame no Uzume not listed above—that is, the act of exposing her private parts. The combined expression of her face and her private parts form a creative power, which accompanies an illusion that makes it seem as though she has two faces.

In *Problems of Art* (1957),[12] Susanne K. Langer argues that in dance, more than in any other art form, illusion plays an important role. The expression is not created by the body movement itself, she argues, but by the illusion created by the body movement that is left behind.

We can apply this to Ame no Uzume, whose exposed private parts themselves do not constitute the creative force; rather, when her private parts are combined with her face, they amalgamate into another face. She is able to create this illusion both with a group, and as an individual.

In today's world, are there sites where we can see such illusions at work? Expressions of sexuality are less restricted in television, videos, weekly magazines and graphic magazines than ever before. Through these media, contemporary Ame no Uzume can perform far more freely than before the war. However, this simply means that expressive forms verging close to complete genital exposure have become commonplace today; these expressions hardly function like Ame no Uzume's did, in the way that she brought the Sun Goddess out of the cave and illuminated the world through her holistic performance.

However, I do recognise sites of Ame no Uzume activity during wartime, in the penis stones and vagina stones folklorist Nakazawa Atsushi (1914–1982) encountered in the mountains of Kōshū (present-day Yamanashi prefecture). Nakazawa, then still in his twenties, turned his back on the nationalist cry of the 'Greater East Asia War'

---

[12] This work is a collection of 10 philosophical lectures on various aspects of creativity, including expressiveness, artistic perception, imitation and transformation.

and spent his free time walking among the mountains in search of *dōsojin* (travellers' guardian deities).[13]

Phallus stones are round stones to commemorate Sarutahiko, who, according to mythological accounts, welcomed and guided Amaterasu's grandson, whereas vagina stones can be regarded as representing his partner Ame no Uzume.

In 1943, in Furuhase, Nakatomi-chō, Minamikoma-gun, in Yamanashi prefecture, a festival to pay respect to traveller deities was held a month later than usual. The locals cooked rice cakes specially for this festival to offer to the deities, in the form of a phallus of fifty centimetres and a vagina of forty centimetres. After the festival the villagers cut the rice cakes into pieces and ate them! (See Nakazawa 1988.)

---

13 In a cabinet decision on 10 December 1941, the Japanese government chose the term 'Greater East Asia War' to refer to the conflicts both with the Western Allies and with China.

Chapter 3
A Light in the Dark Night

In this chapter, Tsurumi begins by exploring evolving notions of beauty through the juxtaposition of Taishō period bromides of film stars with the common-looking characters Okame and Hyottoko featured in *kagura* shrine dances. He then highlights how the advent of television prompted Hollywood producers to introduce more 'accessible' roles such as the Funny Face character, which in Japan reminded viewers of Ame no Uzume. Tsurumi argues that unlike the gossipy middle-aged Obatarian women, who always chase the latest scandals, Funny Face characters such as Ame no Uzume 'warmly' participate in gossip by filtering out narrative details that could adversely affect their subjects. He ends the chapter by reiterating Ame no Uzume's great ability to change a dark or depressed mood into one of joyful celebration.

There is a Shinto shrine called Sakurada Jinja on the street connecting the house where I was born to the main street where the trams run. It is now hard to see the shrine from the main street, but in my childhood sometimes I could see performances of *kagura* (sacred Shinto music and dancing).[1] In my elementary school days, if there was a performance on as I walked home from school, I would stop and watch it for a while.

Many of these performances featured Okame and Hyottoko dancing together.[2] Hyottoko is not a handsome man, and neither is

---

1 See Chapter 1, note 9.
2 Okame (阿亀, tortoise) and Hyottoko (火男, literally 'fire man') are comical Japanese characters, portrayed using characteristic masks. The Okame mask features a woman with a short nose and plump cheeks, while the Hyottoko mask typically features a male with mismatched eyes whose puckered mouth skews to one side.

Chapter 3

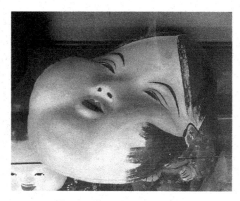

Figure 3.1: Okame mask   **Figure 3.2:** Hyottoko mask
Source: Caito / PIXTA.

Okame a beautiful woman. Even a child could plainly see that they are not known for their looks.

In those days, film star 'bromides' (photographs) were very popular and functioned as standard measures of beauty.[3] That is, we thought we could gauge how good-looking someone was by how closely their face resembled those stars. To me, as a primary school pupil, the benchmark of a beautiful woman was Kawasaki Hiroko (1912–1976),[4] while the male standard was perhaps Ichikawa Utaemon (1907–1999).[5] I wonder when I gave up on this way of measuring beauty.

In any case, even though Hyottoko and Okame are far from good-looking, I must have found them interesting as I stood watching their dance for twenty or thirty minutes. They didn't include obscene gestures, but I gradually understood that Hyottoko's face signified the male genitals, and Okame's the female sexual organ.

---

3 The *buromaido* (ブロマイド, bromide) is a genre of commercial photographic portraits in Japan featuring actors and actresses of film and the stage, as well as sports stars. The term derives from a type of photographic printing paper which is coated in an emulsion of silver bromide. Images are printed on the bromide paper by way of the gelatin-silver process.

4 Kawasaki was a Japanese actress whose career began in 1929. Famous for her portrayals of melancholic heroines, she temporarily retired in 1947 for health reasons, before retiring permanently in 1958.

5 Ichikawa Utaemon was a Japanese actor who was particularly famous for starring in *jidaigeki* (時代劇, period dramas). Initially trained in kabuki, he made his film debut in 1925, and subsequently appeared in over 300 films throughout the course of his career.

A Light in the Dark Night

Figure 3.3: Kawasaki Hiroko
Source: Image courtesy of Jim Clinefelter/
Littlefields Photography Magazine.

Figure 3.4: Ichikawa Utaemon

Once when I went to a friend's house there happened to be a festival on in the neighbourhood, so we decided to go to a nearby shrine, where a street performer was shaking something that looked like a magnet to make dolls on the ground dance. He came over to where my friend (in grade three) was squatting, and chanted, 'Daaance, dance'. Startled, my friend promptly closed his thighs. I think he was terrified of the thought that his private parts might start to dance in front of everyone, controlled by the magnet. On my way home, alone, I was plagued by fears that the magnet might come and find me as well.

According to anthropologist Nomura Masaichi (1942–2017), who specialises in gestures and body language, the early Shōwa Japan of his childhood was still linked to South-East Asia in terms of clothing.[6] At that time, in spring, summer and autumn, the custom of stripping oneself to the waist was still common (Nomura 1983). Earlier, in

---

6 As the Shōwa period spans from 1926 to 1989, Nomura's birth in 1942 places his early childhood in mid-Shōwa rather than early Shōwa as Tsurumi suggests.

Chapter 3

Meiji and Taishō, it was nothing unusual to reveal the upper half of the body and the thighs, not only inside homes but also in public spaces such as train and tram carriages, as well as on the street. Even complete nudity was not that unusual. At company parties people often danced with faces drawn on their stomachs, making their whole bodies into faces. These sorts of customs and body language were still commonly seen in Japanese society. At the same time, the North European and North American custom of revealing only the face to communicate one's intentions was introduced via the upper stratum of society, creating within Japan a conflict with the more traditional communication styles that used the whole body.

One of the games played on New Year's Day in Japan is called *Fuku-warai* (literally, 'the lucky laugh of Otafuku'). A blind-folded child places cut-outs of facial features—eyebrows, eyes, a nose and a mouth—on a sheet of paper that contains the outline of Otafuku's face. Often the child places the cut-outs outside the outline, completely distorting the facial representation. But however disfigured, it is a game that is heartily enjoyed by onlookers who regard the face as a happy one. This makes the game eminently suited to New Year's celebrations.

This Otafuku was used interchangeably with Okame.[7] Their faces may lie outside the norms of beauty, but they make people happy, eliciting smiles and laughter.

I don't know any details about the *kagura* performed at the imperial court by the descendant of Ame no Uzume called Sarume. Parallel to this imperial *kagura*, though, was a commoners' version called *sato kagura*, which included a dance by Okame, who also belonged to the lineage of Ame no Uzume. Far from the standard criteria of film and bromide beauties, the Okame/Otafuku character who appears as the protagonist of *kagura* performances at shrines is an ordinary type of person who works alongside us in our daily lives. There used to be a common expression of humility, 'I'm only an Otafuku', which was not a derogatory expression for being an ugly woman so much as an advocacy of oneself as a companion with an accessible personality and an ability to enjoy life with a partner. At that time, there was still an ethos of being on the alert for any beauties who might force themselves into our everyday lives.

---

7 For Okame, see footnote 2, above.

A Light in the Dark Night

Figure 3.5: *Hannya* mask
Source: Tokyo National Museum.

Otafuku/Okame is clearly different from the hateful *shikome* (ugly woman) character. Similarly, the mask of the *hannya* (female demon) represents a woman crazed by jealousy who is determined to seek revenge on any man who betrays her.[8] The Okame/Otafuku character would never reach such a state of frenzy.

She is also poles apart from the legendary demoness at Adachigahara,[9] O-Iwa from the *Ghost Story of Yotsuya*,[10] and in contemporary manga, the dreaded wife, Onibaba (literally, 'Demon Hag') who appears in Furuya Mitsutoshi's *Dame Oyaji* (literally, 'No-Good Dad', 1970–1982).[11] A prototype of a terrifying demonic woman also appears in Hotta Katsuhiko's manga, *Obatarian* (1988–1998), which follows a narrative of men finding it unbearable to be under constant pressure from middle-aged women.[12]

---

8 The *hannya* (般若) mask is characterised by two bull-like horns and a leering mouth, and is used to represent the soul of a woman so crazed by jealousy and vengefulness that she is transformed into a demon.

9 This cannibalistic demoness was said to haunt a large plain known as Adachigahara in the guise of an old woman. According to legend, a Buddhist monk killed her, and in some versions, her spirit then found peace through the guidance of the Buddha.

10 *Yotsuya kaidan* (四谷怪談, Ghost Story of Yotsuya, 1925) began as a kabuki play, and was later adapted to numerous films in the 20th century. It tells the story of a betrayed woman, O-Iwa, who returns as a ghost to avenge her murder on her former husband and his new bride.

11 *Dame Oyaji* (ダメおやじ) is a manga about an unlucky office worker who is tormented by Onibaba, his tyrannical and abusive wife.

12 *Obatarian* is a manga that satirises common, insensitive and occasionally criminally-minded middle-aged women. Its title is a portmanteau of the two words *obasan* (middle-aged woman) and *batarion* (battalion), the Japanese title of the 1985 American comedy-horror film *The Return of the Living Dead*.

Chapter 3

Figure 3.6: Utagawa Kuniyoshi, *Adachigahara hitotsuya no zu* (The Lonely House on Adachi Moor, 1856)
Source: The Trustees of the British Museum, released as CC BY-NC-SA 4.0.

Figure 3.7: Shunbaisai Hokuei's image of O-Iwa emerging from the lantern (1832)

Figure 3.8: *Dame Oyaji*
Source: Furuya (2017: Cover).

Figure 3.9: *Obatarian*
Source: Hotta (1988: Cover).

Since the advent of television, TV dramas have had quite an impact on movies shown in cinemas. It didn't seem quite right to let prototypical beauties into our living rooms every week, or in some cases, every day. Over time, stars who looked accessible—like a friend or a member of the family—began to increase in popularity. Moreover, beauties don't fit well within the model of airing commercials every fifteen minutes. If they do appear in commercials, those who are able to break away from the stereotypical beauty role and make viewers relax are the ones who prevail.

Another change since the growth of the television viewing audience is that the 'Funny Face' character often plays the role of the central protagonist in films.[13] Although this trend came from the studios of Hollywood, it was also a revival of the indigenous Japanese Ame no Uzume characterisation.

What, then, is the difference between the 'Funny Face' and Obatarian characters?

First of all, there's an age difference between the two, which also affects their clothing. Their topics aren't different, however. The Obatarian talks mostly about gossip, which I guess may also apply to the Funny Face character. At the end of the third volume of *Obatarian* (Hotta 1989), there is an appendix titled 'Obatarian qualification test'. If anyone answers twenty or more of the twenty-five questions correctly, she is regarded as a fully qualified Obatarian. For example,

> Q11: What is the first film that featured Yamaguchi Momoe and Miura Tomokazu together?[14]

> Q12: What is the name of Gō Hiromi's father-in-law?[15]

---

13 The term 'Funny Face' here does not refer to the title of the 1957 American film, but is used as a generic term for those who are not typically beautiful, but whose very imperfections give their faces a unique, attractive quality.

14 Yamaguchi Momoe (b. 1959) is a Japanese former singer, actor and idol whose career began in 1972 with an appearance on a talent show. She retired in 1980 at the age of 21 to marry Miura Tomokazu. Miura Tomokazu (b. 1952) is a Japanese actor who became famous for starring as Yamaguchi Momoe's romantic partner in multiple films and television series throughout the 1970s.

15 Gō Hiromi (b. 1955) is a Japanese singer whose career began in 1971. His provocative performance style earned him a large female fan base. From 1987 to 1998, Gō was married to Nitani Yurie, daughter of the actor Nitani Hideaki (1930–2012).

Chapter 3

Q13: What is the name of Gō Hiromi's first daughter?

Q14: How many children does Chiyonofuji have?[16]

The questions go on. Surely the Funny Face would be able to answer these questions too, but the Obatarian is probably better with gossip about older celebrities.

The Obatarian also likes young stars, especially men, and she is familiar with the details of their private lives. Since she has a richer experience of life, her interest in gossip is somewhat more future-oriented than in the case of the Funny Face. Suppose a popular singer announces on stage:

'I'm getting married.'

'Noooo!'

'You can't!!'

'Hiroshiii!'

Even though the young female fans scream, the Obatarians are unmoved and continue eating their Koma Theatre bento.[17] They stop momentarily to talk to each other.

'Oh, well, they can't do anything about that.'

'Exactly. As his fans, they should be happy for him!'

However, when the star continues with 'I'd like to return what you've given me by becoming happy', the two Obatarians suddenly get annoyed and look at each other:

'What is he talking about!?'

'I know! Surely, if he's so grateful, he'll return the favour by being unfaithful and having an illegitimate child and getting a divorce, so that he's always in our magazines.'

---

16 Chiyonofuji Mitsugu (1955–2016) was a Japanese sumo wrestler whose professional career lasted 21 years. In 1981, he became the 58th *yokozuna* (横綱, the highest title in professional sumo wrestling, literally meaning 'horizontal rope'), a title that he held until his retirement in 1991.

17 The Shinjuku Koma Gekijō (新宿コマ劇場, Shinjuku Koma Theatre) was a major theatre in Kabukichō, Shinjuku, Tokyo. It opened in 1956 and closed in 2008.

Younger would-be Obatarians and incumbent Obatarians may take similar attitudes towards gossip, but the ones with Ame no Uzume's disposition will deal with gossip, especially about their neighbours, in a different manner.

Among people we know, there are some who like gossiping but systematically filter out those stories that could affect the fate of the person in question. These people are trusted, and hence more and more important rumours come their way. What they do doesn't aggravate the wounds of those who are gossiped about, but helps with the healing process, especially in the form of natural healing.

Their behaviour regarding gossip contains something calm, and also something immense.

Oliver Wendell Holmes Jr. (1841–1935), who was a justice of the Supreme Court of the United States in the early twentieth century, said that gossip and philosophy derive from the same materials of everyday life. The difference, according to him, lies in the depth of the view that perceives and processes those materials.

That is, those who view the life of people around them with cold observing eyes are called moralists (i.e. observers of human beings, that is, a kind of philosopher). By contrast, characters such as Funny Face and Ame no Uzume participate in gossip with a sense of warmth. In doing so, what is at work is the ability to select certain information—an ability which is absent in Obatarians (but present in moralists).

A mother who gathers rumours in the neighbourhood like a parabolic reflector before retelling them warmly is an Ame no Uzume. A wife who happily retells the rumour her child has brought home to her late-working husband is an Ame no Uzume. In a way that is so different from the grand goddess Amaterasu, who stands behind heads of state playing the role of one who adds a sense of dignity to the government's policies (though we do not see her figure as often as before the war these days), Ame no Uzume is a goddess who can alight on any small family, any modest party of friends, and redefine the world.

When I open the *Kojiki* again, however, I must admit that there are things that do not support my argument here.

When Ame no Uzume went to the seaside to see off Sarutahiko, she rounded up sea creatures great and small and said,

'You will serve the Heavenly God's child, won't you?'

Chapter 3

Figure 3.10:
Ame no Uzume and sea slug in Kōno Fumiyo's *Bōrupen Kojiki*, vol. 3, p. 32

While the other fishes said 'I will', there was one that kept silent. It was a sea slug. Irritated, Ame no Uzume cried 'There is a mouth that doesn't answer!', and with the knife she had on her belt, she slit open its mouth.

They say this is why the mouth of the sea slug is slit.

This episode seems to tell us that with the authority of the rulers behind her, Ame no Uzume had a side that bullied subordinates. In any case, thanks to this sort of propagandistic work, her clan was highly respected and it became customary that the Sarume no Kimi clan, descended from Ame no Uzume, receives the offerings of the first produce of the season from around the Ise region on behalf of the court.[18]

The vocation of the Sarume no Kimi clan is dance; it is probably because of this vocational path that they have emphasised the loyal aspect of their ancestor, Ame no Uzume.

Kogo shūi (807) is a record compiled by the Inbe clan, motivated by its belief that it deserved a better position and treatment.[19] It narrates the court's legends from the viewpoint of the clan. The Inbes seem to have had been on good terms with the Sarumes as there are favourable descriptions of Sarume no Kimi in the narrative. Similarly,

---

18 The Sarume no Kimi (猿女君) clan claimed descent from Ame no Uzume through Sarutahiko Ōkami, the leader of the earthly *kami*. Both the *kagura* and noh forms of dance originated with this clan.

19 *Kogo shūi* (古語拾遺) is an historical record that Inbe no Hironari compiled from orally transmitted material and presented to Emperor Heizei in 807.

Ame no Uzume is depicted as a capable figure called Ame no Osume, which is said to be the origin of the term '*osushi*', used to refer to a strong woman.[20] According to this text, it was Ame no Osume who wore a wreath of evergreen vine on her head and bound up her sleeves with a length of *hikage* vine. With a bunch of dwarf bamboo leaves in one hand and an iron halberd in the other, she struck an empty bucket placed upside down, in front of the rock-cave door. There she performed, singing and dancing in the light of a brightly-burning fire.

Amaterasu assumed that without her the world would be blanketed in complete darkness, but when she heard the revelry of the deities, she wondered what was happening, and opened the door a fraction to take a look. Then Ame no Tajikarao pulled the door wide open and led her to the seat of honour.

> At this moment the Heavens cleared; as everyone looked around at each other, their faces had taken on a bright white cast. Stretching out their hands, they sang and danced, unanimously chanting,
>
> *Ahare / ana omoshiro, / ana tanoshi, ana sayake, / oke.*
>
> (Yasuda and Akimoto eds. 1976: 45)

Ahare apparently signifies what Amaterasu uttered as she came out of the cave and found the sky clear and bright (*hare*).

Ana is an exclamation from the heart; everyone says it together. *Omoshiro* means that as Amaterasu emerged, the face (*omo*) of every deity looked bright (*shiro*, white).

Tanoshi signifies stretching one's hands out (*ta noshi*) to dance. This is the etymology of today's *tanoshii*, meaning 'merriment' and 'pleasure'.

Sayake comes from the onomatopoeia of rustling dwarf bamboo leaves in the hands of the gods (*sayasaya*), signifying 'purity' and 'clarity'.

---

20 *Osushi* (於須志) is derived from Ame no Uzume's alternate name Ame no Osume (天乃於須女). Her characteristic ferocity and strength are the reasons why the term *osushi* is commonly used to refer to a strong woman.

Chapter 3

All these lines except the last one are part of the song. *Oke*, however, signifies the end of the song, delivered at the same time as the pail (*oke*) is struck with the iron halberd.

In this way, the deep depressed mood changes to one of happy excitement, ending with a great chorus. Ame no Uzume, who brought about this transformation, is like a depressed baseball team's trusty catcher who can cheer up everyone after a bout of disappointments and help restore their enthusiasm.

§

When walking through a dark forest, you and your companions may feel as if an enemy or some sort of beast is about to jump out and attack you. If you listen carefully, suddenly it becomes clear that the noise you can hear is only the sound of leaves rustling in the wind, which is such a relief that everyone laughs out loud. There may also be times when sex jokes that have been suppressed suddenly come out, relieving everyone's tension and bringing a feeling of liberation.

Towards the end of the war, around May 1945, in a large room of the Imperial Navy's General Staff Office then located in Hiyoshi (Kanagawa prefecture), I was once asked:

'I think we're going to lose this war. What do you think, Tsurumi-san?'

The voice was so loud that it was audible in every corner of the room. I became flustered. The person who posed the question was over fifty years old, and the type that didn't get beaten up, because he was good at telling dirty stories.

One of his favourite stories was this: when the ship he was on was wrecked (he had actually worked on merchant ships for a long time, as chief of communications), the crew climbed into a lifeboat and rowed with all their might. After a while, however, no matter how hard they rowed, the boat would not move, and they felt trapped in a thick, soft darkness. Unwittingly, they had sailed into the private parts of a whale.

Stories like this, which made the war seem far away, brought momentary relief to the General Staff Office, where we were translating oppressive news day in, day out. This is how he, Muratani Sōhei, constantly avoided a beating. Mr Muratani had a terrible stutter,

A Light in the Dark Night

which magnified his sincerity and humour, and allowed him some freedom even in the environment of the wartime military.

Since he talked loudly about such things even at the General Staff Office, there can be no doubt that before that, while he was at home as a civilian, he must have been the target of criticism by his children. No doubt he was reproached at the dinner table:

'That's so unpatriotic, Dad!'

At the time, his daughter had not yet reached the stage of respecting her father. After the emperor's radio broadcast about the defeat, she rushed to the square outside the Imperial Palace, kneeled on the gravel, and apologised for the insufficiency of her own efforts. Undeterred by the media's sudden change of attitude to condemnation of the war, she continued to visit the forgotten wounded soldiers, volunteering to wash their bandages and so on.

This young woman then joined the Japanese Communist Party because of her deep sense of justice. Her father did not approve of this decision and told her that she shouldn't be involved in radical activities while she wasn't self-sufficient. To the daughter who was so passionately committed to justice, her father's liberalism appeared half-hearted. Soon she left home, earned a living, got married, and, after several painful experiences of factional conflict, left the Party. It was probably around this time that she began to appreciate her father's thinking. Thereafter her political activities focused on protest against crimes committed by the authorities, such as the Matsukawa derailment incident.[21]

I only encountered her literary works well after these times, and even then I was unaware for a long time that she was a daughter of Muratani Sōhei whom I met during the war.

Her name is Okkotsu Yoshiko (1929–1980). She was involved in a children's literature magazine named *Kodama* (Echo), and published

---

21 On 17 August 1949, a Tōhoku Main Line passenger train derailed and overturned as it was travelling between Kanayagawa and Matsukawa stations in Fukushima prefecture. Three crew members were killed. The incident was one of three that the Japanese government blamed on the Japanese Communist Party and the Japan National Railway Union. Ten workers from the Matsukawa plant and 10 workers from the Japan National Railway were charged, and all 20 were found guilty in the first court ruling on 6 December 1950. The issue continued to be debated over the next decade and new evidence emerged, even reaching the Supreme Court of Japan in 1959. All defendants were finally found innocent in an 8 August 1961 retrial at the Sendai High Court and were awarded compensation in 1970.

Chapter 3

stories such as *Piichaashan* (Beacon Hill, 1964),[22] *Hachigatsu no taiyō o* (The Sun in August, 1966), and *Jūsansai no natsu* (The Summer of a Thirteen Year Old, 1974). Her late work, *Aikotoba wa tebukuro no katappo* (The Password is One Glove, 1978) is an imagined portrait of her father as a young man.

Ms Okkotsu suffered from bone cancer and after a long battle she passed away. Before her death, her father went into her oxygen tent and talked about all kinds of happy memories. At the darkest time of life, any effort to brighten those hours is never in vain. The above scene reminds us of the words from the Indian scripture, *Mahabharata*: 'Death ends death, and hence it is nothing to fear'.

Okkotsu Yoshiko could not complete her final novel, *Piramiddo bōshi yo, sayōnara* (Good-bye, Pyramid Hat, 1980), which, for the first time in her work, shows experimental steps towards surrealism.

What I see in Ame no Uzume is not just the power of the female sexual organ. Just like Uzume, Ms Okkotsu's father, Muratani Sōhei, was a person who created a warm, bright place around him in the darkest days of my life. Such a role is not confined to women.

---

22 *Piichaashan* is set during World War II, and tells the story of the friendship between Takashi, a young Japanese signalman, and Ien Yui, a Chinese interpreter. Through their friendship, Takashi learns of how the Japanese military is selling heroin to Chinese people, and the terrible consequences that this has. In 1965, *Piichaashan* received a special recommendation award from the Ministry of Health, Labour and Welfare Child Welfare Council.

Chapter 4
Laughter and Politics

At the start of this chapter, Tsurumi highlights Ame no Uzume's extraordinary talent to elicit laughter in difficult circumstances by comparing her interactions with Amaterasu to another mythological narrative involving Izanagi and Izanami that does not end so well. Laughter, Tsurumi argues, should be an implicit part of political encounters, along with the freedom to express dissenting views. He highlights the contradiction in the Meiji state's use of ancient Japanese mythology to justify both its own authenticity and the emperor's infallibility. He also points out that this did not align with the way that the combination of laughter and politics, as well as frank descriptions of mistakes made by those in power, are intrinsic to those same mythological narratives.

A powerful sovereign's rule, along with their dignified death, form the main themes of ancient epics. Even if the sovereign is later overthrown and replaced by an assassin, the majestic tone of the epic remains unchanged.

However, the great history of Amaterasu, which predated imperial governance, contains a different nuance of majesty: it includes her hiding in the cave, sulking at her brother's violent behaviour, and then her re-emergence, lured by Ame no Uzume's dance and the myriad deities' roars of laughter.

The sight of a revolving stage run by laughter prompts us to think about the relationship between laughter and politics.[1]

---

1 Revolving stages, or turntables, were developed in 18th century Japan to facilitate sudden scene changes and creative entrances and exits. They were introduced into Western theatre in the late 19th century. Here, Tsurumi uses the revolving stage as a metaphor to highlight the sudden changes of scene and mood in the *Kojiki*.

Chapter 4

Figure 4.1:
Izanami by Kosugi Hōan
(part of his *Kojiki hachidai*
[The Legendary Stories of
Old Japan, 1941])
Source: Idemitsu Museum of Arts.

In *Nihon shinwa no tokushoku* (The Characteristics of Japanese Mythology, 1989: 202), Yoshida Atsuhiko writes that there is a precedent for efforts to call back a goddess who has left this world, although it fails badly. This refers to the case of Izanagi, who visits his deceased wife Izanami in the Underworld (Yomi no kuni), only to flee after seeing her ugly state. The case of Amaterasu and Ame no Uzume presents a stark contrast to this failed precedent: the key to their success was to change the situation through laughter.[2]

The art exhibition of Kosugi Hōan mentioned in Chapter 1 included an image depicting the sorrow of Izanami, who leans against a rock and stares at her husband as he runs away.[3] The image highlights the figure of the wife who is left to carry alone the burden of childbirth, miscarriage and the death of another baby in her care. Her circumstances could not be represented by Ame no Uzume's dance.

I have always been sceptical about the 'loud and prolonged applause' noted after a speech. Actually, seeing such a note after Stalin's speech made me have reservations about his administration.[4]

---

2 Using Lévi-Strauss's notion of 'symmetric and inverse', and referring to earlier studies of Ōbayashi Tarō, Yoshida discusses the 'symmetrical and inverse' relationships between the Izanami-Izanagi episode and the Amaterasu-Ame no Uzume episode (1989: 192–209).

3 Kosugi Hōan, *Kojiki hachidai* (The Legendary Stories of Old Japan), dated 1941, Album, conté on paper, Idemitsu Museum of Arts. The image is included in Idemitsu (2015: 102).

4 Tsurumi refers here to a speech such as the one delivered by Stalin at a Meeting of Voters of the Stalin Electoral District, Moscow, on 9 February 1946. The speech notes read: '(A voice: "Under Comrade Stalin's leadership!" All rise. Loud and prolonged applause, rising to an ovation)'.

I also have reservations about unanimous agreement because I think we should all be able to express our opinions without having to hide any doubts or criticisms we may have. That is, ideally, before deciding by a majority vote, those who hold opposing views should express their opinions freely and openly. For the same reason, it is an important condition that laughter is never suppressed in collaborative scenes involving politics.

Ame no Uzume's dance is central to the court ritual of appeasing the spirit of the dead. Apparently, it is detailed in a book of annual rituals compiled during the Heian period (794–1185). As historian Inoue Mitsusada (1965: 59) describes it, Shinto shrine maidens (*mikannagi*) of the court present deities to the chief shrine officer while a lady-in-waiting brings the emperor's clothes in a box. The *kagura* begins and the shrine maidens dance. The principal dancer steps up on an inverted pail and strikes it with a mallet. For every ten strikes, the chief shrine officer ties a knot in a cotton ribbon. After this, the maidens and Sarume no Kimi dance. Sarume no Kimi belongs to the clan descended from Ame no Uzume.

According to the *Gleanings*, this ritual of appeasing the spirit of the dead was originally handed down by Sarume no Kimi. The dance calls back the spirit. It is the spirit of Toyohirume, who reminds us of Ōhirume no Muchi—that is, Amaterasu Ōmikami. The purpose of this ritual is to stimulate the weakened power of the sun. Given that the festival takes place in November in the lunar calendar, the folklorist Orikuchi Shinobu (1887–1953) regarded it as a rite associated with the winter solstice.[5]

A total eclipse of the sun may seem to match the lore of Amaterasu's hiding in the Heavenly Cave, but Inoue (1965) finds Orikuchi's approach of viewing it as a festival of the winter solstice when the light of the sun is at its lowest intensity a more interesting theory.

> Why, then, is calling back the spirit of the emperor linked to hoping for the regeneration of the sun? It is because [...] the sun and the Founding Deity of the Imperial Family were regarded as one and the

---

5 Orikuchi was also an ethnologist, linguist, novelist and poet. His novel, *Shisha no sho* (translated by Jeffrey Angles as *The Book of the Dead*) and his poems written under the name of Shaku Chōkū are highly acclaimed. His research covers diverse topics including the history of the performing arts and Japanese literature.

Chapter 4

same. At the winter solstice, the light of the sun is at its weakest; in a world where the sun was unified with the Imperial Founder, this meant that the ancestral spirits were leaving the emperor. Therefore, among the rites of the winter solstice, they prayed for the restoration of the sun, and for the return of the spirit of the Sun Goddess. The essence of the festival was thus to raise the power of the sun as well as the spirit of the emperor. (Inoue, 1965: 60–61)

Among the songs sung at this festival was the following:

Horimasu Toyohirume ga mitama hosu (I pray for Toyohirume's spirit high above)

Moto wa kanahoko sue wa kihoko (Originally a metal halberd, now a wooden halberd)

Inimashishi kami wa ima zo kimaseru (The deity who passed away returns now)

Tamahako mochite saritaru mitama (Let us hold the spirit box with the spirit that once left us)

Tama kashi su na ya (Never let it go again)

(Inoue, 1965: 60)

If we consider the legend of the Sun Goddess hiding in the cave to be a winter solstice festival, it can also be found in present-day Japan in the form of *onbe warai* ('burning of talismans and laughing'), which is a traditional festival held in the Kita-Azumi district of Nagano prefecture on the fifteenth night of the new year according to the lunar calendar. In fact, this type of ritual is performed not just in Japan: there are similar ones in California as well as in Assam, India. As for Ame no Uzume, it suits her open-mindedness to think that characters like her were active in various locations. Surely there have been innumerable Ame no Uzumes across the world!

§

In his book *Reflections on Violence* (1908), French philosopher Georges Sorel (1847–1922) discussed two states of the masses: Scylla and Charybdis, named after the monsters of the same names in Greek mythology.[6] Charybdis signifies a state in which the frenzied masses demand justice, denying the present completely for the sake of the future. Scylla, on the other hand, represents a state of apathy that lets the rulers do whatever they like. Needless to say, Sorel's aim was to seek an alternative way, avoiding both of these states. However, the two models of Charybdis (a bloodthirsty and frenzied state seeking cruel judgements) and Scylla (a disenchanted and apathetic state) are thought-provoking when we think about them in terms of human nature.

The state of mass frenzy incited by Ame no Uzume's stage appearance differs in type from both Scylla and Charybdis. What makes the difference is laughter. Because there is laughter in the scene, the deities maintain a flexibility that allows changes in their states towards their indefinite futures.

Mikhail Bakhtin (1895–1975) lived in the Soviet Union and continued to produce treatises even under Stalin's rule.[7] *Rabelais and Folk Culture of the Middle Ages and Renaissance* (1965)[8] analyses the French folk culture of the Middle Ages and the Renaissance that form the basis of Rabelais's works. Through these analyses, Bakhtin indirectly expresses criticism of his contemporary Russia. In this sense, his work offers a prototype unrestrained by temporal or spatial limitations.

According to Bakhtin, carnivals in the Middle Ages in Europe developed over many centuries. Their origins lie in ancient comic rituals (including agrarian festivals) dating back thousands of years. He sees the laughter in carnival as having the following characteristics:

> It is, first of all, a festive laughter. Therefore it is not an individual reaction to some isolated 'comic' event. Carnival laughter is the

---

6 Scylla and Charybdis are mythical sea monsters situated on opposite sides of what scholars generally agree is the Strait of Messina. Since their first mention in Homer's *Odyssey*, the phrase 'between Scylla and Charybdis' has become an idiom for choosing between equally dangerous extremes. In *Reflections on Violence*, an exploration of class struggle, revolution and the role that working class violence plays in contemporary socialism, Sorel uses the Scylla and Charybdis analogy to argue that humanity is perpetually menaced by the competing dangers of weariness/decadence (Scylla) and the despotism of fanatical theorists (Charybdis).

7 Bakhtin was a Russian philosopher, literary critic and scholar whose works inspired other scholars from traditions and disciplines as diverse as Marxism, religious criticism, semiotics, sociology, anthropology and psychology.

8 The English translation by Hélène Iswolsky is published as *Rabelais and His World* (1968); the Japanese translation is by Kawabata Kaori (1973).

laughter of all the people. Second, it is universal in scope; it is directed at all and everyone, including the carnival's participants. The entire world is seen in its droll aspect, in its gay relativity. Third, this laughter is ambivalent: it is gay, triumphant, and at the same time mocking, deriding. It asserts and denies, it buries and revives. Such is the laughter of carnival. (Bakhtin, trans. Iswolsky 1984: 11–12)

According to artist/poet Iida Yoshikuni (1923–2006), the English artist Henry Moore (1893–1986) said that he created his sculptures from forms that he captured from voids.[9] Carnival contains a similar creative experience, where the root buried underground becomes suddenly visible above the ground as a form. The people's whole lives, which are normally governed by politics rather than by the legal system or by various kinds of documents, are now inverted and put on the stage. Unlike a lynching or the ritual of the guillotine, however, in the carnival the people themselves can also become the butt of the laughter.

> Let us enlarge upon the second important trait of the people's festive laughter: that it is also directed at those who laugh. The people do not exclude themselves from the wholeness of the world. They, too, are incomplete, they also die and are revived and renewed. This is one of the essential differences of the people's festive laughter from the pure satire of modern times. The satirist whose laughter is negative places himself above the object of his mockery, he is opposed to it. The wholeness of the world's comic aspect is destroyed, and that which appears comic becomes a private reaction. The people's ambivalent laughter, on the other hand, expresses the point of view of the whole world; he who is laughing also belongs to it. (Bakhtin, trans. Iswolsky 1984: 12)

According to Bakhtin, this laughter in the Mediaeval and Renaissance carnival still retained the ancient rituals of mocking the deity.

---

9 Iida moved from Japan to Europe in 1956 to study painting, but shifted to sculpture after being deeply influenced by an exhibition of Moore's work in Munich. He returned to Japan in 1967.

In his examination of the differences between the *Kojiki* and *Nihon shoki*, Inoue has noted that even though both mention Ame no Uzume's dance, the scene is absent in three of the extant variants of *Nihon shoki*. Refuting the general theory that the parts common to each indicate the original version, Inoue, following the view of mythologist Matsumura Takeo (1883–1969),[10] determines that Ame no Uzume's dance was omitted once it was regarded as 'mere obscenity':

> I find Matsumura's theory convincing as the clan of Sarume no Kimi originating in Ame no Uzume is believed to be older than the Nakatomi clan, founded by Ame no Koyane no Mikoto, and the Inbe clan, whose progenitor is Futodama no Mikoto. (Inoue [1965] 1973: 56–57)[11]

The attempt to excise the obscene dance was targeted at solemnifying the ruler. This decision was linked to the mythology that I learnt at primary school a thousand years later.

Until I started primary school, I had never heard of Amaterasu Ōmikami. Then we were taught about the 'unbroken Imperial line': that is, the authority of the emperor inherited directly from the first Emperor Jinmu, whose ancestor was Ninigi no Mikoto. As Chapter 1 notes, Ninigi no Mikoto, whose line goes back to Amaterasu, descended from the Heavenly Plains.[12] In other words, the authority of the present ruler was justified by his origin, and Amaterasu was placed behind him as an even more splendid being.

---

10 Matsumura was a Japanese mythologist whose writings spanned Chinese, Finnish, Germanic, Greek, Indian, Japanese, Nordic and Persian mythology, as well as language, folklore and fairytales. In 1947, he was awarded the Imperial Prize of the Japan Academy.

11 The Nakatomi and Inbe clans were powerful families that served the Yamato Imperial Court through their involvement in religious rites and services. Ame no Koyane no Mikoto was the ancestral god of both the Nakatomi clan and Fujiwara no Kamatari (614–669), a Japanese aristocrat and statesman who founded the Fujiwara clan. When Amaterasu shut herself away in the cave, Ame no Koyane no Mikoto and Futodama no Mikoto performed a ritual prayer to call her out, while Futodama also used *shimenawa* (a rope used to cordon off an area or as a talisman against evil) to prevent her from going back into the cave again.

12 The Imperial House of Japan is said to have begun in 660 BCE with the accession of the mythological Emperor Jinmu, a legendary figure descended from Amaterasu through her grandson Ninigi. The first historically verifiable emperor of Japan was Emperor Kinmei, who reigned from 539 to 571. Many believe that the Imperial line has remained unbroken since this time.

Chapter 4

The idea that the emperor never errs became common sense in Japan as the wartime conditions intensified. Those who attempted to challenge this position were defeated one after the other, at the Diet and in the newspapers. As a child I never spoke out in criticism of this mindset, but I was very attracted to the autobiography of Pyotr Alexeyevich Kropotkin (1842–1921) after finding it at a bookshop,[13] and began to feel sympathetic towards free thinkers from Alexander Ivanovich Herzen (1812–1870)[14] to Kropotkin who refused to accept the absolutism of the Czar. Since I encountered the European dogma of papal infallibility (adopted on 18 July 1870 by the first Vatican Council), I have regarded it as a persistent stumbling block in our world. Given this background, it was natural for me to doubt the infallibility of the Japanese emperor. I actually thought that the idea of the emperor's infallibility that was regarded as common sense in Japan must have come from Europe. At that point, I had read some Japanese mythology and knew that Japanese deities—from Izanagi and Izanami to Susano'o—clearly made cognitive mistakes and possessed ethical flaws, and were hence a long way off from being infallible. How, then, could the Shōwa Emperor (Hirohito) suddenly become infallible?[15]

Even during the war, I never heard any account that denigrated Emperor Shōwa. Looking back, it seems strange. As for Emperor Meiji,[16] I did hear a story that he was even better at telling dirty jokes

---

13 Here Tsurumi's text reads 'Kuropatokin', which refers to Aleksey Nikolayevich Kuropatkin (1848–1925), a Russian general who served as the Russian Imperial Minister of War from 1898 to 1904. Judging from the context, however, this is likely an error for 'Kuropotokin', a reference to the Russian philosopher, revolutionary, historian, scientist and advocate of anarcho-communism, Pyotr Alexeyevich Kropotkin. Kropotkin's autobiography, *Memoirs of a Revolutionist*, was translated into Japanese by the anarchist Ōsugi Sakae (1885–1923).

14 Herzen was a Russian writer, political thinker and activist who championed agrarian populism and continued to advocate for the rights of the peasantry after the emancipation of serfs in 1861. His autobiography, *My Past and Thoughts* (1870), is considered to be one of the greatest works of the genre in Russian literature.

15 Shōwa Emperor was the 124th emperor of Japan. He reigned from 24 December 1926 until his death on 7 January 1989 and was Japan's head of state before and through World War II, during which time he was venerated as a god. After Japan's surrender and the adoption of the 1947 Constitution, his role became purely symbolic.

16 Meiji Emperor was the 122nd emperor of Japan. He reigned from 13 February 1867 until his death on 29 July 1912, and presided over the Meiji era (1868–1912), a period that saw Japan emerge as a modern, industrialised nation-state.

than the two most notorious elder statesmen, Kido Takayoshi (1833–1877)[17] and Itō Hirobumi (1841–1909).[18] One of the dirty counting songs of the era had a profane verse starting with the line 'When you do it with Her Imperial Majesty', and ending with 'you've got to do it standing to attention'. For soldiers left on the Pacific islands, singing the song drunk was a diversion, an act that drew neither a thrashing nor a lynching. It was only in the case of Emperor Shōwa that the strong will to avoid *lèse-majesté* never buckled, even in a state of extreme drunkenness.

Human beings can make mistakes: in cognition, and in ethics. Rulers can make mistakes too, but their mistakes bring more serious consequences than those committed by people not in power. Such a rule of thumb is useful to have in society. The establishment of a nation-state, however, functions to blur such rules. Japanese mythology clearly records the mistakes of its rulers. Why, then, did the Meiji state use that mythology to justify its authenticity, while at the same time attempt to create the idea of the infallible monarch and then inculcate that idea among the people? The theme of laughter and politics that is inherent in Japanese myths became invisible in the governments from Meiji onwards.

There are times when children remain silent to any question posed to them; the only way that they can break that silence is to utter some obscenity. The existence of taboo words weighs them down, making them feel as if they are restrained and incapable of speaking. If they loudly blurt out a word related to sex or excrement, it enables them to demonstrate their own power, as if they have suddenly become bigger and are able to face down their opponent. Freud analyses jokes this way, but the same sort of change in mood must be at work when repelling the oppression of political power. This attitude is in stark contrast to an extended ovation offered to some authoritative figure.

---

17 Kido was a Japanese statesman who, along with Saigō Takamori (1828–1877) and Ōkubo Toshimichi (1830–1878), is regarded as one of the 'three great nobles of the [Meiji] Restoration' (*ishin no sanketsu*).

18 Itō was a Japanese politician and statesman who served as the first prime minister of Japan from 1885 to 1888, and then for three more terms: 1892–1896, 1898 and 1900–1901. From 1905, when Korea became a protectorate of Japan, he served as the first resident-general of Korea, until he was assassinated in 1909 by a Korean nationalist in Harbin.

Chapter 4

Laughter requires a fair degree of spontaneity. When you go to a toy shop, you might see a can, or rather a bag, of laughter, which when interacted with produces the terribly loud sound of a man laughing. The American comedian Eddie Cantor (1892–1964) was the first to use this sort of thing on the radio.[19] He brought a few cooperative audience members into the studio, and their laughter enlivened the show. It is thought that radio comedies became more engaging after Cantor's innovations. Theoretically this technique could be applied to political scenes as well, but it would be difficult, and I have never encountered any examples.

Iwaki Hiroyuki (1932–2006) travelled extensively to conduct various orchestras around the world.[20] He internalised a catalogue of jokes, collecting them around dinner tables where musicians from different countries tried to relax and enjoy each other's company. Over the years, he developed a reaction of laughing heartily whenever he recognised a joke in the catalogue. One day, when he was dining with his wife in a hotel restaurant in the Belgian city of Brussels, a group of four musicians (Belgian, Dutch, and Danish or Swedish) came and sat at the next table. As is common in such multicultural groups, the topic turned to conventional jokes. Mr Iwaki thought, 'Not again!' but couldn't control his physical reaction:

> Something terrible happened. At the punch line of the joke that I had heard hundreds of times in numerous places and knew back to front, my face went into a spasm of a guffaw. As I was eavesdropping on the conversation at the next table, my civility would not allow me to laugh out loud. And the joke wasn't funny in the slightest. As a matter of fact, I was rather annoyed. I'm sure my eyes were angry. It was just my facial muscles that performed the exercise of a horse's laugh. My wife was shocked.
>
> This episode saddened me. My reaction was a completely pathetic conditioned reflex. (Iwaki: 1984)

---

19 Cantor was an American performer, actor, songwriter and philanthropist. Known for his song-and-dance routines featuring exaggerated eye movements, he was nicknamed 'Banjo Eyes', and appeared in the 1941 Broadway musical of the same name.

20 Iwaki was a Japanese conductor and percussionist. He made his conducting debut in 1956 with the NHK Symphony Orchestra and was later appointed chief conductor of the Melbourne Symphony Orchestra (1974–1997). Iwaki's wife is the Japanese pianist Kimura Kaori (b. 1947).

Forty years ago, I frequented a *manzai* variety hall in Kyoto and recorded the topics included in the performances in a notebook, using symbols.[21] As I listened to them all day, the same topics appeared again and again. It seemed as if while one act was performing, the next one was listening offstage. Although the same topic would not come up immediately afterwards, it would after another four or five acts had finished. What surprised me then was that I could laugh at the same joke on the same day. Since I was still in my mid-twenties, this was by no means anything to do with senility. I was puzzled.

As Iwaki's episode tells us, however, in our daily lives with other people, obligatory laughter does exist. To endure its enforcement and produce expressions of laughter requires patience and acting skills. This is part of political strength in daily life as well.

But beyond such quotidian contexts, there are occasions in which cues for laughter are given in a wider sense.

Towards the end of World War II, in May 1945 to be precise, after Hitler's suicide was reported in Europe, I received a postcard with the following words written in red ink:

> *ima zo ima, Ame no Uzume no mune hadake*
>
> (And now is the time Ame no Uzume bares her breasts)

Some time after the end of the war, I met the writer of this card for the first time. He was living out of the public toilets in a station. Another time he sent me a pamphlet explaining an interesting theory, that human history had completed a stage of solar history and entered one of lunar history. On yet another occasion he sent me some musical notes, with the line 'With your wisdom, I'm sure you can understand what this means', but I had no idea how to decipher it. What impresses me even now is that in 1945, when the war was simmering down, someone sent me a postcard with the message, '*ima zo ima...*'.

---

21 *Manzai* (漫才) is a traditional style of Japanese comedy that originated in the Heian period (794–1185). Comparable to double-act or stand-up comedy, it generally features a serious person (*tsukkomi*) and a funny person (*boke*) who trade quick-fire jokes.

Chapter 5
The Naked Body as Metaphor

In this chapter, Tsurumi starts his exploration into the meaning of nakedness by highlighting the different ways that Ame no Uzume uses her nudity as a performative act. That is, outside the Heavenly Cave, her purpose is to elicit laughter and entice Amaterasu out of seclusion, but at the crossroads of Heaven and Earth where she encounters the stranger Sarutahiko, baring herself is a demonstration of courage as well as evidence that she carries no weapons. Tsurumi explores the idea of nudity as a vehicle to egalitarianism and new perspectives in his discussion of the bathhouse as a space for exchanging ideas, and investigates the etymology of the term *hadaka* (naked) and its various applications. At the end of the chapter, he reminds us that just as we come to life with nothing, we also leave life with nothing.

Ame no Uzume's dance is a winter ritual. The deities gathered outside the cave with her must have been clothed. All the while, deep in a trance with her skirt-band pushed down and her breasts exposed, Ame no Uzume danced and danced, showing her near-naked body. Unlike her audience, she must have forgotten any sense of the cold.

The function of revealing the naked body is the core point here.

Uzume's act of stripping off her clothes in the process of drawing Amaterasu out of the cave was a performance designed to make all the deities gathered there burst into hearty laughter. In the later episode where she faces a giant stranger at the crossroads between Heaven and Earth, the removal of her garments is a performance that shows her courage in meeting her opponent head on, without resorting to the use of weapons. Uzume adopts the same performative pattern in both situations, yet its purpose differs.

Chapter 5

Let us consider the meaning of nakedness.

At the height of the Vietnam War, the anti-war FTA Show for GIs came to Japan.[1] The troupe included celebrities such as Donald Sutherland and Jane Fonda. Their main purpose was to perform at US military bases in Japan, but some members of our Beheiren (Citizen's League for Peace in Vietnam, 1965–1974) invited them to perform at the Student Hall of Dōshisha University in Kyoto.[2] We had a preliminary meeting at a coffee shop near the university with an American woman who came to Kyoto before the troupe. After climbing the stairs to the second floor, we couldn't help but notice that on each wall of the upstairs room there was a huge nude photograph of a White woman. My immediate reaction was to wonder why there were no photographs of Asian and Black people as well. The Caucasian woman I took with me looked uncomfortable seeing the posters, but we got on with the meeting nonetheless. Thinking back on this experience now, it strikes me that it would have been so much better if the walls had been decorated with nude posters not just of women but also men, and not just the young but the elderly too.

Leni Riefensthal, the German film director who found favour with Hitler, not only made films documenting Nazi festivals and the Berlin Olympics, but was active even after the war, publishing a collection of photographs entitled *Die Nuba*.[3] The book presents the masculine beauty of young men, who were her sole photographic subjects even though there were also old people and children in the village where she captured the images. In her approach, I felt the continuation of

---

[1] The FTA Show (also known as the FTA Tour or the Free The Army Tour) was a 1971 anti-Vietnam War road show for servicemen developed by ex-US Army doctor Howard Levy in response to the pro-war USO (United Service Organization) tours. The title of the show was a play on the common troop expression 'Fuck The Army', which in turn parodied the army slogan 'Fun, Travel and Adventure'.

[2] Beheiren, short for Betonamu ni Heiwa o! Shimin Rengō (Citizen's League for Peace in Vietnam), was a socio-political movement that advocated for peace in Vietnam. Formed in April 1965 in response to Operation Rolling Thunder, it staged large-scale non-violent protests, distributed anti-war materials and aided the desertion of American soldiers (see footnote 6). Though the movement eschewed a hierarchical organisational structure, its central figures included Oda Makoto (1932–2007), Kaikō Takeshi (1930–1989) and Tsurumi.

[3] Helene Bertha Amalie 'Leni' Riefenstahl (1902–2003) was also an actress. She directed the Nazi propaganda films *Der Sieg des Glaubens* (The Victory of Faith, 1933), *Triumph des Willens* (Triumph of the Will, 1935) and *Tag der Freiheit: Unsere Wehrmacht* (Day of Freedom: Our Armed Forces, 1935), as well as the 1938 sports film *Olympia*, which documented the 1936 Berlin Olympics.

The Naked Body as Metaphor

the unwavering glorification of the Nazis that characterised her prewar work. As an artist this may support her uniqueness, but as a holistic expression encompassing politics, there is no maturity to her art.

In stark contrast, in a posthumously published essay, Ishikawa Sanshirō (1876–1956) outlined a utopian idea in which old international anarchists who had known each other since the Taishō period got together to hold meetings at public baths in order to debate politics.[4]

"So are you going to have your naked meeting in the bath as usual?"

"Yes. This format seems to have caused some difficulty initially, but now we've met several times, the problem has disappeared. Since this is your first time, you may feel a little embarrassed, but you'll be fine in no time. Western people used to criticise the practice of men and women bathing publicly together, totally naked, but then when they saw the results, they were enlightened. Selecting a bath as a conference room actually has a strategic meaning. You see, here, people of all ethnic backgrounds, and both men and women, can be naked—shedding all religious, traditional and national customs and abandoning all ethnic prejudices—and truly mingle together as one big family. At first, we were accused of being too whimsical, and many others refused to join us, but once they saw the realisation of a true world family congress, the people of the world finally opened their eyes." (Ishikawa 1978: 90)[5]

The emcee who is explaining the details of the meeting in this narrative is 120 years old. As he tells the story, the anarchists' meetings are held at a grand bath in Hakone, which is a mixed bath hosting men

---

4 Ishikawa was a Japanese socialist and anarcho-syndicalist. He was a leading figure in Japan's 20th century anarchist movement, and was involved in the 1946 founding of the Japanese Anarchist Federation. Although Tsurumi calls the piece an 'essay', it takes the form of a utopian novella.

5 The original was written in 1946. Ishikawa was an important inspiration for Tsurumi, who included this piece in his journal *Shisō no kagaku* (Science of thought) in 1966. The piece was also included in a 1978 collection of Ishikawa's works, which is the text used for translating this quotation. The first line of the quoted passage is spoken by a French-Vietnamese anthropologist, Michel, who visits the protagonist of this story, the 120-year-old anarchist Yamagami Noboru, before going to Hakone to attend an international anthropology conference. Michel's grandfather, Jean, is a good friend of Yamagami's.

Chapter 5

and women, young and old. It brings to mind the fairy tale about the emperor having no clothes that is often used as a metaphor in theoretical arguments in the West. In this Eastern essay, however, nudity is the emperor.

Here Ishikawa interprets the custom of bathing naked together as a pattern of action that has the potential to have ideological and political significance in the world. A year after the discovery and publication of this essay I had an opportunity to witness this first-hand.

As part of our anti-Vietnam War movement, the US-Japan meeting passed a resolution encouraging soldiers to desert the front lines. We made fliers and distributed them at the US base in Yokosuka. Not long after, four of them actually deserted.[6] As this was the first time the Japanese anti-war movement actually had to deal with deserters, we decided to make a documentary film about it so that we could ask the soldiers to express their thoughts on the war and on their desertion. After we finished, I took in two of the four deserters at my house.

Hosting deserters was a new experience for me, of course, and this was their first experience of deserting too. They were quite shaken up by it. As they talked to each other, one started saying that he was going to return to their ship. They argued. I did not join in their debate; I just said that each should make his own decision. Eventually they stopped their argument for the night and we went to bed.

The following morning, the one who had wanted to reverse his desertion started preparing to go back to the ship. Because this would be his last chance to have a look at Japan, I asked him if there was anything he wanted to see.

'I want to go to a public bathhouse'.

So the three of us set off. Since I thought the area might be under surveillance, we avoided the closest bathhouse and walked to another one a bit of a distance away. It was a sunny day and our stroll there was very pleasant. When we arrived, the bathhouse was empty because it had just opened for the day. The spacious bathroom was full of sunshine. We were able to take our time, and gradually we all

---

6 The sailors became known as the 'Intrepid Four' because they were from the USS Intrepid. They deserted in Yokosuka on 23 October 1967. After seeking assistance from Beheiren, they were smuggled out of Japan on a Russian-bound ship less than two weeks later, arriving in Sweden on 29 December.

began to relax. As we walked home, the young man who insisted that he was going to return to the ship changed his mind again and decided to continue with his desertion.

After he started talking about going back to the military, I never attempted to dissuade him. But taking off his clothes and soaking in a big bath allowed him to see a new perspective and reconsider his decision.

During the period of the Vietnam War, I had an opportunity to talk with the novelist Takeda Taijun (1912–1976).[7] He proposed the idea that we should produce cans containing the odour of dead bodies and sell them—to remind politicians, and those of us who are involved in politics, that all people eventually die. In his opinion, this would help everyone reach an understanding that stretched beyond fleeting political triumphs and losses:

> **Takeda**: Dead bodies create a problem for the living. The stench of the corpse of the most patriotic resistance activist and the body of a horse are the same. They simply need to be carried away or cremated. If we sold these cans, people would understand the horrible stench of war. Only war creates such a bad smell. Once everyone realises this, no one will ever want to start a war again.
> (Takeda and Tsurumi 1968)

The effect of the naked body is somewhat similar to that of the dead body. Newborn babies are naked. And at the end of their lives, people's clothes are removed from their bodies at least temporarily, and they become naked again. Between these two naked states are our lives, lived in clothes. It is as if we all look back on our lives as dead bodies from our terminal points. José Guadalupe Posada (1852–1913), a lithographer at the time of the Mexican Revolution, put these two states—the naked and the dead—together in his work. His political leaflets feature both leaders from his side and his opponent's side, as well as the masses of people around them applauding, as skeletons (that embody both states). The young men and women dancing

---

7 Takeda was a Japanese novelist and Buddhist monk with an interest in Chinese literature and left-wing politics. His works include the novelettes *Mamushi no sue* (1948) and *Hikarigoke* (1964). The two works were translated by Yusaburo Shibuya and Sanford Goldstein and published together as *This Outcast Generation and Luminous Moss* (1967).

Chapter 5

Figure 5.1: Posada's *Calavera oaxaqueña* (1903)

together at the various balls held in between the revolutionary war battles are also skeletons who shyly face each other. This is a new viewpoint on nakedness that Mexico introduced into its political sphere. In other words, the naked state was used in an unusual way; it makes me think that nakedness (as well as the naked dead body) should be utilised more in our approach to considering politics.

§

The term *hadaka* (naked) is said to come from *hada aka* (literally, 'skin red'), which means the same as *akahadaka*, a term signifying the state of wearing no clothes on the body.

Another etymological theory suggests that *hadaka* is derived from *hada* (skin) and the suffix *ka* as in the verb *hadakaru* (be wide open; exposed).

In any case, *hadaka* signifies 1) the revealing of the whole body; a state without clothing, 2) uncovered and unembellished, 3) having nothing; absolutely no assets or possessions, 4) having nothing to hide, and 5) a bride lacking a trousseau (Shōgakukan's *Nihon kokugo daijiten* dictionary).

The Naked Body as Metaphor

The phrase *hadaka ikusa* (naked battle) apparently means fighting without any subordinates, and even without any armour. There is also the idiomatic expression 'Let's talk to each other [in a state of] *hadaka*'.

The word *hadakamushi* is a derogatory term for all hairless and wingless insects that derives from a Chinese expression. It is used in relation to people as well. For example, the *Liji* (*Book of Rites*)[8] describes human beings as the leaders of *hadakamushi*, and *Kongzi Jiayu* (*The School Sayings of Confucius*)[9] places humans at the top of 360 species of *hadakamushi*. According to the mediaeval Japanese encyclopaedia *Shūgaishō*, humans are placed at the centre and in charge of the 330 *hadakamushi*. Miyake Shōzan's *Haikai kosen* (An Old Anthology of Haiku, 1763) includes the haiku 'rokugatsu no / hito no koto ka ya / hadakamushi' (Does it mean people in June Hadakamushi),[10] where the term means 'the poor without clothes' or 'the children of poor families with no clothes' (*Daigenkai* dictionary, Fuzanbō).

It is interesting to look over the 360 species of hairless and wingless insects and the classification that places humans at the top. It implies that whether a saint or a poor child, everyone is a kind of *hadakamushi* under the taxonomy of 'human being', and that human beings themselves were originally *hadakamushi*.

§

Another idiomatic expression, *hadaka ikkan* (having no capital except one's own body – *Kōjien* dictionary), describes the state of Ranald MacDonald (1824–1894) when he arrived in Japan from the US. On 27 June 1848, the twenty-four-year-old MacDonald asked

---

8 *Liji* (禮記) is a collection of classical Chinese texts that form part of the Confucian canon. The work describes societal and administrative structures as well as ceremonial rites of the Zhou dynasty (1046–256 BCE), as understood in the Warring States (476–221 BCE) and early Han (206 BCE–220 CE) periods.

9 *Kongzi Jiayu* (孔子家語) was written to supplement the *Analects of Confucius*, and gathers together a number of discussions between Confucius and his disciples, as well as sayings by and information on the life of Confucius. The received text was published in the third century.

10 The lunar calendar begins sometime between the end of January and the beginning of February, depending on the year, and is 11 or 12 days shorter than the solar calendar. *Rokugatsu* (June) in the lunar calendar would therefore be around July (midsummer in the northern hemisphere) in the solar calendar.

Chapter 5

a whaling ship to put him in a small boat, which he rowed toward Japan, landing on Rishiri Island off Hokkaido [on 1 July]. The local Ainu people of Nokka village who surrounded him when he arrived were welcoming, but officials took him away, sending him all the way to Nagasaki by palanquin. While one Japanese castaway, Daikokuya Kōdayū (1751–1828),[11] was able to meet Catherine the Great in Russia, and another, Hamada Hikozō (1837–1897),[12] managed to shake hands with President Lincoln in America, MacDonald could neither meet Emperor Kōmei (1831–1867) nor shake hands with Shogun Tokugawa Ieyoshi (1793–1853). He thus had no choice but to return home on an American battleship that came to pick him up in Nagasaki.

For a long time, the story of MacDonald was buried in history, overshadowed by the arrival of Commodore Perry's fleet in Japan in 1853 and the subsequent opening of the country, the war between Japan and the US and the reopening of Japan, the American occupation and the post-war Japanese reconstruction, and also economic friction between Japan and the US. At each of these stages, international people representing their respective governments negotiated with each other. In the process, Ranald MacDonald was forgotten, but in reality he was another type of international person (or rather inter-people person) and his attempts to communicate were another type of international (or people-to-people) exchange.

One hundred and fifty years after MacDonald's landing in Japan, the Friends of MacDonald Society was established, led by Tomita Masakatsu, the president of Seiko Epson Portland Inc.

Japanese businessmen working overseas often feel that their children must go to top schools in Japan. For this reason, many leave their wives and children at home, or, in the case where their families accompany them overseas, they place their children in Japanese schools so that they can continue with their Japanese education. It is true that if these children receive their education from the country in which they are staying, they may not succeed in Japan's entrance

---

11 Daikokuya spent nine years in Russia after his ship landed on the uninhabited island of Amchitka, part of the Aleutian Islands in southwest Alaska. He was given permission to return to Japan after his meeting with Catherine the Great.

12 Joseph Heco, born Hamada Hikozō, was a Japanese interpreter, businessman and publisher who helped publish *Kaigai shinbun*, the first Japanese language newspaper in the US. Heco was the second Japanese castaway to arrive in America, and in June 1858, he became the first Japanese person to be naturalised as a US citizen.

examinations when they repatriate. This in turn could make them feel as if they were lacking in ability, which I'm sure they would find depressing.

Tomita's way of thinking, however, is oriented towards a different ideal that accords with the spirit of the Friends of MacDonald Society. He and his wife have two children, aged three and eleven. The couple don't seem to want their children to prepare themselves for Japan's 'entrance examinations war'. They want their children to live in the same place as them, and to become adaptable to that place. Even if this way of growing up does not suit the Japanese school system, privileging graduates of prestigious universities will not last for long in the Japan of the future. It will change to a society, Tomita says, that values those who are useful in the world and helpful to others, regardless of their alma mater.

In his company in Portland, Oregon, in the US, 950 out of his 1,000 employees are Americans. His confidence comes from managing such a large company.

Ranald MacDonald made up his own mind to visit Japan. His father was a Scotsman and his mother was a daughter of a leader of the native Canadian Chinook people. With this background, it was difficult for him to grow up among Caucasians. Once he had heard the story that his maternal people had lived in Japan, a dream grew inside him to visit this country of Japan, which was then closed to the outside world.

There is another person who went overseas as *hadaka ikkan*, like MacDonald, but in this case, it was not his intention, but rather out of circumstantial necessity. Nakahama Manjirō (1827–1898) sailed out of Usaura in Tosa (present-day Kōchi prefecture) when he was fourteen, with four other crew.[13] In the middle of their longline fishing expedition, they were hit by a storm and drifted to an uninhabited island (Torishima) in the Pacific. When they were discovered by the US ship Howland a month later, they were in a state of *hadaka* without any possessions. As the youngest of the five, Manjirō boarded the whaler and ended up being educated in the hometown of the captain. Eventually he became a crew member on another whaler and was promoted to the position of deputy captain. For this particular

---

13 Nakahama was one of the first Japanese people to visit the US, where he was known as John Manjirō, or John Mung. He played a key role in negotiating the Kanagawa Treaty which effectively ended Japan's policy of national isolation.

Chapter 5

voyage, he received $350 as his share of the catch. Manjirō left the ship and went to California to work in a gold mine, earning $180 per month. From this income, he used $120 to buy a boat, with which he boarded a whaling ship bound for Japan. In his boat, he reached Ryukyu (present-day Okinawa) and from there, he was able to return to Japan.[14]

Manjirō was rescued by the Americans without anything on him. He expressed his gratitude in a letter to his 'Dear Friend', Captain Whitfield. This spirit of equality, with no sense of servility, was exactly what Whitfield wished for Manjirō. In other words, Manjirō returned home with the American ideal of the self-made man. It was difficult, however, to have this ideal accepted in Japan.

Three years before Manjirō's return, MacDonald was forced to leave Japan for the US. The Japanese government (Bakufu) found it strange that the US would send a battleship to fetch this man who had neither rank nor office, and asked how high the rank of the battleship's commander was. MacDonald answered that the people ranked the highest, followed by the president in second place, and that the commanders were positioned in fifth place. The Bakufu officials could not understand the concept that the people were positioned at the top of the hierarchy. MacDonald and Manjirō never met each other but they shared the ideal of holding respect for people with nothing. Here we see the gaze of naked people upon the many nations of Earth.

We come into life with nothing, and we leave life with nothing. In modern life, it is difficult to remember this because we are so preoccupied with obtaining various qualifications. Non-modern cultures, however, developed various ways of nurturing a sensitivity towards death.

I found a Pueblo Indian poem in *Chihōshoku* (The Local Colour, 1990) by Marumoto Yoshio (1934–2008), who specialises in French literature and cooking.[15]

---

14 The Ryukyu Kingdom (1429–1879) was a tributary state of imperial China, ruled by the Ryukyuan monarchy. The kingdom later became a Japanese vassal state, first under the Satsuma Domain (1609), and later under the Empire of Japan in the form of the Ryukyu Domain (1872). In 1879, the Ryukyu Kingdom was formally annexed and dissolved to form Okinawa prefecture.

15 Marumoto was a Japanese writer, translator and culinary researcher. The majority of his works are about cooking techniques and tools, as well as nutrition and health.

Today is a very good day to die.
Every Living thing is in harmony with me.
Every voice sings a chorus within me.
All beauty has come to rest in my eyes.
All bad thoughts have departed from me.
Today is a very good day to die.
My land is peaceful around me.
My fields have been turned for the last time.
My house is filled with laughter.
My children have come home.
Yes, today is a very good day to die. (Wood 1974: 31)

This reminds me of the film *Little Big Man* (dir. Arthur Penn, 1970), which I saw twenty years ago. The protagonist is a short White man who becomes an orphan but is adopted by a Native American's tribal leader. When the chief becomes old, he says that today is the day that he will die, and he takes his adopted son to a light-filled empty space deep in the mountains and lies down. After a while he gets up and says that he won't die that day, and smiles.[16] The two men head back down the mountain together.

The expression of the old man who failed to predict the time of his death was wonderful; it shows his large personality. The character of the chief was apparently played by a real Native American [Chief Dan George (Geswanouth Slahoot) of the Tsleil-Waututh Nation].

The state in which death exists naturally in one's life is a desirable mode of living for human beings. It sounds rather stiff to say that we don't want to forget that we will leave this world sooner or later without anything. So instead, I do want to remember that at any time and in any circumstances something like a *hadakamushi* who has lost his way is living inside of me.

---

16 This scene occurs near the end of the film. After Old Lodge Skins, the Native American chief, declares that 'It is a good day to die', he lies down and prepares to breathe his last, but then it begins to rain. He and Jack, the protagonist, then return to the lodge for dinner.

Chapter 6
Burlesque and Striptease

In this chapter, Tsurumi discusses the first strip show in Japan, staged in 1947, as an introduction to the topic of burlesque. The art of burlesque, performed by both sexes, is often hyperbolic, and can be dry or cruel, with little regard for its subjects. While studying in America, Tsurumi discovered a burlesque rendition of Japan's emperor system in a production of The Hot Mikado, an all-Black jazz adaptation of the operetta The Mikado by Gilbert and Sullivan. Tsurumi extends this discussion to his frequent visits to *yose* variety houses in Kyoto to watch comedic duo *manzai* performances, which always ended with a strip show. He concludes the chapter with the story of the stripper Ichijō Sayuri, who was accused of public obscenity in her 1972 retirement show and jailed for seven months.

In 1947, the first strip show in Japan was shown at the fifth-floor hall of Teitoza Theatre in Shinjuku, Tokyo.[1] No doubt, neither the performers nor the viewers felt that the show was connected to Japanese mythology.

On centre stage, there was a huge picture frame like those used for Western paintings, with two young naked women standing inside.[2] They were not permitted to move. In that sense, the show followed

---

1 The Teitoza Theatre opened on 15 January 1947, with *The Birth of Venus*, Japan's first strip show. Performers appeared in poses from famous Western nude paintings, as well as in various comedy and literary performances. The theatre closed in 1972.

2 See, for example,
https://cultural.jp/en/item/tokyomuseumcolection-topmuseumjbD10005096.
Other related images can be found at:
https://cultural.jp/en/item/tokyomuseumcolection-topmuseumjbD10009117,
https://cultural.jp/en/item/tokyomuseumcolection-topmuseumjbD10014183 and
https://cultural.jp/en/item/photo-00002_00066_0001.

the tradition of *tableau vivant* (living pictures, *katsujinga*) which presented scenes of Christian tales performed by boys and girls at churches from early Meiji to Taishō. Just as *katsujinga* was a performative mode imported by missionaries from the West, this first strip show, called 'Gakubuchi' (Picture frame), employed a Western mode following the style of female nude oil paintings created for art exhibitions in Japan that started in 1893 with *Chōshō* (Morning toilette) by Kuroda Seiki (1866–1924).[3] The show was directed by Hata Toyokichi (1892–1956), who had translated Goethe's *Faust* before the war.[4] On the program it was called 'Masterpiece Album' but as its reputation spread by word of mouth, it was renamed the 'Gakubuchi Show' which remains legendary today.

Such was the beginning of the striptease show in Japan, which swept across playhouses from Shinjuku to Asakusa, driving away the female *kengeki* sword shows featuring top-billing stars of the popular Asakusa vaudeville such as Ōe Michiko (1910–1939)[5] and Fuji Yōko (1912–1980).[6] After the war, a newcomer to the sword show, Asaka Mitsuyo (1928–2020), came up with an innovative 'Strip sword show' to revive the female *kengeki* in Asakusa.

In Europe, the mode of *tableau vivant* was popular from the eighteenth to the nineteenth century. Since there were no movies or magic lanterns (*gentō*), and art museums were not yet part of popular culture, a form of entertainment in which people assumed the guise of an historical figure and performed for their friends or associates became widely popular. *Tableau vivant* gained further acclaim in mid-

---

3 Kuroda was a Japanese painter and educator who played a significant role in introducing Western art theories and practices to the Japanese public. After studying in Paris, he became a leading figure in the *yōga* (literally 'Western-style painting') movement.

4 Hata was a Japanese businessman, stage director, entertainer, writer and translator. Some of his works were published under the name of Maruki Sado, a play on Marquis de Sade. Following his studies of German law at Tokyo Imperial University (present-day University of Tokyo), Hata continued to translate German literature while working for Mitsubishi. He left Mitsubishi to work in the entertainment industry in 1932. Over the course of his career, he was involved with the Tokyo Takarazuka, Nippon Gekijō and Teitoza Theatres.

5 Ōe was a Japanese actress who first drew attention as a film heroine, before turning to the stage. When she died of acute appendicitis in 1939, her protégé, Ōkawa Michiko (1919–2005), adopted Ōe's stage name and continued to perform until the 1970s.

6 Fuji was a Japanese stage actress who helped popularise female swordplay in the 1930s.

nineteenth century England, when music halls were established. At first, out of consideration for the Church, the performances didn't incorporate body movements, but eventually they integrated dance and became increasingly bold, flourishing in the form of strip shows which then expanded to the Continent. In 1920s America, such performances were given the new name 'striptease' as they became a form of entertainment where stripping off items of clothing one by one used rhythm and timing to tease the audience. The *katsujinga* that appeared in Japan immediately after the war took only about a year to become stripteases, skipping the 200 years of the Western history of the art.

The striptease is a dance set to music that publicly emulates sexual intercourse in an exaggerated way. Even though performed by a sole woman, each move of the sexual act is exposed, scene by scene, to the eyes of hundreds of (mainly male) viewers. At times, the performance is interrupted, rolled back, then restarted and continued, and at each step an item worn by the dancer is removed, until finally, to coincide with the climax of the music, the dancer finishes completely naked except for her 'butterfly' (G-string).[7]

This style of dance is probably based on a nineteenth-century American fantasy. Given that in the 1920s and 1930s free heterosexual sex was not strictly repressed, it may have been from around this period that the performances were enjoyed just as a mode of dance. In any case, it is hard to imagine that there were crazed spectators in the audience.

In 1937, when I went to the US to study, what surprised me was that the graffiti in male toilets at the university were almost all concerned with male homosexuality. Taboos on heterosexual sex were clearly much more lenient than in Japan at the time.

I was also surprised when a student at the boarding school[8] I attended started singing the 'Miyasan Miyasan'[9] song out of the blue.

---

7 'Butterfly' is a Japanese term for G-string, used to describe the shape of the material covering the pubic area. Some striptease fans were titillated by the prospect of the string breaking (Ozawa 1977: 43).

8 In 1938, Tsurumi briefly enrolled at the Middlesex School in Concord, Massachusetts, an independent all-boys secondary school for grades nine to 12. He went on to study philosophy at Harvard University the following year.

9 'Miyasan Miyasan' (My Prince, My Prince) was a humorous loyalist song written by Shinagawa Yajirō in 1868, during the Boshin War (1868–1869).

Chapter 6

The school held an annual cultural festival that always included a Gilbert and Sullivan operetta, in which half of the 100 students performed while the other half watched as the audience. The previous year they had put on *The Mikado* and so naturally all the school (except new students like myself) knew 'Miyasan Miyasan'.[10] It was such a part of their everyday school life that when they saw a Japanese person, the song just rolled out of their mouths.

Up until that point I had never watched any Gilbert and Sullivan operettas. I knew nothing about *The Mikado*.

When I went to New York during the summer vacation, I checked to see if there was a performance of *The Mikado*, and found an advertisement for *The Hot Mikado* in a corner of the newspaper.[11] *The Hot Mikado* was my first encounter with the opera. While the Gilbert and Sullivan comic opera used Japanese costumes for satirical entertainment, caricaturing English politicians of around 1885, this performance had been adapted into a Black group dance with jazz music, which was even further removed from Japanese history. The audience was almost all Black; it was clear that this wasn't an entertainment put on by Black people for White people.

According to Allen Woll's *Black Musical Theatre* (1989), the Great Depression of 1929 considerably reduced the population of theatre workers all over the US. As part of the Works Progress Administration (WPA; renamed the Work Projects Administration in 1939), the government proposed the Federal Theatre Project (FTP), which tried to bring about 10,000 actors and directors without jobs back to the stage. Black theatres formed part of this project, and musicals were devised incorporating jazz. The 1938 *Swing Mikado* won the support of the first lady, Mrs Eleanor Roosevelt, who attended the opening

---

10 *The Mikado; or, The Town of Titipu* is a comic opera by Arthur Sullivan (1842–1900) and W. S. Gilbert (1836–1911) that premiered in 1885. It became tremendously popular and remains the most frequently performed Savoy opera today. The opera tells the story of how a poor minstrel (and secret heir to the Mikado), Nanki-Poo, his beloved Yum-Yum and the Lord High Executioner Ko-Ko, navigate the legal technicalities of execution in the fictitious Japanese town of Titipu, where flirting is punishable by death. The opera features the 'Miyasan Miyasan' song, modified as 'Miyasama, Miyasama' (*sama* is a more formal version of *san*).

11 *The Hot Mikado* debuted in 1939 with an all-Black cast. Noted for its wild costuming, *The Hot Mikado* was a hit, and ran for two seasons at the 1939–1940 New York World's Fair. In 1986, it was revived by David H. Bell and Rob Bowman, and has been produced on a number of occasions since.

Burlesque and Striptease

Figure 6.1: Poster for *The Hot Mikado* (1939)

night, and it went on to achieve considerable commercial success.[12] Even though the costumes were changed to emulate the garments of Fiji in the South Pacific, the story was not too far removed from the original English Gilbert and Sullivan version. It was performed by the D'Oyly Carte Opera Company, with about five tunes from the show changed to swing-style jazz music. It was from this context that *The Hot Mikado* was born.[13]

The musical theatre adaptation of *The Hot Mikado* by Mike Todd (1909–1958) appeared on Broadway for the first time in 1939.[14] Since it was produced independently, and had nothing to do with the government's WPA, it was not subject to the restriction of having to use only unemployed performers, and was able to include renowned

---

12 The *Swing Mikado* was an earlier musical theatre adaptation of *The Mikado* set in Fiji and featuring an all-Black cast. The majority of the performance was based on the 1885 dialogue and score, but adaptations included the re-scoring of some music, the addition of some dance sequences, and modifications to some dialogue in order to reflect Black English.

13 The D'Oyly Carte Opera Company is a professional British light opera company founded by Richard D'Oyly Carte (1844–1901) in the mid-1870s in partnership with Gilbert and Sullivan. Carte built the Savoy Theatre to host Gilbert and Sullivan's comic operas.

14 Todd was an American theatre and film producer. In addition to *The Hot Mikado* (1939), he also produced *Something for the Boys* (1943), *Mexican Hayride* (1944) and *Up in Central Park* (1945).

Chapter 6

actors such as Bill Robinson (1878–1949) in its cast.[15] Moreover, the show did not use Sullivan's music, but made its own free music with an African-American rhythm. The libretto was also changed to include lines such as the following, which referred to Roosevelt's possible third-time candidacy:

> If I stand for the third time,
> Vice Mikado will be Joe Louis for sure

Considering that the original version of *The Mikado* alluded to the English politicians of the day, the song in *The Hot Mikado* suggesting that American politicians of the time should make the Black boxer Joe Louis the Vice Mikado certainly carries on the production's original spirit.

The Japanese emperor system was thus relayed from the British to the Americans, from the White to the Black, increasing its metaphorical power in the process.

In *The Hot Mikado*, the emperor system was treated as a burlesque, intended to ridicule through gross exaggeration and comic imitation. This burlesque was performed as a gesture observed from the outside, without any attempt to delve into the minds of those who supported the emperor system. Actions that are usually performed quickly in reality were considerably decelerated, while normally slow actions were accelerated. Burlesques are full of hyperbole, and they can be dry and cruel. In Kenneth Burke's *Attitudes toward History* (1937), he writes:

> The writer of burlesque makes no attempt to get inside the psyche of his victim. Instead, he is content to select the externals of behavior, driving them to a "logical conclusion" that becomes their "reduction to absurdity." (Burke 1959: 54)

The striptease that delays, temporarily interrupts and then reverses the sexual act was also called burlesque. Burlesque is performed by both men and women and is free from any sort of discrimination

---

15 Bill 'Bojangles' Robinson was an American tap dancer, actor and singer, who became the most well known Black American entertainer in the first half of the 20th century. Robinson's career began with minstrel shows and later spanned vaudeville, Broadway, Hollywood, radio and TV.

towards women. *The Hot Mikado*, too, takes the form of the burlesque, which is not limited to sexual topics; what it presented to the audience was a burlesque of the Japanese emperor system that could exist in any place, including the US. It was much later—indeed, more than forty years after seeing this show—that I viewed the D'Oyly Carte Opera Company's version of *The Mikado*, but I felt that as a skeletal image of the emperor system, *The Hot Mikado* was far superior.

According to Burke, when the masses are in a bullish mood, as at the time of the French Revolution, burlesques become popular.[16] He even calls the Declaration of the Rights of Man a burlesque that points only to rights while concealing the duties that should also accompany them.[17]

Japan has many established forms of burlesque, such as kabuki theatre. The techniques of burlesque established before Meiji continue to be seen in performances ranging from festivals and street entertainment to indoor drinking parties. In a 1986 book by *hōkan* artist Yūgentei Tamasuke (1907–1994), there is a section with photographs featuring his one-man comic sketches.[18] Among them are two episodes with a folding screen: one about male-male sex and the other male-female sex, both performed solely by him. Asked about this repertoire, he says:

---

16 Burke writes: 'At the time of the French Revolution, when a "bill of rights" was being drawn, some members of the Assembly suggested that a "bill of obligations" be included to match them. The proposal was voted down by an overwhelming majority. Here the genius of neither tragedy nor comedy was at work, but the genius of burlesque' (1959: 55).

17 Burke does not directly name the Declaration of the Rights of the Man in the text, but as Tsurumi notes, he does mention 'rights': '...the very basis of classic liberal apologetics, the over-emphasis upon freedom, was but a sober way of carrying out the burlesque genius. It *stressed* freedom, and sought to *smuggle* in restrictions. It cried for "rights," enjoying the strategic advantage of this invitation, without considering the corrective feature of ambivalence whereby "rights" also require their unpleasant reverse, "duties" or "obligations"' (1959: 55, emphasis in original).

18 Historically, *hōkan* (幇間), or *taikomochi* (太鼓持ち), were male entertainers who attended feudal lords and princes, rather like court jesters in England. They would dance, tell stories, and assist *geisha* and *maiko* in enlivening events, but were also known to offer strategic advice or fight alongside their lord. The profession has largely disappeared; Yūgentei Tamasuke is sometimes referred to as the last *hōkan*.

Chapter 6

When I was young, my performance of this sort of material was probably immature and obnoxiously affected. But you see, now that I'm eighty I can say anything I like! I've clocked up a lot of experience. Perhaps I shouldn't say this myself, but with age, I've rounded out my sharp spots and I've rusted nicely. Whatever I say now won't sound nasty.

The thing is, if you say something funny in your thirties, it sounds rather offensive. But when I say it, it can't do any harm.

Everyone knows my old fella is of no use anymore. So they know I'm just kidding. (Yūgentei [1986] 2016: 184, 186)

My own method of writing like this, stringing together various materials, is rather like burlesque. If I may refer to my own experience, after moving to the Kansai area in 1949, I was so attracted to *manzai* that on Sundays and holidays I would sit in the same *yose* variety house from morning till night, keeping records of all the performances I watched.[19] After seven or eight acts taking turns one after the other, there was always a strip show (rather than a magic show or something else), which signalled the end of the programme. It consisted of a short play followed by all the dancers (that is, five or six women) appearing on stage and dancing to the music of the 'Yellow Button' song.[20] This was in a theatre in Nishijin Kyōgoku, Kyoto.[21] I was clearly able to see each dancer's individuality; none of them had an overbearing attitude. Never in my life have I seen any strippers as often as these five or six women, so I feel a kind of nostalgia when I think about them. They had none of the deteriorating radiance of Gypsy Rose, whom I read about in a book; instead their charm was somewhat serene and modest.[22]

---

19 See Chapter 4, footnote 21.
20 This song title may be an error, possibly referring to 'She Wore a Yellow Ribbon', a popular US military song that gave its name to a 1949 film featuring John Wayne, or 'The Yellow Rose of Texas', a traditional American folk song.
21 Nishijin Kyōgoku is a common name for a district in Kamigyō Ward, Kyoto. Currently a shopping district and downtown area, in the first half of the 20th century it was an entertainment district that featured many *yose* (寄席, spoken vaudeville), theatres and cinemas.
22 Gypsy Rose was a Japanese stripper (not to be confused with Gypsy Rose Lee, the American burlesque entertainer) who debuted under the name Rose Marie at the age of 15. Known for her exotic appearance and sensual dancing, she became very popular, but began drinking heavily and died of a heart attack in 1967, while still in her early 30s.

The tenth and final issue of *Kikan geinō tōzai* (Quarterly performing arts: Kantō and Kansai, 1977a) edited by Ozawa Shōichi (1929–2012) showcases the theme of striptease by featuring the history of the art in Japan, along with biographies of the main stars, Ibuki Mari, Merry Matsubara, Hirose Motomi, Gypsy Rose (1934/35?–1967), Nara Akemi, Harukawa Masumi (b. 1935), Azuma Kyōko, Fujiwara Midori, Ogawa Kumi, Merry Shinju, Maria Mari, Honey Roy and Shimizudani Tazuko. I have never seen any of them on stage.

There is one performer, however, whom I have never actually seen but who left a vivid impression on me. I discovered her through an LP recording of a live broadcast by Ozawa (1977b).[23]

Ichijō Sayuri (1929–1997) was born in Saitama prefecture on 10 June 1929, and grew up in Kashiwazaki, Niigata prefecture. After the death of both of her parents, she was brought up in an institution in Gotanda, Tokyo. Upon completing junior high school, she became independent, working as a babysitter, a shop assistant in a department store, a ragpicker and a bar hostess. After marrying, her husband tricked her into dancing at a strip house for the first time. Alongside various emerging striptease techniques including the 'chopping board' and the *'tengu'* (long nose), Ichijō's contribution to the art was writhing around while dripping candle wax across her naked body. Strippers use G-strings to hide their private parts but when a dancer accidentally dropped hers in a hall in Shikoku, it created a stir. Soon it became the fashion for one stripper among the group to intentionally let her G-string fall. At first, this was called *tokushutsu* (特出), derived from 'special' (*toku*) and 'performance' (*shutsuen*), but later the same kanji character combination was read *tokudashi*, meaning 'special exposure'. Ichijō Sayuri was famous for her 特出 in both senses of the word. Having worked as a stripper for twenty years, she held a special retirement show at Yoshino Music, Osaka, in May 1972. But, as Ono Nobuyuki writes, 'Her working life as a stripper—capturing the hearts of the masses through the provision of temporary comfort and entertainment—ended with a seven-month jail sentence for public obscenity' (1977).

---

23 Ozawa was a Japanese actor, radio host and singer. He was also an expert on Japanese folk art, and recorded and released *Nihon no hōrō gei* (Japan's Itinerant Arts), a set of seven LP records (1971), which was followed by a further series of records.

Chapter 6

Her crime, according to the prosecution, was exposing her private parts in her retirement show. Let me quote an impression of Ichijō Sayuri as described at the Osaka District Court on 22 August 1972, by one of the defence witnesses, the Chinese literature scholar, Komada Shinji (1914–1994):[24]

> **The Defence Counsel** (Hayami Tarō): Please outline your background.
>
> **Komada:** I graduated from Tokyo Imperial University, that is, present-day Tokyo University, specialising in Chinese literature, in 1940. I had temporary work at the Ministry of Education and the following year became a teacher at Matsue High School. I was then sent to the war. At the end of the war, I returned to the school, which was reformed as Shimane University. I worked there until 1954.
> When I resigned from Shimane University in March that year, I became a writer. At the same time I taught at Tokyo Metropolitan University, Rikkyō University, Meiji University and other places. I'm currently a lecturer at Tokyo University.

In answering a question about Ichijō Sayuri, Komada continues:

> **Komada:** When I first met her, I met her as a stripper, but as I listened to her stories, I realised that she had had an extremely difficult background, experiencing terrible humiliations and tragedies. Despite this, she is very honest and decent, and I was deeply moved by her sincere way of living.
> Let me explain why I was so moved. I, myself, have established a certain social standing, but looking back at my own way of life up until now, I admit I have often deceived both myself and the world around me. In stark contrast, her character is very honest, and she has never led a life of deception. She is different from us ordinary people, living honestly with all her strength, even in the most difficult circumstances. That's what moved me.

---

24 Komada was also a writer and literary critic. He was part of the Japan Romantic School in the pre-war era, and a number of his works drew upon humorous and erotic elements of Chinese literature.

DC: As humans, we shouldn't do things that contravene the law. Don't you agree?

Komada: Well, as for being human, I feel that in order to get some recognition—in my case as a university lecturer, as a writer or as a critic—we are all dishonest by default. To reflect upon my own life again, I think I have gained recognition: it's not a great success story but still, I have gained a certain standing by pretending to be cleverer than I am, or by evasion, which is not quite a crime, but still not entirely transparent. In her case, her human integrity will not allow her to do such things. So when I talk to her, I feel ashamed of myself.

DC: But, Professor, you speak highly of her humanity and her honesty, but are you saying that as a result of her character she ended up in this trial? Is that what you call humanity?

Komada: It is true that she is being tried here, but I believe that what she did is not of the calibre that requires a trial. So I cannot agree with you. (Komada 1976)[25]

The alleged crime was public obscenity; the law that the accused, Ichijō Sayuri, violated is described in the Japanese Penal Code (*Keihō*), Article 175:

> (1) A person who distributes or displays in public obscene objects such as documents, drawings or recording media contained in electronic or magnetic records is punished by imprisonment for not more than 2 years, a fine of not more than 5,000 yen or a petty fine, or both imprisonment and a fine.[26] The same applies to a person who distributes obscene records including

---

25 These extracts are taken from the second trial record of the Osaka District Court's Twenty-third Criminal Division (Keijibu). The participants in the trial included Judge Ōno Takahide, prosecutor Sugimoto Zenzaburō, as well as defence counsel Hayami Tarō and witness Komada Shinji noted above. For further details, see Komada (1976).

26 The amount of the fine was revised in 1947 from 500 to 5,000 yen, which was still current at the time of Tsurumi's writing. In May 1991 the fine was revised significantly to 2,500,000 yen.

Chapter 6

electronic or magnetic records through the transmission of telecommunications.

(2) The same applies to a person who possesses the objects referred to in the preceding paragraph or stores electronic or magnetic records referred to in the same paragraph for the purpose of distributing them for free.

Scholars of legal studies Naka Yoshikatsu (1921–1993) and Sawanobori Toshio (1930–2020) state in an opinion paper used in the trial that having examined similar cases overseas at the time, 'a crime without a victim' such as the present case on trial should not be regarded as a punishable crime except in the case where the crime is committed against 'an unwilling viewer' or against minors. However, their opinion was not accepted by the court, and on 18 January 1975, the Second Small Claims Court of the High Court unanimously settled on a seven-month jail sentence for Ichijō Sayuri.

The aforementioned LPs of Ozawa Shōichi include live recordings of the times when he visited Ichijō in Wakayama Prison, and afterwards, when she ran a bar and appeared on stage in Kisarazu, Chiba in a nude show (although without taking her clothes off). She came out onto the stage dressed in kimono and sang 'The Boat Rowed by a Lone Woman'. Among the fans who gathered there to celebrate the end of Ichijō's prison term, and her twenty-year career as a stripper, were many elderly men. She went out of the hall to buy some sake, and juice for the non-drinkers, as well as some sweets. Her way of interacting with these fans was so gentle and considerate that it was clear that she loved those who frequented her strip shows, even the drunk and shrieking old men. In comparison with laws in other countries, the legal scholars found the Japanese law unfair, since it is concerned only with whether pubic hair is visible or not, and penalises the producers of photographs, books and dances accordingly. Ichijō herself, however, accepted the punitive sanction of her stripshow act as inevitable. Beyond the issue of whether or not the law is appropriate, I felt that there was no doubt that she is a person with a big heart. Her attitude was not akin to giving herself to a pack of wolves out of despair; rather, to borrow her own words, she said 'I want to live like a *daruma*'.[27] Her intention was to share herself with people, even after she stopped performing as a stripper.

---

27 *Daruma* dolls are named after Bodhidharma, a semi-legendary Buddhist monk credited with transmitting Buddhism to China. They are round, hollow dolls that are weighted to prevent them from falling over, symbolising resilience. Ichijō's use of this term suggests that she hopes to remain resilient despite the difficulties she has encountered. As *daruma* dolls are also said to grant wishes and bring good luck, Ichijō may also be suggesting that she wishes to bring good fortune to others.

Chapter 7
Various Forms of Appeasing Violence

Tsurumi begins this chapter with a discussion on the topic of sexual violence, recounting lingering attitudes of victim-blaming in rape cases tried in Japan. Delving into various works analysing rape and its impacts, he notes Ame no Uzume's partially naked encounter with the stranger Sarutahiko could potentially have been a problematic one if Sarutahiko was inclined to consider his strength and ability to rape her an act of heroism in the way that some Victorian Englishmen did in the era of Jack the Ripper. Nonetheless, in terms of political gain, he concludes that in exposing herself without any sense of shame or violence, she was able to bring about her desired result of transforming a racial/ethnic conflict into a peaceful outcome. He ends the chapter with an analysis of two pacifist communes in the US, the Shakers and the Oneida Community, which had radically different approaches to the question of sexual exchange.

After the appearance of Jack the Ripper in England in late 1888, several incarcerated men confessed before breathing their last that they were the infamous serial killer. Even today, more than a hundred years later, we don't know the killer's true identity. However, the fact that some men, thinking themselves heroic as they lay near death struggling to breathe, identified themselves as Jack the Ripper provides us with a glimpse into the deepest ideals of Victorian era Englishmen. On the one hand, their confessions signify an attitude of male pride regarding the ability to rape, while on the other, they support a cowardly worldview that shifts the blame to seductress women as the sources of evil.

On several occasions during the war, I encountered men actually boasting of their ability to rape. For example, there was an old soldier who had fought in China and Singapore before he was admitted to

Chapter 7

the hospital where I was being treated. Out of boredom, he told the younger soldiers stories of his experiences while out on expeditions; he would rape then kill his victims to erase all evidence before heading out on another march. His stories were, like poorly written pulp fiction, so conveniently staged around himself that I found it difficult to swallow everything he said. At the very least, however, it was clear that he wanted to brag about his raping prowess.

I did not have any sympathy for the way he felt. Around that time, I had this constant feeling of terror that women might think of me as a man who could commit rape.

Ochiai Keiko's novel *The Rape* (1982) depicts this sort of view of rape among men (actually, women are caught up in it too) that survives in Japanese society today.[1] The defence lawyer speaks in court to a woman who chose to forgive her rapist:

> **Kurose (lawyer):** Let's change the topic. In former times, some women whose virtue was violated chose to kill themselves. What do you think of them?

This question speaks to a lifelong concern of mine. There are many people in real life who talk like the lawyer in this novel. During the war, they shouted out against the 'Western (American and British) brutes' and advocated 100 million Japanese choosing death rather than surrender. After Japan's defeat, these same people thought it natural to be tied to America, and believed that Japan was a world leader along the same lines as the Western countries. It never occurred to them that this way of thinking oppressed and killed not only Americans but also Koreans, Taiwanese, Chinese, Filipinos and Singaporeans. Nor do they ever hold themselves accountable for not committing suicide in order to be true to their own ideology. In this particular case, the defence lawyer accuses a woman of not killing herself to protect her chastity. This is all because of his sense of reassurance that he has immunity from being attacked by the entire

---

1 Ochiai (b. 1945) was a successful radio personality in the 1970s whose career expanded to include work as an author, translator, bookstore and restaurant manager, activist and social commentator. A vocal feminist and supporter of Japan's anti-nuclear and anti-war movement, Ochiai has authored over 100 novels and essays. *The Rape* (sometimes referred to as *The Second Rape* in English, due to the theme of the book) was made into a Japanese film in 1982.

nation of Japan for his wartime ultranationalism. In Japan, this is the way that the apparatus of covering up rape accusations continues to work.

In *The Rape*, the victim's lover identifies with this apparatus and leaves her. Her colleagues at work, too, frown upon her accusation against the perpetrator.

As long as people maintain the custom of regarding women who publicly take their rapists to court as impertinent and too assertive, such customs will continue to hold a power that is stronger than the laws of everyday life. This is characteristic of Japan today. However, the number of rape cases is much larger in the US. People move around much more than in Japan, where people speak the same (Japanese) language and tend to maintain relationships with the same neighbours for generations. Exposed to constant fear, American women such as Jean MacKellar (1975, Japanese translation 1976) have produced corroborative studies based on criminal statistics.[2]

Regarding women's views of rape, psychoanalyst Stephanie Demetrakopoulos writes:[3]

> [Women's deep spiritual connections to and reverence for her body make clear why a woman undergoes such deep repugnance and existential nausea when she suffers rape or incestuous abuse. A modern depth psychologist, James Hillman, says that rape is a forcing together of two ontologically different realms;] to a woman, her body is literally a temple that reflects or even *is* sacred process, and to suffer rape is an assault on her metaphysics. Women never fully recover from rape and often brood over it all their lives. Men find this inability of women to simply forget an experience of rape puzzling; a modern male writer guesses that rape is simply being out of control and fearful for one's life for half an hour (Timothy Beneke, "Male Rage: Four Men Talk about Rape," *Mother Jones* VII (July 1982: 20)). The experience of rape is a terrible knowledge of

---

2 MacKellar is an American writer whose works include *Hawaii Goes Fishing* (1956), *Rape* (1975) and *Way Out Here* (1988).

3 Demetrakopoulos (b. 1937) is a former Western Michigan University professor whose research focuses on women's studies and Jungian psychology. She is the author of *Listening to Our Bodies: The Rebirth of Feminine Wisdom* (1983), quoted here, and co-author of *New Dimensions of Spirituality: A Biracial and Bicultural Reading of the Novels of Toni Morrison* (1987).

Chapter 7

nihilism that can never be truly understood or accepted as part of life. (Demetrakopoulos 1983: 27)[4]

§

What sort of gesture was it then when Ame no Uzume loosened her dress and revealed her naked body to a man who stood at the place where Heaven and Earth parted?

She actively exposed her naked body in front of a man who may have considered his ability to rape her as a characteristic of heroism. Here the mention of the name of Mahatma Gandhi (1869–1948) may seem odd, but Uzume's gesture towards a stranger reminds me of him. Gandhi had a jealous personality and demanded celibacy of the boys and girls under his care. He writes that when these young people went to bathe, he would accompany and watch them. The depths of his heart contained an act of violence against his own sexual desires, and a reaction to that violence in the form of moral oppression forced upon his wife and children, as well as the other young people he looked after (Erickson 1969). Despite this difference, Gandhi is rather like Ame no Uzume in exposing his naked body to an unknown opponent. In terms of political effectiveness, both were able to achieve their desired result with their attitude, as long as their opponents possessed certain characteristics.

In 'Reflections on Gandhi' (1949), George Orwell (1903–1950) claims that Gandhi's non-violent struggles in the South African Union and India remained effective because they did not understand the nature of totalitarianism and were simply directed against the British government.[5]

Gandhi was assassinated by a Hindu fanatic in January 1948. Orwell (1949) writes:

---

[4] Tsurumi's quotation of Yokoyama Sadako's 1987 Japanese translation begins after the semi-colon, but we have quoted Demetrakopoulos's original text. The text in square brackets has been added from Demetrakopoulos (1983) for additional context.

[5] This essay was written in response to Gandhi's autobiography, *The Story of my Experiments with Truth* (1925–1929). Along with his impressions of the style and content of Gandhi's autobiography, Orwell argues that Gandhi's non-violent approach, while politically successful, would not be effective in a totalitarian society that lacked civil rights. 'Reflections on Gandhi' was Orwell's last published essay.

Various Forms of Appeasing Violence

It is curious that when [Gandhi] was assassinated, many of his warmest admirers exclaimed sorrowfully that he had lived just long enough to see his life work in ruins, because India was engaged in a civil war which had always been foreseen as one of the by-products of the transfer of power. But it was not in trying to smooth down Hindu-Moslem rivalry that Gandhi had spent his life. His main political objective, the peaceful ending to British rule, had after all been attained. As usual the relevant facts cut across one another. On the other hand, the British did get out of India without fighting, an event which very few observers indeed would have predicted until about a year before it happened. On the other hand, this was done by a Labour government, and it is certain that a Conservative government, especially a government headed by Churchill, would have acted differently. But if, by 1945, there had grown up in Britain a large body of opinion sympathetic to Indian independence, how far was this due to Gandhi's personal influence? And if, as may happen, India and Britain finally settle down into a decent and friendly relationship, will this be partly because Gandhi, by keeping up his struggle obstinately and without hatred, disinfected the political air? That one even thinks of asking such questions indicates his stature. One may feel, as I do, a sort of aesthetic distaste for Gandhi, one may reject the claims of sainthood made on his behalf (he never made any such claim himself, by the way), one may also reject sainthood as an ideal and therefore feel that Gandhi's basic aims were anti-human and reactionary: but regarded simply as a politician, and compared with the other leading political figures of our time, how clean a smell he has managed to leave behind!

The deep jealousy inside Gandhi made him a narrowly focused and resilient political activist. By contrast, Ame no Uzume's humanity is liberated from such a repressed revulsion toward sex, helping to bring forth change from the darkness caused by Amaterasu's hiding away, and becoming the force to transform racial/ethnic conflicts into peace. There are many things we can learn from the allegorical meaning of having a striptease dancer as one of our ancient political leaders.

Chapter 7

Politics, of course, is not confined to the political speeches of politicians. Nor is politics limited only to the nation-state's instruments of violence or the forms of mass violence that protest against them.

John Rutherford Alcock (1809–1896), who was both the first British Consul-General of Japan and later the first Minister Plenipotentiary of Japan, was originally a surgeon who had learned how to draw due to his need to study anatomy. In 1859 he went to Japan. Two years later, on 23 April 1861, he set off on a walking tour of the Kyushu countryside, accompanied by the artist Charles Wirgman (1832–1891).[6] In *The Capital of the Tycoon*, Alcock writes:

> At Urisino [Ureshino, Saga prefecture] in the morning, and Takeiwa [Takeo, Saga prefecture] in the evening of the third day we found some hot sulphur baths. The first we visited was open to the street, with merely a shed roof to shelter the bathers from the sun. As we approached, an elderly matron stepped out on the margin, leaving half a dozen of the other sex behind her to continue their soaking process. The freedom of the lady from all self-consciousness or embarrassment was so perfect of its kind, that one could not help recalling the charitable exclamation of John Huss when he saw a pious old woman bringing a fagot to his stake, '*O sancta simplicitas!*' O holy simplicity, which has no fears of a censorious world, is vexed by no arbitrary code of conventional proprieties, and feels no shame in the absence of covering. She had washed, and was clean; and with the consciousness alone that she had accomplished a duty, evidently saw no reason why all the world should not know, and see it too, if they chanced to come that way. There were great crowds of men and women luxuriating in them; and I suppose it is the force of habit, but they certainly bear parboiling, both men and women, better than any people I ever met with. (Alcock 1963: 70, 75)

Perhaps Alcock tried this hot spring himself later and was surprised to see how hot it was. In any case, to him—who like Jack the Ripper

---

6 Wirgman was an English artist and cartoonist. In 1861, he moved to Japan as a newspaper correspondent and remained there until his death. During his time in Japan, Wirgman created *Japan Punch* (1862–1887), a satirical magazine that used cartoons to critique Meiji period politics. He also taught Western-style drawing and painting techniques to several Japanese artists.

had been brought up in Victorian England with strict taboos about female sexuality—it was undoubtedly a shock to encounter women in country Japan with absolutely no sense of shame about nudity.

Within half a century of Alcock's account, the custom of mixed bathing in Japan declined, thanks to the rigid attitudes imported from the West regarding the naked bodies of women.

The Chief Abbot of Hōnen'in Temple and scholar of ethics, Hashimoto Mineo (1924–1984), re-evaluated the bathing custom in connection with the religious sensibility of Japanese Buddhism.[7] Where he wished to revive mixed bathing, he had thought through, in his own way, a logical ideal:

> In stark contrast to Christianity's tendency to suppress bathing, Buddhism treated the custom as a way to gain virtue, and hence included it as part of meritorious and memorial events. The change of the bathing medium from steam to hot water must have had some significant meaning.
>
> The pleasure of bathing in hot water is the ecstatic skin sensation caused by the hot water seeping in through the pores, which erases the distinction between skin and water, that is, the inside and outside. Or alternatively we could call it that feeling of being enveloped by hot water. There is even a saying that the water of a bath that no one else has soaked in feels hard on the skin. This suggests not only the physiological process of perspiring amidst the steam, but also the psychological pleasure of one's internal and external self *mingling* together.
>
> I cannot help but think that this is one typical example of the sensualisation of Buddhist philosophy. (Hashimoto 1977)

Public baths are the type of place where anyone who pays the entrance fee is welcome. Everyone is naked, and no one uses violence. Everyone shares the bath, and after a while each person leaves. The order of things at the bathhouse has a form that reflects social customs developed over a long period of time. It is a form of customary law that is set without legislation. The forms contained in

---

7 Hashimoto was the 30th chief abbot of Hōnen'in, an independent Pure Land Buddhist temple located in Kyōto. He also taught philosophy and ethics at Kobe University.

these customs are more fundamental than written morals and more fundamental than laws set by the government of the time. In cultures where there are no public baths, there may be a form in group dance, for example, that is equally moral and legal because of a rule that allows anyone to join in the dance. Sudden violent actions such as rape and homicide may be curtailed by learning about the forms that drive the customs of public bathing and group dance.

After returning from the US, the wellness guru Okada Torajirō (1872–1920) founded during the Taishō period a method of sitting still (*seizahō*) for physical health and mental tranquillity.[8] He gained inspiration for this method while living in America—especially through watching dance. He remarked that had he been in America, he would have based his method on dance, but because he was in Japan, he chose the action of sitting still.

The foundation of the United States of America, with the participation of groups including the Puritans carried there on the Mayflower, was driven by an intention to build a new society governed by a new set of rules. After the establishment of the nation, various smaller communities were developed. The book *Communalism: From Its Origins to the Twentieth Century* (1974) examines what has happened to some of these idealistic communities. According to its author, Kenneth Rexroth (1905–1988), only a few of the communes that started with their own rules and regulations have survived, and even those that seem to be still active have changed in nature and have lost their founders.[9] Many communes have disappeared altogether.

Outstanding in this general regard was the Shakers' community established in 1776 in Niskayuna, Watervliet, near Albany in New York

---

8 Okada was also a Japanese agricultural researcher and philosopher. He graduated from an agricultural college and spent several years working to improve rice yields, before moving to the US to pursue his philosophical interests. Okada returned to Japan after nearly four years to enter into an arranged marriage that later fell apart due to disagreements with his father-in-law.

9 Rexroth was an American poet, translator, critical essayist and political activist. Known in his lifetime as the Godfather of the Beat Generation (an association that he disliked), Rexroth's interest in world literature and his translation of Japanese and Chinese poetry into English helped open American poetry to Asian influences. His works include *The Phoenix and the Tortoise* (1944), *Thou Shalt Not Kill: A Memorial for Dylan Thomas* (1955) and *The Heart's Garden, The Garden's Heart* (1967).

State.[10] The founder, Mother Ann Lee, prohibited sexual intercourse, and after a day's work and supper, when sexual desire was at its peak, she got the members to start dancing and to continue until they were so exhausted that they went home to their own beds. They therefore had no children of their own, but established a large orphanage to adopt and raise children who had lost their families. The members carefully trained these children in the ways of refined agriculture, furniture making and carpentry, and let them leave the commune without forcing them to become believers. As a result, the commune disappeared, leaving behind only beautifully crafted furniture. By the mid-twentieth century, the commune that had had twenty villages and six thousand villagers just a century earlier was reduced to around 100 elderly people.

The dance they performed, unique to the Shakers, was preceded by a minister's sermon and some hymns. Men and women would stand on opposite sides of a large hall and sing hymns as they approached each other, dragging their feet and stretching their arms straight forward. As they passed each other, they would become excited and exchange foreign-sounding words, and then hug and kiss each other before repeating the process again. The most passionate form of love was exchanged here, filling the room with a heated atmosphere. The session would conclude with irregular dances such as the jitterbug.

In another commune founded by John Humphrey Noyes (1811–1886) in Oneida, Vermont, in 1846, everyone shared their property and sexuality.[11] Noyes recognised two purposes of sex: propagation and pleasure. He advocated not only oral sex but also what he called 'male continence' [aka coitus reservatus]—that is, for men to hold ejaculation during sex to elicit a satisfied response from their partners. As part of this arrangement, there were not to be any boys,

---

10 The Shakers, or the United Society of Believers in Christ's Second Appearing, are a millenarian restorationist Christian sect that was founded in mid-18th century England and spread to the United States in the 1770s and 1780s. Membership peaked at around 2,000 to 4,000 believers across 18 major (and numerous smaller) communities in the US, though only Sabbathday Lake Shaker Village in Maine is active today. It has three members.

11 Noyes was an American preacher, religious philosopher and utopian socialist who believed that the second coming of Christ had already happened and that true Christians—such as himself—were perfect and free of sin. When he founded the Oneida Community, he sought to realise Jesus's millennial kingdom by practising communalism, complex marriage (free love), male continence and mutual criticism in order to eliminate undesirable character traits.

widows or older women who had difficulties in obtaining sex. This system of sexual practice had a form that mitigated violence within the community. However, the strict rules Noyes imposed on sexual intercourse were in reality managed by the community. This custom of communal sex made Oneida famous all over the US, bringing in tourists with curiosity but no belief in communal sexuality. Eventually, young people including Noyes's own descendants began to oppose his teachings, and he fled the community when he was sixty-eight. Free sex was abandoned, and the utopian communalism ended on 1 January 1881. However, the custom of diligence that was upheld for a century became the foundation of a silverware company, which continues to hand down its communalism to this day (Kuratsuka 1990).

Both the Shakers community and the Oneida community are based on pacifism; the latter presented their own 'Declaration of Independence' to the US as a protest against slavery. Oliver Wendell Holmes Jr. (1841–1935), who grew up in these times, fought as a lieutenant in the Union Army during the Civil War that divided the country into two for the first time since its independence.[12] In his military career, he was wounded three times, experiences that greatly impacted his thinking as a lawyer. Holmes served as Justice of the Supreme Court in his nineties. In his belief that 'The life of the law has not been logic: it has been experience', he opened a new avenue in US jurisprudence by arguing that even the Constitution was not written in anticipation of everything that would happen in the future, and that what was felt to be necessary at different points of time should be incorporated into the operation of the Constitution. His view as a jurist was that experience has form and that that form, once extracted from experience, ought to be immersed in new experiences and given new practical applications. The forms of human relationships integrated into public bathing and dancing ultimately derive from the foundations of this nuance of the law.

---

12 Holmes was a jurist and legal scholar. He served as a Supreme Court Justice from 1902 until his retirement in 1932. A civil libertarian and fierce advocate of the First Amendment, he remains one of the most commonly cited and influential American common law judges in history.

Chapter 8

The Day Japan Became Naked

In this chapter, Tsurumi explores the nakedness of Japan following the country's surrender to the Allied Forces and its subsequent demilitarisation. Arguing that the defeat created a blank space in the Japanese belief system, he presents various reactions to the demise of the empire, including the fascinating story of Kitamura Sayo, who established a dancing religion in Japan in 1944 that gained a widespread following in the wake of the war. Initially, Kitamura was a staunch supporter of national goals, but as a deity infiltrated her thoughts, she adopted an increasingly confrontational stance towards the secular 'maggot world' of the emperor, the bureaucracy and the intelligentsia. Tsurumi charts the intensity and vastness of Kitamura's ambit, from her petitions to her followers to cleanse themselves to her descriptions of modern Japan as 'shit' and the Japanese as 'maggot beggars'. He then draws from cellular theory to argue that Kitamura's dancing religion represented a movement which gave individuals the freedom to retrieve the 'microcosm' of human existence from the bottom of their guts. At the end of the chapter, Tsurumi observes that Kitamura's Japanese believers granted her the same kind of trust that Ame no Uzume received from her fellow deities.

In 1945, as houses burned down in continuous air raids, the Japanese were driven to live almost naked lives. They were hoping that the Combined Fleet would be mobilised, unaware that it no longer existed.

On 23 June, the battle of Okinawa drew to a close. Then on 15 August, the war officially ended. The Allied Forces' Supreme Commander, General Douglas MacArthur (1880–1964), landed in mainland Japan on 28 August, and five days later, on 2 September, two Japanese

Chapter 8

government representatives signed the document of surrender.[1] Japan was thus demilitarised, and became a naked nation.

In the lead up to this day, there were some people who wondered if there was perhaps another way.

In 1942, Sakaguchi Ango (1906–1955) wrote in his essay 'Nihon bunka shikan' (A personal view of Japanese culture) that it would pose no problem if the Hōryūji and Byōdōin temples were razed to the ground.[2] After the defeat, in his essay 'Darakuron' (Discourse on decadence, 1946) and his fictional work 'Hakuchi' (The idiot, 1946), he urged that the Japanese make a fresh start based on the body and physicality (*nikutai*) [rather than ideology or spirituality]. By contrast, Yamagishi Miyozō (1901–1961) discovered the importance of paying attention to the bare necessities of life from his experience of poultry farming.[3] He went on to establish an agricultural community, and developed a method of study that used the fewest words possible. These ideas did not disappear as temporary fads of post-war Japan, but rather, became rooted and evolved into a movement that embraced physical language within the framework of a rapidly growing economic power.

In the early morning of 4 May 1944, a farmer woman in Tabuse-chō, Kumage-gun, Yamaguchi prefecture by the name of Kitamura Sayo (1900–1967)[4] got out of bed, offered prayers to the *kamidana*[5] shrine, and went to her husband's futon and kicked his pillow out from under his head. Then the voice of another spoke from inside her:

---

1 Foreign Minister Shigemitsu Mamoru and General Umezu Yoshijirō signed what was called the Japanese Instrument of Surrender on the deck of the USS Missouri in Tokyo Bay on 2 September 1945.

2 The essay has been translated into English by James Dorsey. Sakaguchi was a Japanese writer of short stories, novels and essays, and a leading figure in modern Japanese literature. His works also include the short stories 'Sensō to hitori no onna' (1946, translated by Lane Dunlop as 'One woman and the war') and 'Sakura no mori no mankai no shita' (1947, translated by Jay Rubin as 'In the forest, under cherries in full bloom').

3 Yamagishi was a farmer and founder of the Yamagishi movement, a network of egalitarian agricultural communities whose members lived without money and with only minimal material possessions.

4 Kitamura Sayo was first introduced in Chapter 1, footnote 11.

5 *Kamidana* ('god-shelf') are small household altars dedicated to *kami*, often local deities or ones associated with particular professions. Family members typically cleanse their hands or mouth before offering prayers, food and flowers at the altar.

The Day Japan Became Naked

Figure 8.1: Kitamura Sayo

"Hey, Seinoshin, your wife O-Sayo has been purifying herself with cold water despite the chill of the mid-winter morn and noon, and her heartfelt prayers have most certainly reached Heaven! And yet, look at you! You are also my child, but all you do is just sleep, without any praying! Get up at once and pray!" (Tenshō Kōtai Jingūkyō ed. 1951)

Until that point, Kitamura Sayo had been a hardworking farmer. Married to the thirty-seven-year-old Kitamura Seinoshin, who did exactly what his mother told him to do (including divorcing five previous wives), Sayo, as his sixth wife, worked without a word of complaint until her mother-in-law died at the age of ninety.

Sayo's way of thinking, typical of the average Japanese person of the period, prioritised the nation-state, teaching its militarism to children without any sort of modification. However, once the deity infiltrated her, she started to speak out freely and coarsely. The deity, at first, shouted the same lines as the government—that is, 'Fight for Japan, sacrifice your own life for the country'—at the top of her voice, to everyone she met. In autumn 1944, however, as the war was simmering down, she suddenly began to speak ill of the imperial family.

> On 28 September, the Founder Sayo went as usual to the Hachimangū Shrine in Yawata on her bicycle, and then visited Mr Hirai [Tsurumi's note: Hirai Kenryū (or possibly Nobutatsu)], a graduate

105

Chapter 8

of Hiroshima Higher Normal School, who worked for the Ministry of Education. He had built a small shrine as the Yoda branch of the Inari Association attached to the Fushimi National Shrine of Major Grade and it attracted many members).[6]

There she spoke ill of the Emperor, as her gut told her to do.

Unlike today, this was a time when the entire country served His Imperial Majesty, who was regarded as more important than the nation. Mr Hirai was thus very surprised when she bad-mouthed him, and said to her:

'If the deity made you say such things, there's nothing to be done about it, but you must absolutely avoid speaking ill of the Imperial family like that. It's far too dangerous.'

His advice was out of concern for her safety. However, the Founder turned red and shouted at the top of her voice:

'Shut your mouth! O-Sayo, even as a woman, is resolutely determined to carry out sacred deeds. Stop your grumbling!'

She then stood up and left Mr Hirai's house. On her way home, the voice in her gut spoke to her again.

'O-Sayo, if you keep on wandering around, saying bad things about the Imperial family, you'll be caught one day and executed. Yoshito [her eldest son, who was in the military] will feel responsible and commit *hara-kiri*. Seinoshin will go crazy and die. Whatever pitiful assets you have will be shared by your relatives.'

She began to wonder if this was the voice of an evil god, so she sat to attention at the altar and prayed. Then she asked: 'Am I being used by an evil god or by a virtuous god?', to which the one in her gut replied, 'To tell the truth, I am a virtuous god, but unless someone sacrifices themselves, this country cannot be saved. What do you think of that?'

The Founder said to herself: 'All right, if I die, and my family members die, and our pitiful assets are lost—if just these things can save this country, then please, feel free to use me now.'

---

6 With the establishment of Japanese Kokka Shintō (State Shinto), official Shinto shrines (with the exception of the Ise Grand Shrine) were divided into *kanpeisha* (官幣社, Imperial shrines) and *kokuheisha* (国幣社, National shrines). *Kokuheisha* are subdivided into minor, medium and major shrines. Fushimi National Shrine of Major Grade is a reference to Fushimi Inari Shrine in Kyoto.

'There! That is the true essence of worship', said the voice, and the Founder's body was raised about two *shaku* [approximately 60cm] into the air.

The founder was absolutely determined to devote her life to the deity and save the country. (Tenshō Kōtai Jingūkyō ed. 1951)

What was inside Sayo's gut was not against the government initially. Needless to say, before this deity started to speak out, Sayo's position was one of contributing to the sacred war, exactly as the government demanded. The sudden change in her position in autumn 1944 opposing the government—first appearing in the deity inside her, and then inside herself—does not demonstrate the same sort of consistency as seen in cases such as the late Edo founder of Tenrikyō, Nakayama Miki (1798–1887)[7] or the founder of Konkōkyō, Kawate Bunjirō (1814–1883).[8] Since the *Seisho* scripture does not attempt to conceal this change in Kitamura Sayo, it can be regarded as reliable.[9] Moreover, the fact that her neighbours accepted this change indicates a characteristic of Japanese culture that does not emphasise consistency.

According to the *Seisho*, Kitamura Sayo was born on 1 January 1900 into a farming family located in Ōsato, Hizumi-son, Kuga-gun (present-day Yanai-shi), Yamaguchi prefecture. Sayo was the fourth daughter of her father Ekimoto Chōzō and her mother Ura. When she was twenty, she was married to Kitamura Seinoshin of Hano, Tabuse-chō, Kumage-gun, Yamaguchi prefecture. At around the age of sixteen or seventeen, Seinoshin had decided he wanted to emigrate overseas, and so went to Hawaii where his uncle lived. For seven or eight years he worked there. In 1910, with considerable savings in hand,

---

[7] Nakayama was a Japanese farmer and religious leader who founded Tenrikyō (天理教). Her followers believed that Nakayama was the Shrine of God, through which God revealed divine intent. The religion aims to promote *yōki yusan* (陽気遊山, 'Joyous Life', also known as *yōki gurashi* 陽気暮) through acts of charity and mindfulness.

[8] Kawate was also a farmer and religious leader who founded Konkōkyō (金光教), a Shinto sect whose followers believe that *kami* are present within the world, and that human life can be bettered by living virtuously and appreciating all things.

[9] Tenshō Kōtai Jingūkyō (天照皇大神宮教) is the name of the movement. The quoted passages come from the scripture published by the movement called the *Seisho* (生書 The book of life), which is a homophone of the Japanese word for Bible (聖書 lit. Holy book). All quotations from this source below are shown as Tenshō Kōtai Jingūkyō 1951. Page numbers are not included in Tsurumi's quotations.

Chapter 8

he returned to Japan, built a house and lived with his parents. As I mentioned earlier, Sayo was his sixth wife. At the time, the Kitamuras owned more than a hectare [10,000 square metres] of rice paddies and 2 or 3 ares of vegetable patches [200–300 square metres], which in this region was quite a large-scale farm.

Sayo worked hard in the rice fields and vegetable patches until her mother-in-law, Take, trusted her even more than her own middle-aged son Seinoshin, and handed her the bank passbook and wallet. For more than twenty years, everyone in the neighbourhood knew how hard Sayo worked. The trust she built up with her neighbours was key to their continued support of her even after she came to be regarded as insane. Both prior to and soon after the onset of her insanity, the thoughts she expressed publicly were completely loyal and patriotic. But at the point where her loyalty to government policy became the most intense, she launched a counterattack criticising government policy using precisely the same principles.

Let me quote Sayo's letter dated 27 July 1944, addressed to a teacher at Hizumi Elementary School, Matsumoto Chie, copied verbatim in the *Seisho*. It reflects the sort of typical public ideological stance held by an average Japanese person at the time. The only difference here is that Sayo's version of the ideology took an extreme form, which she sincerely believed. This is where her criticism of Japanese bureaucrats and civilians began, as they did not adhere to her extreme ideology.

> As we are old and don't even read the newspaper, we don't really know anything, but they say that the flowers were blooming in Saipan. Yoshito wrote to us saying he was happy to find a place to bury his twenty-three-year-old bones, so wherever he dies, it will conform to his wish.
>
> We, too, made up our minds to give our son to the country. We don't expect him to be able to come home alive in such a big war. We are willing to give our son to the country, and we are not attached to our house or assets.
>
> My only wish is that this precious land of Imperial Japan, with its history of three thousand years, will continue to shine throughout the world for all eternity. I have been praying for this, and only this.
>
> Now is the time to abandon ourselves, and for each one of us to serve His Imperial Majesty. (Tenshō Kōtai Jingūkyō ed. 1951)

The long letter continues.

> To think that in the middle of this great war, there are some people who are only concerned with making profits for themselves through the black market. I'm convinced that if I were a god, I would find and kill each one of them.

From about here, the spirit in Sayo's gut wanted to drag her out of Japan to make her see the other countries of the world.

Her mother-in-law died on 10 November 1940. Her eldest son joined the army in January 1942. Two years later, on 4 May 1944, whatever had crept inside her started to speak out.

To begin with, the voice said:

> Be an honest person. Pray, and be honest. Everyone in Japan, be honest. If every Japanese person becomes honest, Japan will definitely win the war. (Tenshō Kōtai Jingūkyō ed. 1951)

It was on 28 September 1944 when the voice inside Sayo's gut started to speak ill of the emperor:

> Two thousand six hundred and five years ago, the *kami* knew exactly where on earth to descend.[10] Just as the *mikoshi*[11] shrine serves as the sacred resting place during the Maggot Festival,[12] the *kami* knows where to come to rest, and O-Sayo is it for now. (Tenshō Kōtai Jingūkyō ed. 1951)

From the position of the temporary resting place for the *kami*, the government's order for one hundred million people to die in honour of the national polity (i.e. the emperor) looked evil.

---

10 *Kenkoku kinen no hi* (建国記念の日, National Foundation Day), formerly known as *Kigensetsu* (紀元節), is an annual celebration held on 11 February, to mark the accession of Emperor Jinmu, the legendary first Emperor of Japan (see Chapter 4, footnote 12). Since 660 BCE is supposed to mark the first year of the foundation, 1944 would be the 2605th year.

11 *Mikoshi* (神輿) are sacred religious palanquins that transport Shinto deities between main and temporary shrines during festivals, or when deities are moved to a new shrine.

12 The Maggot Festival is named after the final part of the festival procession, during which the participants lie at random on the ground, resembling maggots.

Chapter 8

The descendant of the Emperor who was told to govern the Land of Roots[13] is now boxed in, surrounded by the Double Bridge, the Quadruple Bridge and even the Sextet Bridge,[14] nailed in, sealed up, thrown up to the ceiling, and made into an ornament—that's the current maggot Emperor! He isn't a living god or a god incarnate. He's nothing. (Tenshō Kōtai Jingūkyō ed. 1951)

The defeat in the war created a blank space among the neighbours. What they believed in was lost, leaving a giant hole in their lives. In the middle of this hole stood Kitamura Sayo, completely devoid of fear. Her thunderous voice resounded in people's hearts at the time.

"Maggot beggars, wake up! Beggars, traitor beggars, wake up! The Heavenly Cave door is open!" (Tenshō Kōtai Jingūkyō ed. 1951)

This formed part of the song-sermon delivered on 16 August, the day after the defeat, at the assembly hall of Kumage High School.

The meeting was supposed to start at ten in the morning, but the group was told that without police permission, no one could use the venue for a lecture. So they all agreed that instead of a lecture, they would have a song-sermon. Sayo's performance lasted for an hour, with no pauses.

"Now is the time for great changes in Heaven and on Earth. Wake up, quickly, wake up! I have given the key to O-Sayo to enact changes, but you probably don't understand this. You see, O-Sayo has a divine wireless machine attached to her, so that she can see everything from up above in Heaven right down to the Land of Fire, and everything in between. If you want to know about fate and destiny, about making life in this world, about *kami* and Buddha,

---

13 Ne no kuni (根の国, Land of Roots) is a netherworld in Japanese mythology, though its relationship to other worlds such as Yomi no kuni (黄泉の国, Land of Darkness) and Tokoyo no kuni (常世の国, Eternal Land) remains unclear. Here, the reference is to Amaterasu instructing Ninigi to descend from Takamagahara (see Chapter 1, footnote 5) and govern the land below.

14 The Double Bridge is a reference to Nijūbashi in front of the Imperial Palace Main Gate. The name comes from the bridge's double structure to support the original wooden bridge. There is no Quadruple Bridge or Sextet Bridge, although the palace is surrounded by a moat with gates and bridges.

she will teach you for free any time, as long as you polish your spirit..." (Tenshō Kōtai Jingūkyō ed. 1951)

After Sayo's death, I visited the main shrine of the Tenshō Kōtai Jingūkyō where I participated in a ritual and listened to the tape recording of the founder's song-sermon. Her granddaughter, Kitamura Kiyokazu,[15] took over the leadership of the religious group, but the core of the ritual was listening to the Founder's recordings. Although the base of the music was like *naniwabushi*, or rather more like its original form *deroren saimon* or *ahodara-kyō*, it deviated from any existing genre of music. In the middle, the Founder often changed her voice modulation and randomly inserted something, so that sometimes it sounded like a modern popular song, *ryūkōka*, or a traditional-type *enka*, or even like the *katsuben* narrator of silent movies or a *shigin* recitation.[16] In short, it was a continuous flood of sounds.

Takahashi Kazumi (1931–1971) depicted a dancing religion in his novel *Jashūmon* (The Heretic Faith, 1966).[17] I'm not sure if he ever met Kitamura Sayo, but he took note of the fundamental tone of her verbal expressions, and was impressed by her method of describing modern Japan using the metaphors of 'shit', 'shit pot' and 'maggots' which were familiar elements of everyday life for any Japanese at the time. For example, Kitamura writes:

> "I tell you what maggot beggars are. They are in the shit pot, trying to crawl up above the others, trampling on their fellow maggots. You see maggot beggars struggling to get stature, honours and

---

15 Kiyokazu (清和) is unusual for a woman's name.
16 *Naniwabushi* (浪花節) is a form of traditional Japanese narrative singing, often accompanied by *shamisen*. It is based on *deroren saimon* (デロレン祭文), a performing art involving the blowing of conch shells, and *ahodara-kyō* (あほだら経), light-hearted folk songs. *Ryūkōka* (流行歌) is used today to refer specifically to popular Japanese music in the early part of the 20th century. *Enka* (演歌) is a popular Japanese musical genre that is thought to bear a stylistic resemblance to traditional Japanese music. *Katsuben* (活弁), also known as *benshi* (弁士), were Japanese performers of live narration for Western and Japanese silent films. *Shigin* (詩吟) is a form of poetry recitation.
17 Takahashi was a Japanese novelist and scholar of Chinese literature. Although Tenshō Kōtai Jingūkyō was nicknamed *odoru shūkyō* (dancing religion), Hinomoto-kyō, the religion in *Jashūmon*, was probably modelled after Deguchi Nao's Ōmotokyō.

Chapter 8

Figure 8.2:
Self-effacing dance
Source: *The Sun Photo Times* (25 September 1948), Mainichi Newspapers Company.

wealth, using all sorts of backhanded and sideways methods, scuffling around and even resorting to using boxes of cakes for bribery." (Tenshō Kōtai Jingūkyō ed. 1951)

In a similar vein to Takahashi, Mori Hideto (1933–2013), the author of the first biography of Kitamura Sayo written by a non-believer, titled his book *Uji no kojiki yo me o samase* (Wake up, Maggot Beggars!, 1975).

During the war, Sayo sang the songs that emerged from her gut, and told the people around her to sing, too. Even they thought they couldn't possibly sing themselves, somehow songs came out their guts too. And this was in the middle of the war!

Eventually Sayo's body began to shake and she started to dance as instructed by the *kami*, and then the people around her followed. When Sayo went to Tokyo after the defeat, this self-effacing dance gathered huge crowds in the square outside the station, and the group became famous as the 'dancing religion'.

From the late stage of the war to the immediate post-war period in Japan, when there were not enough medical facilities or medicines, the group's closed-eye dancing rite performed *en masse* in open spaces, free from social shackles, offered a means of therapy for neuroses and psychoses, and helped to cure many psychogenetic illnesses. Through physical exercise, the image of one's inner self permeates the whole body and psyche in order to restore health. It is an effective folk remedy.

The Day Japan Became Naked

In reference to Lynn Margulis's 'Symbiosis in Cell Revolution' (in *Microcosmos: Four Billion Years of Evolution from Our Microbial Ancestors*, 1986),[18] the anthropologist Fujioka Yoshinaru (1924–1991) writes:

> Human beings live as such since the earliest biological form during the age of the primordial Earth, according to Lynn Margulis. At the end of her Introduction, she writes:
> [...] there is evidence to show that we are recombined from powerful bacterial communities with a multibillion-year-old history. We are part of an intricate network that comes from the original bacterial takeover of the Earth. (Margulis 1986: 24)
> Human wisdom, therefore, is nothing but the wisdom of all the living creatures on Earth; to say that man stood on the moon amounts to a sense of heroism and anthropocentrism. Margulis remarks that objectively speaking, "with respiring mitochondria and spirochetal secret agents dividing their cells, communities of the microcosm have alighted—if briefly—on the moon" (Ibid. 228). According to her way of thinking, it is arrogant of human beings to talk about the protection of the Earth since if all humans ceased to exist because of environmental pollution, life on Earth as a whole would not be affected in the slightest. All human beings can do is try to maintain the environment for themselves. [...]
> We are, to use Margulis's words, a group of organisms that have existed since the primordial Earth age, and for this reason—to express this in East Asian philosophical terms—we are nothing more than a fragment of a microcosm. Where we come from "exists" in our bodies now, as it did originally. (Fujioka 1989)

The song and dance emerging from the bottom of the gut which Kitamura Sayo expressed during the war represented a movement from which each individual could retrieve the freedom of the microcosmic world inside their bodies. From this point of view, the watershed of the

---

18 Margulis (1938–2011) was an American evolutionary microbiologist and leading figure in the development of modern symbiogenesis, the theory that eukaryotic cells developed from prokaryotic organisms through endosymbiosis. Margulis was also a key proponent of Robert Whittaker's five-kingdom classification system, and co-developed the Gaia hypothesis with the British chemist James Lovelock.

Chapter 8

defeat in the war was a trifling matter, as was the entry of foreigners into Japan. Kitamura went to Hawaii on 15 May 1952, and two years later, on 18 February 1954, she started a tour of the US in that state, before moving on to San Francisco, Boston, Chicago, Washington DC, New York and Los Angeles.

The photographic collection *Kami no kuni* (The Divine Country, Tenshō Kōtai Jingūkyō 1966) includes a photograph of Kitamura landing in Chicago with a meek expression in her eyes. There is no trace of an inferiority complex, nor the opposite, a sense of arrogance, which was a typical Japanese reaction towards the Americans at the time.

Addressing Ame no Uzume, Amaterasu said '[...] you are [the type of] deity who can face and overwhelm [others]. Therefore go alone and inquire' (Philippi 1968: 138). The Japanese (at least the believers) granted the same kind of trust to Kitamura that Uzume had received. She never feared different races, even during the war.

Not only during the war, but after the defeat too, newspapers and magazines belittled and attempted to undermine Kitamura's activities. Most of the reports on the 'dancing religion' were only half serious—a situation that was not unrelated to the fact that from the beginning of Shōwa, journalists were all university graduates. During and after the war respectively Nazi Germany's militarism and Western democracy were treated as legitimate thought systems; no serious reporter was going to take up the idea of maggots put forward by Kitamura, who had only finished primary school. The idea of the maggots, however, contained a viewpoint that crossed wartime boundaries and linked Japan to Asia, even though Japan was divided from the rest of Asia following the war. The media were so engrossed in looking at the Occupation Forces that they had no idea that during the war, while they were following the military government around, Kitamura was transposing herself by listening to the voice inside her gut.

In Japan, where flush toilets were gaining widespread popularity, preaching about maggots became increasingly unrelatable. Japanese youths today are so used to cleanliness that when they travel to New York on group tours and go without a shower for three days, they develop skin problems. Psychologist Ōhira Ken's (b. 1949) book, *Yutakasa no seishin byōri* (The Psychopathology of Affluence, 1990) vividly describes the process of development of a culture among young people where they encase themselves in brand clothing and accessories and talk endlessly about them. This new language is at odds with the governing powers that manage contemporary Japanese society through a quantitative grasp of numbers. However, unlike either of these cases, the language used in the narrative of the maggots still survives today as a link between Japan and the rest of Asia. The Yamagishi movement, which became active at about the same time that Kitamura Sayo began her religion, has become a large community by taking advantage of increases in land prices. They continue to engage in agriculture in the age of industrialisation, taking consignments of land from people who have lost interest in ploughing the fields. Even in an age when second-generation farmers abandon the unprofitable farming industry and sell their land, what sustains human beings is not that different from Kitamura Sayo's preaching.

Chapter 9

Painting the Body in Two Colours

This chapter delves into the topic of individuals as political activists who attempt to live outside the norms of Japanese society. By way of example, Tsurumi introduces various socialist and anarchist figures of the early twentieth century before discussing the Buddhist nun and feminist Setouchi Jakuchō at length. Setouchi became a prolific writer of fiction and non-fiction after divorcing her husband in 1950 and moving to Kyoto. In 1973, she took the tonsure, but did not step back from her outspoken stance on public issues, continuing to advocate for causes she believed in. Tsurumi highlights how Setouchi creates a colour division within herself: in one of her essays, the narrative plays out through a conversation between her pre- and post-tonsure selves (Setouchi Harumi and Setouchi Jakuchō respectively), who have opposing viewpoints on topics such as sex. He concludes the chapter by nominating Setouchi as a successor of Ame no Uzume.

In 1985, at the United Nations Decade for Women conference in Kenya,[1] the Catholic sister and educationalist Watanabe Kazuko (1927–2016)[2] talked about Setouchi Harumi (aka Setouchi Jakuchō, 1922–2021) as a Japanese feminist. I admired her choice of this public figure. Since Setouchi was a Buddhist nun, her case probably

---

1 Tsurumi's note: Following on from the International Women's Year in 1975, a global conference was held in 1985 in Nairobi, marking the final year of the International Decade for Women. Participants included government representatives from various countries, as well as representatives from many NGOs.

2 Watanabe was a member of the Sisters of Notre Dame de Namur, a Catholic institute of religious sisters that was founded to educate the poor. She served as president of Notre Dame Seishin University, as well as administrative director of the Japanese Federation of Catholic Schools, and received the Order of the Rising Sun in 2016.

Chapter 9

impressed the delegates gathered from all over the world too as an example of feminism that was not incompatible with religion in Japan. Setouchi was a supporter of Fuji Shigeko, who was accused and found guilty of the Tokushima Radio Merchant Murder Case.[3] Fuji continued to protest her innocence both during her incarceration and after her release, following the completion of her sentence. Setouchi joined the movement that was organised as an attempt to open the way to a retrial of the case. Even though Fuji's adopted daughter had given evidence attesting to her stepmother's innocence, it was dismissed by the authorities as nothing more than the unreliable statement of a minor. The police also covered up the fact that the young employees working at the shop had amended their statements in support of the prosecution. As these facts came to light, they cast doubt on Fuji's guilt. It was widely suspected that the police and the detectives in charge of the case harboured ill feelings toward Fuji due to her de facto relationship with the radio merchant, as well as her liberated way of living, and it was suspected that they had asked the young workers leading questions.

However, once the guilty verdict was passed down, the court was unwilling to change its judgement, and it was difficult to find an opening for a retrial. When Fuji died [in 1979], her family took over the responsibility of appealing for a new trial.

In 1973, Setouchi suddenly joined a Buddhist order, shaved her head and became a nun. Against any expectation that this might mean the end of her social commitments, she continued to support the retrial request, right up until Fuji's innocence was proven [in 1985] after her death.

---

3 Tsurumi's note: On 5 November 1953, Saegusa Kamesaburō, a 53-year-old radio store owner in Tokushima, was stabbed to death. The Tokushima District Public Prosecutor's Office arrested 43-year-old Fuji Shigeko the following year, in August 1954. Despite Fuji's claim to innocence, the first trial sentenced her to 13 years' imprisonment. The second trial returned the same result, leading Fuji to abandon her appeal. However, in 1959, a request for a retrial was filed after two youths (aged 16 and 17) who worked in the store and lived at the house at the time, and whose testimony was a decisive factor in the conviction, confessed to perjuring themselves out of their fear of the police. [Fuji was released in 1966.] Fuji died on 15 November 1979, but her siblings carried out her final wishes by pressing on with the appeal, and in December 1980, the Tokushima District Court reopened the case. On 9 July 1985, Fuji was acquitted. This verdict marks the first posthumous acquittal in Japan (Watanabe 1983).

Figure 9.1:
Setouchi stands in support of Fuji's family as they announce her verdict of innocence
Source:
Jiji Tsūshinsha
(9 July 1985).

Women who hold their heads high, free from concerns about what other people think of them, are often labelled impertinent; in Fuji's case, the detectives did not miss the chance to bully the accused. In response, Setouchi tried to protect Fuji's free way of living—an attitude that did not change after she took the tonsure. In the Meiji period, there were cases where religious figures were also political activists, such as one where the Buddhist priest Uchiyama Gudō (1874–1911) was implicated in the High Treason Incident of 1910.[4] In the following Taishō and Shōwa periods, however, taking Buddhist vows meant pledging obedience to the government of the time. Unlike almost all of the professional priests who belonged to Buddhist organisations during Shōwa, Setouchi never tried to force young people to obey the government. She dared to do things that nuns normally shunned—such as serialising '"Sei" no funshoku kessan' (Closing an embellished account of 'sex') in the magazine *Shinchō 45* (August 1989–May 1990, published in book form as *Waga sei to sei* [My life and my sex life 1990]). This way of life is linked to her support of Fuji Shigeko and shows her true nature.

---

4 Uchiyama was a Sōtō Zen Buddhist priest and anarcho-socialist activist who was outspoken in his support for redistributive land reform, democratic rights for all, the mass desertion of conscripts, and overturning the Meiji emperor system. The High Treason Incident was an alleged anarcho-socialist plot to assassinate Emperor Meiji. Following a mass arrest, 26 defendants were brought to trial, of whom 11 (including Uchiyama) were eventually executed on 24 January 1911.

Chapter 9

As a forerunner of Setouchi, Kinoshita Naoe (1869–1937) also comes to mind.[5] He was against the emperor system of the Meiji period and participated in the formation of the Social Democratic Party. In addition, at the time of the Russo-Japanese War (1904–1905), he was a central figure in the Heiminsha (Commoners' Association),[6] which adopted an active anti-war stance. In 1906, after the war, Kinoshita withdrew from socialist party politics, devoting himself instead to Okada Torajirō's 'sitting still' meditation.[7] During this time, however, he continued to participate in the movement led by Tanaka Shōzō (1841–1913) that campaigned against mining pollution in Yanaka-mura.[8] After Tanaka's death, Kinoshita kept up his support of the residents of Yanaka and even kept records until their departure from the village. In his texts, Kinoshita wrote on the Buddhist philosophers Nichiren, Hōnen and Shinran; in his younger days he had also been influenced by Jesus.[9] The teachings of these religious figures appear in his later writings. In a collection of essays published after Okada's death, *Kami, ningen, jiyū* (God, Human Beings, Freedom, 1934), he nominated various religions as 'stars', and formulated his own religion, whose principal practice was gazing at the empty spaces amongst the constellations of the night sky.

The Manchurian Incident (or Mukden Incident, 1931), which demonstrated imperialist absolutism in its rawest form, renewed

---

5 Kinoshita was a Japanese Christian socialist activist and author. He supported women's rights as well as environmental and anti-war movements in a series of magazines and novels, including the anti-war novel *Hi no hashira* (*Pillar of Fire*, 1904–1906, trans. Kenneth Strong), which the Japanese government banned in 1910.

6 Heiminsha was nominally a newspaper company that promoted socialist ideals, but it was also a key central organisation that brought together supporters of the socialist movement, including Kōtoku Shūsui (1871–1911) and Sakai Toshihiko (1871–1933).

7 See Chapter 7.

8 Tanaka was a Japanese politician, as well as a social and environmental activist. He was particularly vocal in his support for rural residents near the Watarase River, whose health and livelihoods were increasingly damaged by pollutants from the Ashio Copper Mine from the 1870s onwards.

9 Nichiren (1222–1282) was a Japanese Buddhist priest and philosopher whose writings formed the basis of Nichiren Buddhism. Hōnen (1133–1212) was a religious reformer who founded Jōdo-shū, the first independent branch of Japanese Pure Land Buddhism. Shinran (1173–1263) was one of Hōnen's pupils and the founder of Jōdo Shinshū, a school of Pure Land Buddhism.

Kinoshita's engagement with current affairs.[10] One example is the clear articulation of his critical views in a letter to Morito Tatsuo (1888–1984)[11] following the imprisonment of Kawakami Hajime (1879–1946).[12] The letter, dated 24 July 1936, is reproduced in Kawakami's autobiography. Interestingly, in Sōma Kokkō's (1876–1955) autobiography *Tekisuiroku* (A Record of Waterdrops), the Kinoshita of the Shōwa period (i.e. 1926 until his death in 1937) is depicted with contempt; nevertheless, her sketches have provided me with a key to understanding the strength of Kinoshita's political ideology.[13] Postwar scholars of intellectual history regarded Kinoshita after 1906 as a figure who abandoned all criticism of power, but this interpretation only reveals the narrow-mindedness of viewing politics along socialist and communist party lines. During the second decade of Shōwa (i.e. 1936–1945), what attracted me to Kinoshita most was his combination of nihilism and political criticism.

§

Setouchi Harumi was born on 15 May 1922 (the eleventh year of Taishō) in Tokushima city, to a merchant house selling all manner of Buddhist and Shintoist altars and goods. She had one elder sister. After graduating from Tokushima Girls' High School, she enrolled in the Japanese Department at Tokyo Women's Christian University. In 1943, Setouchi married, and in September that year she graduated

---

10 On 18 September 1931, in the Chinese city of Mukden (now Shenyang), a Japanese lieutenant detonated a small quantity of dynamite near a South Manchuria Railway line. The Imperial Japanese Army attributed the explosion to Chinese dissidents and then used the incident as a pretext for the 1931 invasion of Manchuria.

11 Morito was a Japanese economist, politician and educator who served as Japan's Minister of Education under Prime Minister Katayama Tetsu (1887–1978). He was also the first president of Hiroshima University.

12 Kawakami was a Japanese writer and economist. He was dismissed from his professorship at Kyoto Imperial University for his participation in the March 15 incident (a 1928 governmental crackdown on socialists and communists), and was later imprisoned for joining the then-outlawed Japanese Communist Party. Upon his release, he translated Marx's *Das Kapital* into Japanese.

13 Sōma was a Japanese entrepreneur, philanthropist and patron of struggling artists and writers. She and her husband founded the Nakamuraya bakery in Shinjuku, and also supported the pan-Asian movement.

from the university early due to the war. She then moved to Beijing where her husband worked.

1944: Setouchi's daughter was born. After the defeat, in 1946, the family of three returned to Japan, and from 1947 lived in Tokyo.

1948: Moved to Kyoto on her own and worked first in a publishing house and later at the paediatrics research institute attached to Kyoto University Hospital, before finding employment at the hospital's library. During this period she joined a coterie magazine and began to write novels.

1950: Got divorced. Earned money for the first time through the submission of manuscripts.

1951: Moved to Tokyo.

1957: 'Joshidaisei Chui Airin' (Qu Ailing, the female college student; fiction).

1958: *Kashin* (The Centre of a Flower; fiction).

1961: *Tamura Toshiko* (biographical novel).[14]

1963: *Natsu no owari* (*The End of Summer*, trans. Janine Beichman; fiction).

1965: *Kanoko ryōran* (biography of Okamoto Kanoko).[15]

---

14 Tamura Toshiko (born Satō Toshi, 1884–1945) was a Japanese novelist and feminist whose works include *Akirame* (Resignation, 1911) and *Miira no kuchibeni* (Lipstick on a Mummy, 1913). After her death, Tamura's royalties were used to establish the Tamura Toshiko Prize, an annual literary award that recognises outstanding works by female writers.

15 Okamoto Kanoko (1889–1939) was a Japanese author, tanka poet and Buddhist scholar. Her works include short stories 'Tsuru wa yamiki' (The dying crane, 1936), 'Kingyo ryōran' (A riot of goldfish, 1937, trans. J. Keith Vincent) and 'Rōgishō' (Portrait of an old geisha, 1938, trans. Kazuko Sugisaki).

1966: *Bi wa ranchō ni ari* (*Beauty in Disarray*, trans. Sanford Goldstein and Kazuji Ninomiya; biography of Itō Noe).[16]

1970: *Tōi koe* (Distant Voices; biography of Kanno Suga).[17]

1971: *Odayakana heya* (A Calm Room; fiction).

1972: *Yohaku no haru* (Springtime in the Margins; biography of Kaneko Fumiko).[18]

1973: 14 November, takes the tonsure at Chūsonji temple in Hiraizumi. Buddhist name: Jakuchō.

1974: *Izuko yori* (Whence; autobiography). Moved to Kyoto. Sixty-day training at Yokawa, Hieizan. Received the four-step esoteric training (*prayoga*). Founded an independent temple in Saga Toriimoto, Kyoto.

Of the many works of fiction Setouchi wrote, I like *Odayakana heya*.

> Looking down from her room on the seventh floor, the swell of the rooftops in the metropolis became a sea of grey that expanded to the horizon. Here and there among the waves of rooves, high rise buildings stood out conspicuously, looking like ships on a voyage; the various television towers and monuments scattered among them had the appearance of masts with their sails down.

---

16 Itō (1895–1923) was a Japanese anarchist, social critic, feminist and editor-in-chief of the feminist literary magazine *Seitō* (Bluestocking). In September 1923, shortly after the Great Kanto Earthquake, she was murdered along with her partner, anarchist Ōsugi Sakae (1885–1923) and his nephew by military police led by Amakasu Makahiko (1891–1945).

17 Kanno Suga (aka Kanno Sugako, 1881–1911) was a Japanese journalist and anarcho-feminist who advocated for freedom and equal rights for men and women. She was hanged for her alleged involvement in the High Treason Incident, becoming the first female political prisoner to be executed in modern Japan. See footnote 4, above.

18 Kaneko (1903–1926) was a Japanese anarchist and nihilist who was convicted of plotting to assassinate members of the Japanese imperial family, together with the Korean anarchist and independent activist Pak Yol (1902–1974). She was reported to have committed suicide in prison in 1926.

Chapter 9

> On rainy days and foggy days, the city looked even more nautical.
> Viewing the cityscape from her room, she felt lonely, as if she, too, was in a solitary cabin of a ship on a long voyage, drifting about the wide sea. (Setouchi 1971)

The novella depicts the flamboyance of an insincere man who visits this room, but the story is filled with the calm feeling of the woman who expects very little from him.

Before this work was published, Setouchi's real life was full of raw instances of being betrayed, as well as her own betrayals, in the triangular and quadrangular romances that are depicted in her autobiographical novel, *Izuko yori* (Whence). During these years, her estranged ex-husband and daughter rebuild their lives together, and after a long separation, they meet the author again. The novel ends with a story of the ex-husband, his new wife, and the daughter, who is now under the stepmother's care. The text depicts both the heroine, who lives out her life true to her feelings, and those around her, who endure the consequences of her actions, as they go about their own lives. The dexterity of this group portrayal is testament to the capacity of the author to write biographical novels.

Tamura Toshiko, Okamoto Kanoko, Itō Noe, Kanno Suga and Kaneko Fumiko: the women Setouchi Harumi chose as the protagonists of her biographical novels also lived their own lives, protecting their true feelings against contemporary society. There were people that they trampled on in the course of their lives, but naturally those people had their own lives too. Setouchi's biographical novels have a depth that is reflected in her ability to observe the people who were impacted by her triangular and quadrangular relationships in *Izuko yori* and other works such as *Natsu no owari* (The End of Summer).

After all these experiences, she reached the decision to become a nun.

> Before my tonsure, my mentor, Master Kon Shunchō (aka Kon Tōkō, 1898–1977), listened to my request to take Buddhist orders, and asked:[19]

---

19 In addition to being a high priest of the Tendai sect of Buddhism, Kon was also a novelist and, from July 1968 to July 1974, a member of the House of Councillors. His novel *Ogin-sama* (1956) won the 36th Naoki Prize.

"What will you do with your hair?"

I instantly replied:

"I'll have my head shaved."

I feared that a slovenly person like me might return to where I started soon after taking the orders unless I followed the ritual forms strictly. Master Kon very gently said:

"Well, you don't have to, you know."

I grinned without saying a word. Then he asked again:

"What about the lower half of your body?"

"I'll give it up."

My answer was easy. I was actually surprised by this question.

"I see, but you don't have to give it up, you know," muttered the Master. The topic was never again raised between us.

The above is an extract from the aforementioned 'Closing an embellished account of "sex"' (in Setouchi 1990). After this episode, Setouchi wonders if she was too hasty in her answer, which makes the autobiography all the more convincing.

The narrative takes the form of correspondence between Setouchi Jakuchō and Setouchi Harumi, which brings to mind a tribal custom in Africa.

According to Dominique Zahan, 'the first "monument" offered to color is the human body and... the first "canvas" for the artist was his own skin' (Zahan and Grieco 1970: 100).

The Greek arts divided the body into the upper and lower halves, creating the half-human half-beast Centaur, Silenus, Satyros, Gorgon, the Sirens and the griffin. By contrast, in Africa they chose the division of the right and the left, rather than the upper and the lower.

> Africa shows us a whole conception of the human being and his destiny in the ritual, vertical, color-division of the human being. Half white, half black, man is symmetrically divided in his very being into left and right, masculine and feminine, heaven and earth. (Zahan and Grieco 1970: 115)

Chapter 9

Setouchi applies a similar colour division to herself: her viewpoint as a nun comes from Setouchi Jakuchō, whereas her viewpoint prior to tonsure derives from Setouchi Harumi. The balance between these two determines how light is shed upon their mutual past concerning sex. In other words, this balance is based on the way she views her tonsure: when she became a nun, her secular self died and thereafter she looked upon herself as dead; yet, as she was still alive, her feelings as a nun did not constitute all of her self. This brings to mind a question I encountered in Okada Seizō's (1913–1994) novel *Teinengo* (After Retirement, 1975):[20] 'Can't we regard the dead body as matter that has completed living?' This extraordinary question was put by the protagonist to the coroner who conducted an autopsy on his sister, who had committed suicide. Priests may regard themselves as deceased and yet they are by no means 'matter that has completed living'. Rather, they are a form of living matter. Hence, even on the topic of sexuality, one that has already been clearly settled, a form of correspondence between the two perspectives of the priest and the non-priest emerges.

Long before becoming a nun—in fact, even from her primary school days when she had just begun to read—Setouchi Harumi would go to the pharmacy across the road from her house to indulge in reading erotic books from around the world.[21] From late Taishō to early Shōwa it was illegal to collect, translate or publish erotica from other cultures; anyone who engaged in these activities had to be prepared to face fines or imprisonment. For that reason, those who were prepared to take the risk were interested not only in financial gain but were seriously committed to disseminating the work as well. This sincerity is clearly reflected in the style of the promotional fliers distributed at the time, which Setouchi Harumi collected at Setouchi Jakuchō's request.

---

20 Okada was a Japanese novelist and journalist. His short story *Nyū Giniya Sangakusen* (New Guinea Mountain War, 1943), based on his experiences as a war correspondent, was awarded the 19th Naoki Prize in the first half of 1944.
21 This pharmacy specialised in contraceptives and other sex-related goods, though the books Setouchi read were not for sale, but part of the pharmacist's personal collection. The works included translations of the *Kama Sutra*, *Jin Ping Mei* (*The Plum in the Golden Vase* or *The Golden Lotus*), *One Thousand and One Nights*, the *Decameron*, and *Memoirs of a Woman of Pleasure* (popularly known as *Fanny Hill*).

Born in the morn, perish in the eve, all those **sham erotica** bookstores! Don't be fooled by them! All they do is spread their samples and never actually send any books. Don't be deceived by the sweet words of these shameless swindlers!

Look at the glorious history of our association,

Fighting through numerous oppressions!

Bacillus of erotica land! Bringing dishonour to us all

With firm determination to purge all the **swindlers**, we return to the world of erotica!!

Absolutely fed up with all the swindlers?

Come to us! Our resurrected association is an **oasis** in the **Gobi** Desert [Emphasis in original.]

The experience of reading such books with a serious curiosity as a primary school student formed both the background of Setouchi Harumi's literature and the foundation of 'Closing an embellished account of "sex"' after she became a nun. Through the works of people such as Umehara Hokumei (1901–1946)[22] and Koike Mubō (1895–1986),[23] who ventured to publish translations in this dangerous period, Setouchi Harumi stored a catalogue of sexual love in her memory from an early age, and later wrote about the facts of sexuality that she experienced, saw, heard and classified, including in the period after she entered the order. Since I have skipped over the graphic descriptions in this chapter, it may not be terribly interesting, but Setouchi also outlines various reports on how far into old age it is possible to have sex, before concluding:

---

22 Umehara was a Japanese writer and editor who played a prominent role in early-Shōwa *ero guro nansensu* culture, which saw the popularisation of literature, magazines, news articles and music that dealt with erotic grotesqueness. Notably, he published the magazine *Grotesque*, which was banned on several occasions between 1928 and 1931.

23 Koike was an artist, essayist and social commentator. After moving to Tokyo, he became involved in cultural projects, working with theatre companies and assisting with the establishment of buildings such as the Ichiyō Memorial Museum and the Shitamachi Museum.

Chapter 9

(From Harumi to Jakuchō): What is sexual love? Now I think I vaguely understand the profound meaning of Buddha's insistence on renouncing desire. Perhaps this is a result of ageing.

I congratulate you from the bottom of my heart for renouncing the world at age fifty-one and retiring from sexual love.

Many people still ask me leading questions about whether Jakuchō is hiding a lover or say that it would be impossible to give up sex with her level of vitality. What stupid things to say!

I feel I understand your current peace of mind more than anyone in this world.

I know why you couldn't help writing about the platonic love practiced by both Ryōkan and Saigyō.[24]

I still adore sexual love and can of course sympathise with people who indulge in it. If there was any man who said he was besotted with me even as I am now, I'd feel very happy and excited.

On the other hand, if I imagine myself engaged in sex now, my heart sinks.

I think your becoming a nun is, ultimately, an attainment of your aestheticism.

With sex, too, I just cannot think of it without aestheticism. A beautiful man's body, a male sexual organ full of youthful power—to women's eyes, these are the most beautiful things in this world.

An ageing body and an ageing sexual organ may be things that need to be perceived as beautiful. But in my eyes, as a secular person who is not ordained, the ugliness of old age still looks ugly.

(From Jakuchō to Harumi): Perhaps it is a good time to close this correspondence. A female journalist came to my temple the other day on business and told me she has been gaining much pleasure from reading this series. For your aestheticism as well, it's best if we close the curtain while it's still popular. Thank you for reminding me of various things.

---

[24] Ryōkan Taigu (1758–1831) was a Sōtō Zen Buddhist monk who lived most of his life as a hermit, writing poetry and calligraphy inspired by nature. Saigyō Hōshi (1118–1190) was a Buddhist monk and poet whose works are included in the imperial anthology, *Shin kokin wakashū* and many other collections, including his own *Sankashū* (Collection of a Mountain Home). His poetry and life have inspired many other poets, artists and performers.

> Finally, I have reached the point where I am able to think that sex between old people is beautiful.

Harumi and Jakuchō thus keep their disagreement right until the end regarding sex in old age.

A letter from Harumi to Jakuchō just prior to the one above quotes a late work by Tanizaki Jun'ichirō (1886–1965), *Fūten rōjin nikki* (1961; *Diary of a Mad Old Man*, trans. Howard Hibbett).[25] Tanizaki was seventy-five when he wrote this novel whose protagonist is a seventy-seven-year-old man with paralysis. I saw a stage production of it on television. The lead actor Hanayagi Shōtarō (1894–1965) was quite old at the time, although I'm not sure exactly how old he was.[26] As the old writer-protagonist, he has a Buddha's footprint made [for his grave], modelled after the foot of his daughter-in-law (played by Mizutani Yaeko 1905–1975).[27] I found the part where he imagines himself being trampled by her after his death, and trembles with pleasure, deeply moving.

Jakuchō writes that during the sixty-day training at Hieizan, she found the esoteric ritual of *goma (homa)* burning erotic.

> The sword changed into the Great Sacred Acala (Immovable Lord). His skin is coloured dark blue; his countenance is serene even though his body is enveloped in flames.

---

25 Tanizaki was a writer of novels, short stories, plays, essay and silent film scripts, and is widely regarded as one of the most important modern Japanese novelists. His innovative approach to literature saw him continually combining new and traditional approaches in his writing, from his literary debut in 1910 until his death in 1965. Many of Tanizaki's works, including 'Shisei' (The Tattooer, 1911, trans. Howard Hibbett), *Tade kuu mushi* (*Some Prefer Nettles*, 1929, trans. Edward Seidensticker), *Manji* (*Quicksand*, 1928–1930, trans. Howard Hibbett) and *Sasameyuki* (*The Makioka Sisters*, 1943–1948, trans. Edward Seidensticker), have been translated into English and other languages. Tanizaki also wrote an acclaimed modern translation of *The Tale of Genji*.

26 Hanayagi was primarily a stage actor whose career flourished in Tokyo from the 1920s to the 1950s. He made his film debut as a kabuki actor in *Zangiku monogatari* (The Story of the Last Chrysanthemums, 1939), and was designated a Living National Treasure for his contributions to drama in 1960.

27 Mizutani was a famous Japanese theatrical actress who played a central role in the development of *shinpa* (new school) both as a theatrical genre and, later, in films. Her daughter Yoshie, also an actress, took over the esteemed name Yaeko in 1995 to continue her legacy.

Chapter 9

For Jakuchō, performing symbolic Buddhist signs with her fingers was an erotic act. Because she associated Acala with an erect phallus, she was reminded of the Tachikawa-ryū cult (originating from Esoteric Buddhism), whose adherents achieved nirvana through sex.[28]
How fascinating Buddhism is!

§

When I was teaching at a university, there was a get-together of one of my seminar groups in which a female student from Tokushima showed us the hand gestures of her hometown's *Awa odori* dance.[29] As we watched her lone dance, a male student stood up and joined her. His own natural response to her dance movements made me feel as though a new age had begun.

I think the spirit of the traditional *Awa odori* must dwell in the notion of looking down upon oneself as a fool during the dance.

When Satsuma Jirohachi (1901–1976), who donated the Maison du Japon to Paris,[30] lost everything in World War II, he returned to Japan and married a stripper from Asakusa. After he had a stroke, this former stripper returned to her hometown and supported her renowned dandy of a husband with her sewing machine. Shishi Bunroku (1893–1969) included in his biographical novel *Tajima Tarōji den* (1967) a scene in which she takes good care of her paralysed husband and takes him to the venue of an interview with a journalist

---

28 Tachikawa-ryū (立川流) was a branch of Shingon Buddhism founded in the early 12th century. In addition to its heterodox approach to sexual intercourse, the cult was criticised for rites involving skull worship, and was eventually dissolved during the Edo period.

29 *Awa odori* (阿波踊り) is an annual dance festival that forms part of *bon* festival celebrations in Tokushima prefecture (formerly Awa province). Participants wear traditional *bon* dance costumes and parade the streets as they dance, chant and sing to the music of traditional Japanese instruments. The verse includes the famous lines: 'odoru ahō ni miru ahō, onaji aho nara odoranya son son' (dancers are fools, onlookers are fools, if both are fools, it's a shame not to dance).

30 Satsuma was the grandson of a wealthy Japanese spinning merchant who supported Japanese artists living in France before World War II, including Léonard Tsuguharu Foujita (1886–1968), Takasaki Takeshi (1902–1932) and Kōno Misao (1900–1979). In 1927, Satsuma financed the construction of Maison du Japon (Japan House), a residence in Paris for promising Japanese students.

from Tokyo.³¹ Both this woman, and Setouchi Harumi, look like successors of Ame no Uzume to me.

---

31 Shishi Bunroku was the pen name of Iwata Toyo'o, a Japanese writer whose works include *Etchan* (Little Etsuko, 1936), *Jiyū gakkō* (*School of Freedom*, 1950, trans. Lynne E. Riggs) and *Musume to watashi* (My Daughter and I, 1956). Iwata also directed the Bungakuza Theatre in Tokyo under his real name.

Chapter 10
Ame no Uzume in the Home

In this chapter, Tsurumi discusses the fiction and non-fiction works of Tanabe Seiko, a native of Osaka. In Tsurumi's view, a number of Tanabe's works contain figures who approximate the character of Ame no Uzume in their free and amusing natures, and in their ability to enjoy their own company. Tanabe and her husband's daily life at home—hers as a writer in her study, and his as a doctor in his surgery—also relies on mirth: at the end of each day, the two crack jokes at each other while they have drinks, before moving on to singing and dancing. The interior of their home is thus an expansive space, devoted to making a living, raising children and entertaining themselves. They also enjoy observing the political world from the comfort of their home, reflected in the dialogue of one of Tanabe's most famous characters, Kamoka no Otchan (Uncle I'll-bite-you).

Even a master of the *naginata* (Japanese halberd) is not able to use a well-crafted weapon freely in a low ceilinged, six-mat tatami room.[1] However, the same is not true of a dancer, who isn't bound by any tools and can make the most of her skills, even in a tight space such as a room in a house.

The works of Tanabe Seiko (1928–2019), which include both fiction and essays, contain various examples of Ame no Uzume figures who are enclosed inside their homes and yet live freely.[2]

---

1 The *naginata* (薙刀) is a weapon comprised of a 30–60cm curved, single-edged blade that is attached to a wooden or metal pole. Since the Edo period, *naginata* has been associated with women's self-defense and martial arts.

2 Tanabe was a Japanese writer who used the Osaka dialect to great effect in many of her literary works, including the ones discussed in this chapter. Her biography is discussed in the second half of this chapter.

Chapter 10

A favourite phrase of a little old man nearing eighty, the uncle of the protagonist in 'Busu guchiroku' (A record of grumblings about ugly women, 1986, in Tanabe 2005), is 'Amusing women are the treasures of this world'. This phrase encapsulates one of his thoughts on life. In his view, the amusing side of women in their twenties and thirties does not fade with age, whereas beauty and intelligence are fluctuating variables. In fact, even living closely with amusing women for forty or fifty years will not deplete this part of their character. It is the same for Ame no Uzume: her amusing nature is revealed not only in her famous outdoor dance but also in her everyday gestures, which derive from her attitude toward making the world a more amusing place, rather than her skill in performing those gestures. She has the power to amuse herself even when she has no other option but to be alone.

In a different story, 'Nakijōgo no tennyo' (The sentimental drinker angel, 1986, in Tanabe 2016), a forty-two-year-old man named Nonaka meets another customer, Tomoe, at a run-down bar. After a few chance meetings there, on one occasion he encounters her crying.

> "It's good while you can still cry", said Nonaka, and poured whiskey into her glass from his bottle.
>
> Perhaps Tomoe had grown tired of weeping; she cheered up, wiped her tears away and blew her nose, announcing [in her earthy Osaka dialect],
>
> "Well, I'll give some singing a bloody good go then!"
>
> She turned the pages of the bar's song books. The way she spoke was pretty rough for a woman but it sounded pleasant to Nonaka's ears.
>
> The wizened bar madame encouraged her, "Yeah? Go on, have a bloody good go!" The two women seemed like good friends from long ago. Nonaka liked Tomoe because she looked as though she was happy to entertain herself like that, and also because there was no hint of flirtation when she looked at men. This absence of coquetry was in all likelihood the key to her being able to enjoy her own company.
>
> Actually, Nonaka found Tomoe's rough and unrestrained style of speech shockingly refreshing and was instantly attracted to her.
>
> Tomoe's rough talk may perhaps be how she cultivated resilience in her daily life. That realisation made Nonaka feel like cheering her on. (Tanabe 2016: 18–19/361)

Ame no Uzume in the Home

On the evening of *setsubun* (the last day of winter),[3] Nonaka invites Tomoe to the lantern festival of Nara's Kasuga shrine[4] before they eat *yudōfu*[5] together at a restaurant-inn and stay the night there. Her Osaka-style pronunciation of tōfu as 'otofū' with a rising intonation reminds Nonaka of his mother, who was also from Osaka, which he finds amusing.

"This otofū is a little too soft, I think. The firmer *momen* variety is better for yudōfu, don't you think?"
"Yeah, I agree."
"The hard ends of *momen* are so delicious."
"Sure are."
Nonaka was deeply moved. It was not that he disliked young women, but who could discuss tofu connoisseurship with them? (Tanabe 2016: 28/361)

Nonaka was quite fussy about women's clothes, but he felt he could always feel comfortable with whatever Tomoe wore.

And speaking of wearing things, Tomoe's expressions were just wonderful. When she smiled, he felt his body and heart completely sucked in. Her expressions were so profound that they could not have been developed in a day: they would be impossible for a woman in her twenties or thirties, he thought. Up until then Nonaka had a strong dislike of middle-aged women in their forties or fifties, regarding them as shamelessly pushy, but once he heard that Tomoe was forty, he changed his entrenched opinion instantly and completely.

Tomoe carefully savoured everything she ate. She even ate the garnish accompanying the sashimi. Although Nonaka was a fussy eater himself, he liked women who ate everything with care and

---

3 *Setsubun* (literally 'seasonal division') is the last day of winter according to the old Japanese calendar. It falls in the period 2–4 February, and involves rituals for driving out the bad fortune of the previous year and welcoming in the new year.

4 Setsubun Mantōrō is an annual ritual held on 3 February at Kasuga Taisha Shrine in Nara, during which 3,000 stone and bronze lanterns are lit at nightfall. Participants are able to write wishes on strips of paper that are placed over the lanterns.

5 *Yudōfu* (literally 'hot water tofu') is a Japanese dish that consists of tofu that is boiled (often with a piece of *kombu* seaweed) and eaten with a soy sauce-based *dashi* (stock).

appreciation. When Tomoe took off the cover of Nonaka's tofu pot or passed over the little dish with seasonings, or when she picked out crab meat from the shell for him, her hand movements were gentle and attentive, just as she was when she put food in her mouth.
That was a sign of a true food lover. (Tanabe 2016: 30–31/361)

The two started living together. Tomoe told him that she worked at a futon company, but some time after she moved in with him, she stopped working there. About a year and a half later, when Nonaka said, 'Why don't we get married? It's about time', she disappeared the following day.

The note she left said: 'Thank you for everything. I know this is selfish, but please do not look for me. There is tofu for your dinner tonight in the fridge'.

Nonaka tried to ring around all the futon shops he could think of but none of them knew a 'Higashiura Tomoe' until the very last company, whose receptionist reported: 'Ms Higashiura no longer works here'.

"When did she resign?"
"She retired last year."
"Retired?"
"Yes, Ms Higashiura turned sixty last year."
"How long did she work with you?"
"The record says thirty continuous years."
(Tanabe 2016: 45–46/361)

After a while, a letter was forwarded to his house from her previous address—which Nonaka checked, but she had moved out of course. It was an invitation to a ceremony to celebrate the erection of a stone monument commemorating the members' loved ones at a temple in Kyoto. The participation fee, including lunch, was 7,000 yen.

Nonaka went to Kyoto in the hope that he might find something. About 200 women were there, but Tomoe was not. To his question about why it was called 'Monument to Women Living Alone', he was told that it was built by women who had lost their partners in the war. Immediately following the war, Tomoe must have been around twenty years old.

§

The author Tanabe Seiko was born on 27 March 1928 in Kami-Fukushima, Konohana-ku (present-day Fukushima-ku), Osaka City. Her father ran a photographic studio. She graduated from Shōin Women's College, majoring in Japanese literature. For about seven years she worked in a small firm, which gave her insights into the psychology of Osaka's merchants.

1956: *Niji* (Rainbow); novel, received Osaka Citizens' Literary Award.

1964: *Sentimental Journey*; novel, won the Akutagawa Prize.

1974: *Subette koronde* (Slipped and Fell); novel.

1976: *Yūgohan tabeta?* (Have You Eaten Dinner?); novel.

1977: *Shiteki seikatsu* (Private Life); novel.

1978: *Rāmen nieta mo gozonji nai* (You Haven't Even Noticed that the Ramen is Ready); essay collection.

1982: *Shinkozaiku no saru ya kiji* (Monkeys and Pheasants Made of Rice-Flour Dough); autobiographical novel.

1982–1983 [sic]: *Tanabe Seiko chōhen zenshū* (Tanabe Seiko's Collected Full-Length Novels) in eighteen volumes, published by Bungei Shunjū.[6]

---

6 The publication date for the 18-volume collection should be 1981–1982. Like Setouchi Jakuchō, Tanabe continued to publish prolifically for many years after Tsurumi wrote this chapter. More recent collections of her works include: a six-volume compilation of selected short stories (1993) published by Kadokawa Shoten; *Tanabe Seiko zenshū* (2004–2006), a collection comprising 24 volumes and one supplementary volume from Shūeisha; and an eight-volume collection of selected works (2008–2010) published by Popurasha (Popular Publishing Company).

Chapter 10

Privately, she became the second wife of a doctor by the name of Kawano Sumio in 1966. He and his late wife had four children. At the time of their marriage, Tanabe was thirty-eight and Kawano was forty-one. He was transformed into Kamoka no Otchan (Uncle I'll-bite-you)[7] in Tanabe's essays and became an exceptional partner not only in real life but also in her works.

Besides essays and interviews, she has written numerous books on classic literature such as *Konjaku monogatari*,[8] *Genji monogatari* (*The Tale of Genji*),[9] *Makura no sōshi* (*The Pillow Book*)[10] as well as old *senryū*.[11]

---

[7] This is the nickname given to the partner in the essay series. *Otchan* and *ossan* are colloquial renderings of *ojisan* in the Osaka dialect, though the former suggests greater familiarity. While *ojisan* literally means 'uncle', it can also be used as a general term for middle-aged men. The same applies to the female *obasan*, or aunt (*obahan* in the Osaka dialect). Kamoka is the Osaka dialect equivalent of *kamō ka* (嚙もうか), which literally means 'Shall I bite you?', but is more commonly associated with the image of a monster threatening to bite children.

[8] *Konjaku monogatari* is a collection of over 1,000 tales gathered from India, China and Japan that was written in Japan during the late Heian period (794–1185). Selected translations into English include *Ages Ago: Thirty-seven Tales from the Konjaku Monogatari Collection* (1959, trans. Susan W. Jones), *Tales of Times Now Past: Sixty-two Stories from a Medieval Japanese Collection* (1979, trans. Marian Ury), *The Konjaku Tales* (1986–1994, trans. Yoshiko Kurata Dykstra), *Tales of Days Gone By* (2003, trans. Charles De Wolf) and *Of Birds and Beasts, Fish and Fowl: Japanese Tales of Times Now Past* (2017, trans. Charles De Wolf et al).

[9] *Genji monogatari*, by the noblewoman and lady-in-waiting Murasaki Shikibu, was written in the early 11th century and tells the story of Hikaru Genji, the son of a Japanese emperor, and the women he loves (a low-ranking concubine). The work depicts the lifestyles of aristocrats during this period, paying particular attention to Genji's romantic life. It is sometimes considered to be the world's first novel (or first psychological novel) and has been adapted into multiple films, manga, anime series, theatre performances and even an opera. It has been wholly or partially translated into English by translators including Suematsu Kenchō (1882), Arthur Waley (1925–1933), Edward Seidensticker (1976), Helen Craig McCullough (1994), Royall Tyler (2001) and Dennis Washburn (2015).

[10] *Makura no sōshi* was written during the 990s and early 1000s, by Sei Shōnagon, a lady-in-waiting to Empress Consort Teishi. It is a collection of private essays, anecdotes, poems and descriptive passages inspired by moments in Sei Shōnagon's daily life. Selected translations into English include those by Arthur Waley (1928), Ivan Morris (1967) and Meredith McKinney (2006).

[11] *Senryū* are 17-syllable Japanese poems that like *haiku* follow a 5-7-5 syllable pattern. They differ from *haiku* in that they do not generally include a *kireji* (punctuation words such as '*ya*' or '*kana*') or *kigo* (season words). *Senryū* also tend to be more cynical or satirical, and often make use of this humorous element to highlight the foibles of human nature.

This is an example of an everyday exchange between the couple, who both work from home—Kawano in his surgery and Tanabe in her study:

> I, for one, believe that we should be merry and make jolly noises when drinking. At our home, a party begins every evening after eight (as our Ossan works at the surgery until then).
>
> Our professions do not get along with each other. A doctor and a writer represent egoism and arrogance. After work we both look glum; we couldn't survive without the drink. And once we have drinks in our hands, it's stupid not to be merry.
>
> As I want to be in high spirits as soon as possible, I finish work at six, start preparing dinner, and give the children theirs first before arranging the food for the adults. Ossan comes in at his usual time, greeting us with a "Good evening". I respond with "Welcome! You are diligent visiting us every evening!"
>
> "I always intend going home, but my feet just come straight here. But Obahan, why don't you employ a pretty young girl? It's always just you here, Obahan. Your customers may up and leave you."
>
> Unless we indulge in this sort of folly, it gets boring since it's always the same cast of characters, every evening.
>
> Even so, as we drink, we do get merry. At first it's out of desperation that we joke and pretend to be jolly, but gradually the feeling becomes genuine. (Tanabe 1980)

In the course of drinking, another person appears within; then two become four, and the number continues to multiply. This is how parties build.

Conversations become increasingly lively, and then the dancing starts. This topic arises in a dialogue between Tanabe and Tomioka Taeko (1935–2023).[12]

---

12 Tomioka was a Japanese feminist poet, novelist, literary critic and translator. Her works, which include the novels *Oka ni mukatte hito wa narabu* (Facing the Hills They Stand, 1971), *Meido no kazoku* (Family in Hell, 1974) and *Hibernia tō kikō* (Traveling to Hibernia Island, 1997), have received numerous literary accolades, including the Yomiuri Prize, Noma Literary Prize, Murasaki Shikibu Prize and Mainichi Publishing Culture Award. Her works available in translation include: *See You Soon: Poems of Taeko Tomioka* (1979, trans. Hiroaki Sato) and *The Funeral of a Giraffe: Seven Stories by Tomioka Taeko* (1999, trans. Kyoko Iriye Selden and Noriko Mizuta). Tomioka was presented with the Award of the Japan Art Academy in 2004. Like Tanabe, Tomioka was from Osaka. She uses the Osaka dialect in this quotation.

Chapter 10

Tomioka: You sing, don't you, Tanabe-san? I heard that you like singing with your husband rather than discussing difficult issues.

Tanabe: Yes, and once we start singing, we can't help dancing.

Tomioka: What sort of dancing?

Tanabe: Everything, from the go-go to anything we feel like.
(Tanabe 1977)

Inside the house, there are not only spaces for each of them to make a living through their work, but also to bring up the children, and room enough for their singing and dancing. These spaces are not cut off by thresholds, but expand outwards.

The novel *Dansu to kūsō* (Dance and Fantasy, 1983) presents Tanabe's theory on urban spaces in its depiction of an idealised Kobe.

The city of Kobe, according to the novel, is like a coterie magazine. Since it was developed at the beginning of Meiji as a port city to take in foreigners, the locals had ample opportunity to observe them firsthand. Seeing the way that foreigners strode along with their backs straight, for example, the people of Kobe became more conscious of their own way of walking and improved their posture.

In the city many people, including Japanese, were introduced to the art of kabuki through the 'Canadian Kabuki' performed by students at an international high school, the Canadian Academy.[13] As part of their Japanese lessons, the students (from thirty-seven countries) got together to learn kabuki. Every year at the city's Culture Hall, they performed classical repertoires such as *Kanadehon chūshingura* (The Treasury of Loyal Retainers),[14] *Kanjinchō* (The Subscription List)[15] and *Sukeroku*.[16]

---

13 The Canadian Academy is a private, co-educational, international school for pre-kindergarten to grade 12 students in Kobe. It was founded in 1913 as the Canadian Methodist Academy, before changing its name to the Canadian Academy in 1917.

14 *Kanadehon chūshingura* (1748) is a *bunraku* (traditional puppet theatre) play that tells a fictionalised account of the revenge of the 47 *rōnin*. The kabuki adaptation appeared shortly thereafter.

15 *Kanjinchō* (1840) is a kabuki dance-drama based on the noh drama *Ataka* (1465). It tells the story of the loyalty and devotion of the warrior monk Benkei towards his master Yoshitsune, as they attempt to pass a guarded gate together without revealing Yoshitsune's identity.

Their performance was full of genuine feeling, and the students really understood the characters they were playing. They even seemed to understand the shackles of the "floating world" (*ukiyo*), and the continual dilemma of *giri* (duty) and *ninjō* (compassion).

We could see how much they had dedicated themselves to their performance; as we watched, our faces became flushed, and we felt tears welling up. It reminded us that humans can do whatever they want to if they are determined enough. The students taught us about our own traditional culture, rather than the other way round, which is a bit embarrassing. But still, we were so happy to experience Japanese feelings understood and expressed like this. What a funny place Kobe is. [...]

Only, the students are very tall. Some playing the merchant and samurai roles are almost two metres tall. They have small and slender faces, marking quite a difference from the real kabuki actors, but because they're all between sixteen and nineteen, their skin is beautiful and the white kabuki makeup enhances their beauty, in both boys and girls. Every year the senior students graduate and take off in all directions overseas, so there are no continuing star actors. But there is depth to their performances and the people of Kobe always look forward to the next Kanadean Kabuki.[17] (Tanabe 1983)

This kind of culture is difficult to nurture in places like the millennium capital, Kyoto. In a survey of six major Japanese cities developed by Kitamura Hideo, Yamamoto Akira and others in the 1960s, the most popular city as voted by its residents was Kobe, and the runner-up was Kyoto. In the case of Kyoto, residents' families tend to have been there for generations, and so the city is eminently liveable for them. In stark contrast, many Kobe residents are from other places; their judgement that Kobe was a liveable city was based on a comparison with those places. The reasons the Kobe citizens gave included

---

16 *Sukeroku* (1713) is a kabuki play, based on *Soga monogatari* (The Tale of the Soga Brothers, or The Revenge of the Soga Brothers), in which two brothers avenge their father's death by searching for the wielder of Tomokirimaru, their father's sword.

17 Kanadean is an alternate spelling of Canadian that is derived from the kanji 仮名手庵. It is a play on Kanadehon (仮名手本), the first part of the title of the famous play *Kanadehon chūshingura* (see footnote 14). The name of the kabuki group was changed in 1982 to International Japanesque Kabuki.

Chapter 10

the lack of neighbourhood meddling, a respect for privacy and the establishment of parks, libraries, concert halls and other public facilities that residents can freely enjoy.

Kobe is a stage on which citizens go out and walk around. It is also a place that values rest and entertainment. Naturally, the city is more fashion conscious than Kyoto and Osaka as well.

Dance and Fantasy is a novel about ten or so women (all around an average age of thirty-four or thirty-five) who work in the fashion industry and related fields. Each one of them runs a shop. Together, the group is named 'Belle Fille', meaning beautiful girl. They show little interest in finding out about each other's private lives, instead concentrating on supporting the work of each member. In the process they become a driving force for festivals, events and parties, thus influencing the city's direction.

Their parties always include dancing, in which men and women, old and young participate. Everyone enjoys the food, the fashion, the atmosphere and the conversation.

> "Kobe is such a comfortable place that I fall asleep".
> "That's great—we can all fall asleep together. It's a city where we can happily grow old". (Tanabe 1983)

Observing world politics from the comfort of home is Tanabe's style of everyday domestic conversation. The following is Kamoka no Otchan's view:

> "I used to vote for the Communist Party. For several years after the defeat, when the Communist Party was still very weak and held very few seats, I supported them because I thought we needed people like them. Oh, where's the sake bottle? It's OK, I'll pour it."
>
> "Shut up! Don't stop in the middle of an important topic. So you were a Communist before. What about now?"
>
> "Well, sometimes I voted Communist, sometimes Socialist, depending how I felt on the day, but one thing was always definite: I could never vote for the conservatives; I always supported the reformist parties. ... This sake is just right, if you heat it any more, it'll boil."

Otchan seemed to be concerned only about the temperature of the sake.

"So are you still a reformist supporter?"

"Well yes, that's true, but things have changed subtly. As the Communist Party is much stronger now, I feel a little hesitant."[18]

Otchan filled my sake cup and then his.

He savoured his sake without haste—he isn't the type to gulp his drinks.

"Whether to support the reformists or not is a different matter, but now the conservative party has variety ranging from the left to the right within its ranks, so that's great. It's also wonderful to have debates and variety about political views among different factions within the one party. The Communist Party, however, is scary: one party with a singular view alarms me. It would be a problem if such a party gained a huge amount of power. That's my feeling anyway."

"So you support the conservatives now? You're switching your allegiance?"

"Well, that's what I meant by being subtle. I do get cross though, if young people say they support the conservatives right from the start."

"But then you're half making eyes at the conservatives, aren't you Otchan?"

"Nonsense! My eyes took a long detour with many twists and turns. It's the result of decades of watching and comparing the changes within the parties. Youngsters, on the other hand, opt for a shortcut and quickly reach their decision. I get annoyed with those kinds of simplistic conservative supporters. What are they thinking!"

"So you think it's all right if they support reformists?"

"No, you can't trust those who simply shout reforms, either. If it was one country one party, that'd be terrible too."

"So what is it that you want?"

---

18 The militant approach of the Japanese Communist Party (JCP) during the 1950s contributed to the party's 'scary' image, which it gradually distanced itself from throughout the 1960s. In the general elections held on 10 December 1972, the JCP won 38 seats, making it the third-largest party in the Diet and the second-largest opposition party. JCP membership peaked by about 1980, and its subsequent decline led the party to modify its policies along more traditional democratic socialist lines.

Chapter 10

"How would I know? Don't look at me like that. My point is we middle-aged people cannot say incisive things, like two times two equals four. It's like your wife is fine, but other women are attractive as well. Only the middle-aged can appreciate both sides of things." (Tanabe [1978] 2000: 134–136/325)

The state of the body, the naturalness of human interactions and a calm state of mind when making judgements—all these things form the yardstick of political discussions at this house. These discussions, in turn, are reflected in Tanabe's portrayal of Otchan:

"Oh, I heard that soldiers on the battlefield get erections when they die. Their comrades feel so sorry for them that they cover them up with their helmets..."

"I think I've heard that story before," said the stupid bar madame with tears in her eyes. "So the helmets sway in the wind for a while." "It stands to reason," replied Kamoka no Otchan, "as the blood goes down from the head, it seems natural that it would collect down there."

"Really? I doubt it..."

"When blood moves up to the head, they say, Banzai to the Emperor. But when the blood goes down, it becomes O-Sei-san [i.e. his wife, Tanabe Seiko] Banzai!" (Tanabe [1978] 2000: 86/325)

Let me quote a few examples from the household's home-made *iroha karuta*:[19]

<ho/bo> *boke to yobarete mada mitsuki* (only three months since I was called senile)

<nu> *nuide kara kotowarare* (rejected after removing clothing)

<o> *onna ni teinen nashi* (women never retire)

<na> *naien ni rikon nashi* (no divorce for de facto couples)

---

19 *Karuta* (from the Portuguese 'carta', meaning 'card') are Japanese playing cards. *Iroha karuta* are a version of *karuta* used in children's games. They consist of a set of cards with each of the *hiragana* characters printed on them, and a corresponding set of cards with proverbs that begin with each of those characters. Players must select matching cards from the array before their opponent.

<mu> *murete wa ōgoe* (becomes loud in a group setting)

<se> *sewa nyōbō wa jiritsu no taiteki* (a good caring wife is a huge enemy of independence)

Tanabe's comments on 'women never retire' reads:

> Women are active until they die. It is their wish to remain young and beautiful forever. That's the essence of this line. (Tanabe 1985)

If the sentiment of 'women never retire' were used in politics, I believe the world would be a better place. But perhaps this could be realised only in combination with the courage of men who could accept being 'rejected after removing clothing'. Tanabe Seiko's eighteen volumes of full-length novels and several dozen essay collections form a grand corpus supported by the energy generated by the couple's continuous daily conversations over several decades.[20]

---

20 The 18-volume collection refers to the 1981–1982 publication by Bungei Shunjū.

Chapter 11

Japan and Abroad

In this chapter, Tsurumi explores the body and its relation to the sense of smell. He discusses how his revulsion towards the smells produced by his own body gradually changed over many years after discovering the pleasure Walt Whitman derived from his own mysterious bodily odours. Tsurumi recounts the stench of human waste while cleaning latrines on a wartime ship, an experience that reminds him of the world of excreta in the *Kojiki*, where deities are born of tears, urine and grime. He links this discussion to the decline and onset of human history, in turn connecting human life to the topic of dance as described by Havelock Ellis. Tsurumi then turns to Japanese dance, examining the meanings and usages of the terms *odori* and *mai*, and the custom of *odori nenbutsu* (a Buddhist incantation using chanting, drumbeating and dancing), which dates back at least to the time of the tenth century monk Kūya. The ancient practice of calling on the spirits of the deceased with song and dance forms the origin of many Japanese performing arts. Tsurumi ends the chapter thinking about whether Ame no Uzume's dance may be related to that of the Hindu deity Shiva.

In February 1943, when Japan's defeat began to seem certain, I boarded the blockade runner Burgenland, which operated between Japan and Germany.[1] The ship was equipped with machine guns. Occasionally we practised some manoeuvres so that we would be able to endure bouts of limited fighting and also break through the

---

1 Despite their initial success, the Japanese were not able to drive the US Navy from the Pacific. The June 1942 Battle of Midway and the Guadalcanal campaign, which Japan lost in February 1943, marked a turning point in the war, as the Japanese were rapidly outstripped by the United States in their ability to replace losses in men and resources.

Chapter 11

blockade network to reach Germany by sailing around South America and entering the Mediterranean Sea. When it came down to it, however, this plan never materialised.

For several days before the voyage, I was on standby at a Kobe inn with three others. The city was laden with books, new and old, in European languages, presumably left behind by foreign residents when they returned to their home countries. Since I was about to board a ship, I wasn't in a position to load myself down with a lot of things, but I did buy several small books that didn't weigh too much; among them was *The New Spirit* (1890) by Havelock Ellis (1859–1939).[2]

I knew Ellis's name but had never had a chance to read his work properly. At first he discussed Diderot, as a man who wished to be no one, and as the originator of the new spirit. The brilliance of Ellis's argument left a lasting impression on me.

For his study, Ellis selected those whom he believed to represent the new spirit, regardless of their chronology: Diderot, Heine, Whitman, Ibsen, Tolstoy and Huysmans.[3] His view of Whitman, especially, was clearly different from any of the lectures on him I had previously encountered.

The way Whitman felt about his body was different from any other writer; he worshipped his own smell and the mystic atmosphere it produced.

I was astounded by the several lines illustrating Whitman's view. It was not that his words immediately changed my sense perceptions; rather, my astonishment was a result of the realisation that it was possible to theorise in this way. Over the next few decades, a change in my sense perceptions gradually occurred, and honestly, I doubt whether this would have happened had I not read *The New Spirit*.

Ever since I can remember, I have found the smells emitted by my body objectionable. This feeling was at the core of my self-existence throughout my early childhood and teenage years. It was my ideal to erase this sense of self-existence somehow.

---

2 Ellis was an English physician, writer, intellectual and social reformer. In addition to publishing the works detailed below, Ellis studied psychedelics and served as vice-president of the Eugenics Society from 1909 to 1912.

3 The French writer and art critic Joris-Karl Huysmans (1848–1907) is not included in the editions of *The New Spirit* that we have found. Tsurumi may be referring to another edition.

The turning point in this self-myth was born around this time. My voyage on the blockade runner ended in Jakarta, but for the remainder of the war, I continued to board other transport ships. The stenches I encountered once aboard, along with my anxieties about dying, formed the basis of my experience and memory of the war. When a ship with people packed into the hold was stalled for many days due to an enemy attack, temporary latrines were erected on the deck. Every few days, when it was time for cleaning, the filth flowed all over the deck, releasing a human world of stench under the blue sky. As we washed it all away with a hose, I had a sense of exhilaration (for me, the sense of the realisation of a new society), for this was far better than killing or being killed.

When I re-read the *Kojiki*, this world of excreta returned.

The intellectual Seki Hirono (b. 1944) remarked that after two total wars and the appearance of the atomic bomb, it is no longer valid to plan for the future by using a yardstick of civilisation based on a left- or right-wing state.[4] Instead, he proposed that we should focus on the possible extinction of human beings and devise ways of thinking that include this process of annihilation. Dying in our own sewage is not just a personal future but a future shared by all humans.

> Next, when the land was young, resembling floating oil and drift—like a jellyfish, there sprouted forth something like reed-shoots. From these came into existence the deity Umashi Ashikabi Hikoji no Kami. (Philippi 1969: 47; romanisation modified)

This excerpt, which begins the narrative of the *Kojiki*, fits well with the idea of a declining human history, just as it does with the beginning of human history. Deities born of tears, urine and grime, and the world of the gods they create await us in the future.

In my childhood I looked at the world from the other side of life, that is, from what I imagined to be the side of the dead. To view this world we inhabit from the perspective of the (imagined) dead, we can create an image of the world that makes sense. If, on the other hand, we look at the world of the living from within, it soon shows signs of

---

4 Seki is an historian and commentator who has critiqued the confrontational binary system between the left and the right. He also refutes popular humanism and a unilinear, progressive view of history.

Chapter 11

strain, no matter how hard we try to balance the account. To those who dance, the world dances, too.

To Havelock Ellis, the word 'dance' was important to the way he thought about the world. At sixteen, he quit school in England and went to Australia, where he worked as a primary school teacher, and at one time a headmaster, among other things. He spent a lot of time out in the open by himself, and became impressed by such things as the effortless way kangaroos hopped. Around that time, he was attracted to *Man and His Dwelling Place* (1859) and *Life in Nature* (1862) by James Hinton (1822–1875), and devised two plans: the first, to study religion using the suggestions in Hinton's works, and the second, to study sexuality.[5] He chose the latter as his life's work, authoring seven volumes of *Studies in the Psychology of Sex* because there were no precedents for this kind of research. However, he also maintained his other interest in nature and religion throughout his life and wrote an introduction to his wife Edith Ellis's (1861–1916) last work, *James Hinton* (1918).[6]

When he was nineteen, Ellis returned to England, and upon visiting the surviving family of the late James Hinton, agreed to organise the manuscripts that the physician Hinton had left unpublished. At the same time, with the support of Hinton's friends, Ellis studied medicine for eight years at St Thomas' Hospital. However, despite obtaining the qualification to become a medical practitioner, he never actually practised medicine. Instead, he continued his research on the psychology of sex, mainly through questionnaires, and made his living as an author. *My Confessional* (1934) consists almost entirely of his responses to letters. *The Dance of Life* (1923), like *The New Spirit*, testifies to his belief in nature. In this work, Ellis tries to view all kinds of art forms as dance, regarding life itself as dance too. When viewed in this way—as a dance with certain particularities—the respective

---

5 Hinton was an English author and aural surgeon. As a writer, he frequently discussed contemporary social and moral problems, in addition to publishing multiple papers on aural surgery. Hinton was also a radical advocate of polygamy. His son, the mathematician and author Charles Howard Hinton, was convicted of bigamy.

6 Edith was an English writer and women's rights activist whose works include *Seaweed: A Cornish Idyll* (1898), *Attainment* (1909), *The Imperishable Wing* (1911) and *The Mothers* (1915). Though married to Ellis, Edith was a lesbian; the two had an unconventional, open marriage which Ellis discusses in his autobiography, *My Life* (1939).

features of human life and the arts become clearly visible. Dying is a kind of dance, too. After death, the spirit and the flesh scatter in different forms and continue to exist. Ellis never relinquishes his idea that human existence is itself dance.

Even though dance was so important to Ellis, he could not dance. The author of the seven-volume *Psychology of Sex* was too shy to face anyone and look into their eyes (Calder-Marshall, 1959). Nevertheless, from Ellis's viewpoint, life itself was dance. He planned to have his body cremated and his ashes sprinkled on a hill on a sunny day, and thus become part of the soil, plants and flowers—he died imagining these things with joy. According to a statement dated 27 November 1913, 'it is essential to the human dignity of a truly civilised society that it should hold in its hands not only the Key of Birth but the Key of Death' (Ellis 2007: n.p.) During his lifetime, he was put on trial for authoring obscene books, and was subjected to persecution for more than half a century. But now, he who was once so notorious is all but forgotten.

§

Putting the translated (Chinese) term *butō* aside for a moment, the terms *odori* and *mai*, which both mean 'dance' in Japanese, are distinct from each other.[7] A monograph by Ogasawara Kyōko, *Izumo no O-Kuni* (O-Kuni of Izumo, 1984)[8] states that until O-Kuni was called to the court to perform *yayako odori*,[9] all the dances performed at the court had been variations of *mai*. In other words, the history of official dance before O-Kuni was the history of *mai*; *odori* was not an art performed by professional performers, but something

---

7 *Butō* is an imported term from the Chinese *Liji*, or Book of Rites (see Chapter 5, footnote 8). In ancient times, the term referred to ceremonial acts of worship in the Imperial Court, but it was later used as a translated term for 'dance' in the Meiji period (1868–1912). In the contemporary context, *butō* is a form of dance initiated by modern avant-garde dancers in the post-war period.

8 Izumo no O-Kuni (c.1578–c.1613) was a Japanese *miko* (see Chapter 2, footnote 7) who is thought to have invented kabuki when she and her all-female theatre troupe began performing in a dry riverbed in Kyoto's Kamogawa River.

9 *Yayako odori* (literally, 'dance by children') was a type of dance performed by girls and young women from the late medieval and early modern period. The term was used to broadly describe three forms of entertainment: a type of *bon odori* (see footnote 17); a type of dance performed by O-Kuni before the emergence of kabuki dance; and an early kabuki dance repertoire.

Chapter 11

Figure 11.1: Kūya
Source: Rokuharamitsuji temple, Kyoto, Japan.

that the general public engaged in and enjoyed.

The verb *mau*, from which the noun *mai* derives, comes from *mawaru* (to turn), a verb that signifies the act of quietly moving around and in the process calling upon a centrally placed object representing a divine spirit: it was performed by professional *miko* (shrine maidens) and gave a rather stiff and formal impression. By comparison, people found *odori* attractive, because of the enjoyment of performing outdoors in a large group, without being restricted by any particular forms. Gradually *odori* came to be used for entertainment at parties in conjunction with *mai*, to the extent that O-Kuni and another girl were invited to the court to perform *yayako odori*.

Odori itself existed much earlier for people's enjoyment. According to Gorai Shigeru's *Odori nenbutsu* (Dancing prayer to Amitābha, 1988, Heibonsha Library edition 1998),[10] in the time of Kūya (903–972),[11] monks would surround him and perform a dancing prayer. It is uncertain as to whether Kūya himself started the dance, or even if he danced himself. In any case, much earlier, around the time of Gyōki (668–749), it is thought that groups of several thousand people

---

10 This work has not been translated; here Amitābha has been chosen for the service translation as he is the principal Buddha of Pure Land Buddhism. The expression *odori nenbutsu* is used to describe a form of Buddhist incantation that uses chanting, drumbeating and dancing.
11 Kūya was an itinerant Buddhist monk ordained in the Tendai Buddhist sect who was credited with adding music and dance to his prayers. This *odori nenbutsu* was thought to deliver the dead to the Pure Land (the celestial realm of a buddha or bodhisattva in Mahāyāna Buddhism). Kūya's efforts helped to promote the spread of Pure Land Buddhism in Japan.

Japan and Abroad

Figure 11.2: Nenbutsu odori in *Illustrated Biography of the Itinerant Monk Ippen*
Source: National Diet Library Digital Collections (https://dl.ndl.go.jp/pid/2591579/1/30)

would gather together to engage in wild dancing.[12] After Kūya, Ippen (1239–1289) was also well known for *odori nenbutsu*.[13] The place of origin of this version is identified in the famous scroll *Ippen hijiri e* (Illustrated Biography of the Itinerant Monk Ippen) as Usuda-machi, Nagano prefecture, but in another version of the scroll, *Ippen Shōnin ekotoba den*, as Nozawa-machi, Saku-shi, Nagano prefecture.

With various versions of prayer dances developed in many different places over the centuries, O-Kuni, according to Gorai, started to dance *ko-uta nenbutsu*[14] as the *kanjin miko*[15] of Izumo Taisha[16] shrine.

---

12 Gyōki was a Japanese Buddhist priest, possibly of Korean descent, who travelled the country contrary to the regulations of the time, teaching commoners about Buddhism and organising public works projects, including the building of 49 monasteries and nunneries that operated as hospitals for the poor.

13 Ippen was an itinerant Buddhist preacher and founder of the Jishū (時宗) school of Pure Land Buddhism. The school taught that individual salvation could be achieved by calling upon Buddha's name rather than through individual efforts or even through faith.

14 *Ko-uta* were songs comprised of short verses (often secular love poems) that were particularly popular during the Muromachi period (1336–1573).

15 *Kanjin* (勧進, temple solicitation) is a Japanese term used to describe various methods used by Buddhist monks to solicit donations, often for the construction or repair of temples. The term has also been used in Shinto, and to describe fundraising for public works projects.

16 Izumo Taisha (Izumo Grand Shrine) is an ancient (possibly the oldest) Shinto shrine in Japan. Located in Izumo, Shimane prefecture, the shrine is dedicated to Ōkuninushi, a god linked to nation-building, agriculture, marriage, medicine and protective magic, as well as Kotoamatsukami, a collective name for the first gods that came into existence in Takamagahara when the universe was created.

Chapter 11

Figure 11.3:
O-Kuni and Sanza
Source: Kyoto National Museum.

The love songs of *odori nenbutsu* and *bon odori*[17] were in fact songs to welcome the spirits of the dead, and then to see them off. In kabuki dance, love songs are called *shinobi odori*, derived from longing for (*shinobu*) the spirits of the dead. (Gorai 1988/1998)

In an early kabuki play, O-Kuni appeared on centre stage and danced a *shinobi odori*, clothed as a man in a happi coat, a pair of pantaloons and a woven hat, with a small gong in one hand and a wooden bell hammer in the other. In response, the spirit of the dead woman played by Nagoya Sanza stood up from the audience to face O-Kuni.[18] His hair was arranged in the *kirisage-gami* style and he carried a *nenbutsu* gong on his chest.[19] A *Nara ehon* illustrated manuscript titled *Kabuki no sōshi* apparently contains this scene.[20]

---

17 *Bon odori* is a type of folk dance that is performed during Obon (or Bon), a Japanese festival during which the spirits of departed ancestors are said to return to visit household altars. It is performed to welcome these spirits. The music and dances differ from region to region.

18 Nagoya Sanza (short for Sanzaburō) was a legendary man of the 16th century, possibly a samurai, who is said to have founded kabuki alongside O-Kuni. In this play, O-Kuni, a woman, plays a man, while Sanza plays the spirit of a dead woman.

19 The *kirisage-gami* or *kiri-kami* hairstyle was worn by upper-class widows during the Edo period (1603–1868) and the Meiji period (1868–1912). It involved tying up the hair and trimming the ends, so the ponytail remained at neck level or higher. The use of this hairstyle emphasises how both O-kuni and Sanza are cross-dressing.

20 *Nara ehon* are illustrated manuscripts dating from the late Muromachi period (1336–1573) to the early Edo period (1603–1868) that depict short stories.

Figure 11.4: *Kiri-kami* hairstyle (another name for *kirisage-gami*) Source: Shinmura (2018: 787).

Some of the *ko-uta* songs that belonged to the *shinobi odori* lineage are included in the collection *Matsu no ha* (Pine Needles, 1703).[21] The background to this is that the *bon odori* is a surviving form of the ancient *kagai* (or *utagaki*), as evidenced by a song in *Matsu no ha*, 'Wait for the Twenty-third Moon'.[22]

An example of *shinobi uta* song that calls back a spirit can be found in the *ko-uta odori* dance of female shamans (*kuchiyose miko*) that eventually connects with the *odori nenbutsu* of Izumo no O-kuni. The song begins with the metaphor of drawing a bow and develops into the typical pattern that involves a spirit emerging. Quoting again from Gorai (1998: 23):

> *Michinoku no azusa no mayumi wa ga hikaba yōyō yoriko shinobi shinobi ni*
> (When I draw a bow made from the *azusa* tree of Michinoku, come closer and closer, secretly) *Kagura*[23] *uta*
>
> *Michinoku no Adachi no mayumi wa ga hikaba sue sae yoriko shinobi shinobi ni*

---

21 *Matsu no ha* is a collection of *nagauta* (長唄, literally 'long songs'), traditional Japanese pieces played on the *shamisen* and used during interludes and to accompany dance in kabuki theatre.

22 *Kagai* were ancient Shinto ritual gatherings, closely associated with harvest rights and fertility, during which participants would sing, dance, eat, recite poetry and engage in free sexual intercourse. The practice seems to have originated in the late fifth century but became particularly popular during the Nara period (710–794).

23 For *kagura*, see Chapter 1, note 9 and Chapter 3.

Chapter 11

> (When one draws a bow made from the *mayumi* tree of Adachi in Michinoku, both ends come close; when I draw you, come close like the bow drawn closer, till the end [future], secretly) *Kokinshū*[24]

In ancient times, calling on the spirit of the deceased with song and dance, and dancing together with the dead, were regarded as among the enjoyments of this world. This was the origin of kabuki. Other dances such as *bon odori* and *Awa odori* were also derived from this lineage and survive to this day.[25]

> Common to almost all variations of *nenbutsu odori* throughout Japan is the travel attire of the dancers. In "Kanko odori", for example, covers for the back of the hand and wrist, as well as gaiters and straw sandals, all signify travel. The idea of dancers as travellers is based on two points of view. First, it indicates the lineage of travelling sages [...] holding major *nenbutsu* meetings in different places for the local spirits of the dead, and teaching villagers how to perform the prayer dance.
>
> The other view is that the dancers are the spirits of the dead who have returned to this world from Paradise, travelling one trillion miles, and will dance back all the way after the memorial service. For the dead, a straw hat to hide the face and a straw raincoat were akin to a uniform. (Gorai 1998: 189–190)

Gorai travelled across many parts of Japan to see and record *odori nenbutsu*. Based on this research, he claims that many Japanese performing arts were born out of this tradition.

In *odori nenbutsu* the dead stand close by the living, like their shadows, showing the quality of joy that characterises this dance.

---

24 *Kokinshū* or *Kokin wakashū* (古今和歌集, *A Collection of Poems Ancient and Modern*, trans. Laurel Rasplica Rodd and Mary Catherine Henkenius) is an anthology of Japanese *waka* poetry, dating from the Heian period (794–1185) and compiled by four court poets (Ki no Tsurayuki, Ki no Tomonori, Ōshikōchi no Mitsune and Mibu no Tadamine). Michinoku, otherwise known as Mutsu or Ōshū, was an old province of Japan in the Tōhoku region, while Adachi was a town located in this area (present-day Fukushima prefecture). Bows made from the *mayumi* trees from this region were well-known even in the capital, Kyoto.

25 See Chapter 9, footnote 29.

Sansa shigure ka kayano no ame ka
oto mo sede kite nurekakaru
Shongaina
(Sansa, late autumn shower or rain on the sedge field /
comes suddenly without a sound and rains on / shongaina)[26]

What 'comes suddenly without a sound and rains on' is a reference to the dead. It is pure joy to dance shoulder to shoulder with deceased loved ones. Thus the *nenbutsu odori* was linked with the *bon odori* and became the *shinobi odori*, which in turn succeeded the pre-Buddhist *utagaki* customs. Folklorist Yanagita Kunio's 'Seikōkan aishi' (The tragic history of the Seikokan Inn, 1926, included in *Yukiguni no haru* [Spring in the Snow Country], 1929) describes a *bon odori* that includes the formation of small circles under the moonlight, which is regarded as a vestige of an old *utagaki* passed down in Taneichi-mura (then called Okonai in Kunohe), Iwate prefecture. The song used in this event contains the phrase:

naniya to yaare / naniya to nasarenō

which Yanagita interpreted as 'Do whatever you like, you can do whatever'—in other words, as a love song from a woman to a man.

Gorai (1998: 226) cites the Book IX: 1759 poem of the *Man'yōshū*[27] as an example of an ancestral festival permitted by the mountain gods in ancient religions that predate Buddhism.

> Maidens and men, in troops assembling,
> Hold a *kagai*, vying in poetry;
> I will seek company with others' wives,
> Let others woo my own;
> The gods that dominate this mountain
> Have allowed such freedom since of old
> (Keene and Nihon Gakujutsu Shinkōkai, 1965: 222)

---

26 *Sansa* and *shongaina* are *hayashi kotoba*, speech-like phrases and exclamations that have no meaning, but which are used to make songs more rhythmical. *Sansa shigure* is a celebratory folk song thought to have originated in the Tōhoku region in the mid-Edo period (1603–1868), before spreading to other parts of Japan.

27 *Man'yōshū* (万葉集, literally, Collection of Ten Thousand Leaves) is a collection of over 4,500 Japanese *waka* poems, compiled sometime after 759, although

Chapter 11

After this custom was mixed with Buddhism, *bon odori* were always performed between the ritual *odori nenbutsu* dances, as exemplified in the Dainenbutsu and the Hōka Dainenbutsu dancing events of Mikawa province (eastern Aichi prefecture).[28]

In terms of the origins of kabuki, the pivotal figures were the avant-garde performers called *kabukimono*, who assumed a leading role in attempting to subvert the public morals of the time.[29] The kabuki tradition has continued for 400 years, since the time of O-Kuni—first in the form of the female-only Onna Kabuki, which was banned in 1629, and thereafter in inverted form, with men playing women's roles.

§

The city of Edo that nurtured the dance theatre in Japan had a better sewage system than contemporaneous London or Paris, and its civic facilities were highly developed as well. In the Taishō period Tokyo of my childhood, horses and cows traversed the streets, leaving their manure everywhere. At that time, the toilets were privy-style, following the Edo tradition, and the wagons of night soil collectors could be seen on the streets. From the Shōwa period, however, people began to regard privies as backward, especially when compared to the big cities of the US. In the current Heisei period, the sense of hygiene has become even more sophisticated.[30] Viewed from the present time, pre-war Japan seems utterly filthy, and the conditions of Edo even more unbearable. This is typical of the way olden times are so often regarded as pathetically backward. However, eighteenth-century Paris, which formed the basis of today's Western

---

some poems may have been composed as early as 600. Several poems deal with Confucian, Taoist and Buddhist teachings, but the majority echo ancient Japanese themes, particularly Shinto virtues.

28 Dainenbutsu are large-scale Buddhist chanting rituals. In the Hōka Dainenbutsu event at Shinshiro in Aichi prefecture, participants shoulder enormous *uchiwa* fans and tie *taiko* drums to their waists as they dance and chant.

29 Kabuki derives from the verb *kabuku*, which means 'to lean' or 'to be out of the ordinary'. Thus, kabuki was not just a form of song and dance, but an unusual avant-garde theatrical form. *Kabukimono* ('strange things' or 'the crazy ones') in the late 16th century signified gangs of samurai or men who had once worked for samurai families and dressed flamboyantly and subverted social customs.

30 Tsurumi first published this work in 1991, the third year of Heisei.

civilisation, was even less hygienic than contemporaneous Edo. In the 'Translator's Afterword' to Patrick Süskind's (b. 1949) novel, *Das Parfum: Die Geschichte eines Mörders* (originally published in 1985; English translation by John E. Woods, *Perfume: The story of a Murderer* in 1986; Japanese translation by Ikeuchi in 1988), Ikeuchi Osamu mentioned that when an offensive odour was being investigated along the Seine in March 1782, a laboror fell off a ladder into the river. By the time they managed to pull him up, all he could do was gasp, and amidst the stench he succumbed to oxygen deprivation. Eight years after this incident, on 14 February 1790, a group conducting another similar investigation made a return journey of ten kilometers around Pont Neuf. The entire group had difficulty breathing, and as they panted with gaping mouths, their tongues began to swell up. This episode is apparently mentioned in French historian Alain Corbin's (b. 1936) *Le miasme et la jonquille: L'odorat et l'imaginaire social, XVIIIe-XIXe siècles* (1982, trans. John E. Wood, *The Foul and the Fragrant: Odor and the French Social Imagination*, 1988).

The protagonist of *Perfume* lived in this period.

> At the age of six, he had completely grasped his surroundings olfactorily. There was not an object in Madame Gaillard's house, no place along the northern reaches of the rue de Charonne, no person, no stone, tree, bush or picket fence, no spot be it ever so small, that he did not know by smell, could not recognize again by holding its uniqueness firmly in his memory. He had gathered tens of thousands, hundreds of thousands of specific smells and kept them so clearly, so randomly, at his disposal, that he could not only recall them when he smelled them again, but could also actually smell them simply upon recollection. And what was more, he even knew how by sheer imagination to arrange new combinations of them, to the point where he created odours that did not exist in the real world. (Süskind and Woods 2003: 27)

Plato discussed the power of smell in evoking memories. Up until Plato's age, the ability that living creatures had to recognise, remember and predict through smell must have been constantly maintained by human beings as well. Thousands of years later, perfumer Nakamura Shōji described in his book *Kaori no sekai o saguru* (Adventures in the World of Perfume, 1989) the extraordinary 'nose' and sixth

Chapter 11

sense of the leading perfumers in contemporary Paris, and how they honed and developed these skills. Such an ability may return to the Japanese, who in ancient times invented incense games. Unless we recoup at least some of this ability, it will be difficult for five billion—and soon ten billion—people to cohabit this earth, negotiating with each other side by side.

When we move to different social conditions, the abilities we had before lose their validity. However, if we remember how African Americans were uprooted from their home cultures and moved to the American continent—where despite their enslavement they were able to maintain their indigenous rhythm for 200 years under the dominating Anglo-Saxon culture and create jazz—we can understand that rhythm possesses a much stronger continuity than any written ideology.

If we could view the whole globe with a telescope, Ame no Uzume's dance, Izumo no O-Kuni's dance and *bon odori* could all possibly be seen as branching out from the dance of Shiva.[31] In Indian religions, dancing deities are placed at the centre of those religions as their symbols. Shiva has many manifestations and appears in diverse dances in various regions. Viewed in this way, the words of the Indian philosopher Ananda K. Coomaraswamy (1877–1947) declaring that there is no special category of people called artists so much as each person is a special artist seem particularly profound.[32]

---

31 Shiva, the creator and destroyer of all things, is a Hindu god and part of the holy trinity (trimurti) of Hinduism, together with Brahma and Vishnu. He is frequently depicted as a divine cosmic dancer, and different variations of his dance are associated with creation and destruction. Though Shiva is a male deity, in Tsurumi's context, Shiva appears to take multiple forms.

32 Coomaraswamy was a metaphysician, historian and philosopher of Indian art, who was largely responsible for introducing Indian art to the West. Several of his metaphysical writings highlighted the unity of the Vedanta (a school of Hindu philosophy) and Platonism, as well as the close relationship between Hinduism and Buddhism.

Chapter 12
Past and Present

In this chapter Tsurumi observes the Japanese past and present through inspirational figures that come to mind, highlighting how humans incorporate particular traditions into their own lives. The discussion of the models and heroes of his childhood leads into the topic of Ame no Uzume and her successor, the legendary figure Izumo no O-Kuni, who is thought to be the originator of kabuki. Tsurumi discusses several modern cultural representations of O-Kuni. He closes the chapter with his observations on discourses of Japanese culture and questions surrounding the myth of Japanese 'uniqueness' and gender issues. In conclusion, he declares his desire to mimic the attitudes of Ame no Uzume in seeking out equality rather than exclusivity, friendly diplomatic relations between Japan and foreign lands and an open mindset that questions the rigid ideologies of those in power.

In the Taishō era (1912–1926) of my early childhood, the first Sino-Japanese War (1894–1895) seemed like a thing of the past but memories of the Russo-Japanese War (1904–1905) were still fresh in people's minds.

> *Ri Kōshō no hage-atama, **manjū** kutte kawa nokosu*
>
> (Li Hongzhang's bald head, eating a bun but leaving its skin)

I had no idea what this phrase of a *shiritori* verse meant but I still found it funny.[1] It refers to Li Hongzhang (1823–1901), who was sent

---

1 *Shiritori* (尻取り) is a Japanese word game, in which players must say a word that begins with the final syllable of the previous word. *Shiritori uta* (shiritori song) are folk songs in which the syllable or word used to end one line is used to begin the next line. This verse is from one of many variations of a popular *shiritori* song that deals with themes of the first Sino-Japanese and Russo-Japanese Wars.

Chapter 12

as the Qing representative to negotiate with the Japanese victors in Shimonoseki, Japan.[2] The verse, which must have been written in 1895, was still commonly known around 1922 (i.e. the eleventh year of Taishō), when I was born. However, the songs about Lieutenant Colonel Tachibana and Commander Hirose from the Russo-Japanese War were far more enthusiastically received.

> Over the fortress of Liaoyang the night wears on
>
> The wan morning moon shines brightly
>
> ('The Song of Lieutenant Colonel Tachibana')[3]
>
> Guns roaring, bullets flying
>
> Raging waves washing the deck ('The Song of Commander Hirose')[4]

As a three- or four-year-old child, with the encouragement of the older children around me, I performed renditions of the final battles of Lieutenant Colonel Tachibana Shūta (1865–1904) of the Imperial Japanese Army and Commander Hirose Takeo (1868–1904) of the Imperial Japanese Navy many times every day. I must have created certain images in my mind and most likely performed with great passion. In my own way, I vividly felt the scenes of the vast plains of Liaoyang and the seascape outside Port Arthur with my own body.

There is no doubt that to my young self, Commander Hirose and Lieutenant Colonel Tachibana were model figures worth looking up to.

But why could my ideal person not have been a woman? Thinking about it now, it is strange. I think I must have been influenced by the narrowly defined Taishō era customs of gender division.

---

2 Li was a Chinese politician, general and diplomat who played a significant role in protecting Chinese interests in negotiating a series of unequal international treaties with the Western powers, as well as the Russian Empire and the Empire of Japan.

3 Tachibana died at the Battle of Liaoyang (31 August 1904), when he refused to take cover and charged the Russian position. His death was immediate and futile but was glorified in wartime propaganda. 'The Song of Lieutenant Colonel Tachibana' paints a picture of a bleak, war-torn Liaoyang, with Tachibana bravely facing his death for the glory of the army.

4 Hirose died during the Battle of Port Arthur, looking for other survivors when the cargo ship that he commanded was hit by coastal artillery. His death was heroically depicted by the Ministry of Education in 'The Song of Commander Hirose'.

Prior to school age, finding ideal characters from the Japanese past led me to Lieutenant Colonel Tachibana and Commander Hirose. Once I was of primary school age, however, my focus shifted to characters who appeared in movies. These included heroes in samurai movies such as Mikazuki Jirokichi and Tsukigata Hanpeita[5] who were played by Bandō Tsumasaburō (1901–1953), Ichikawa Utaemon (1907–1999) and Kataoka Chiezō (1903–1983).[6] Then later I gradually began to identify with outlaw heroes such as Sōma Daisaku and Yanagawa Shōhachi[7] who appeared in the written versions of *kōdan*[8] narratives. Thus, after beginning primary school, I never again aspired to become any sort of military man.

Since the recounting of Japanese mythology was the exclusive preserve of the Imperial family and the government, I listened to the narratives as episodes that had nothing to do with me. The only scene that left a lasting impression in my mind was from a textbook that described how Ototachibana-hime, praying for the success of her husband Yamatotakeru's mission, threw herself into the stormy sea. However, distanced by the sense of awe that I had at the time towards the Imperial family, I could not feel her determination as my own.

The figures that appeared in folk stories were much easier to identify with. Having sensed the horrifying power of war, I found solace in a film produced by the Takarazuka Revue, *Utau tanuki goten* (Singing Racoon Palace, directed by Kimura Keigo, 1942).[9] The *tanuki*

---

5 Mikazuki Jirokichi and Tsukigata Hanpeita were legendary figures who featured heavily in popular kabuki, films and theatre productions. The former originated in the early Edo period and the latter in the late Edo period.

6 Bandō Tsumasaburō (a.k.a. Bantsuma) and Kataoka Chiezō were prominent actors who starred in *jidaigeki* (時代劇, period dramas). Bandō in particular was famous for the unique, fast-paced sword fighting in his films. For more on Ichikawa Utaemon, see Chapter 3, footnote 5.

7 Sōma Daisaku was a popular figure and model of an ideal samurai, while Yanagawa Shōhachi was something of a 'lone-wolf' samurai who rebelled against the warrior class.

8 *Kōdan* (講談), or *kōshaku* (講釈), is a style of traditional Japanese oral storytelling. It originated in the Heian period (794–1185) as a way of lecturing nobles on historical, literary or religious topics, before gradually being adopted over the centuries by samurai and then commoners. *Kōdan* was largely phased out by the end of the Edo period (1603–1868).

9 The Takarazuka Revue is a Japanese all-female musical theatre troupe that was founded in 1913 in an attempt to capitalise on the growing popularity of Western song and dance shows and draw business to Takarazuka in Hyōgo prefecture. The Revue is divided into five troupes, each performing in different styles and with different materials.

Chapter 12

Figure 12.1: Scene from *Utau tanuki goten*

(racoon dogs) who disguised themselves as young women seemed to me to be a metaphor for escapism [from the oppressive nature of contemporary society]. According to the philosopher Ōmori Shōzō (1921–1997), understanding other people involves animism. In the context of the human world at the time, when it was regarded as normal for humans to kill other humans, putting one's hope in the existence of a non-human world was an effective way to sustain oneself.

As I was thinking about the notion of tradition used in one's own life, I felt the most important thing for me was the tradition of animism, which is the idea that the objects alongside us are alive. If I reframe my thinking from this point of view, it feels like the *Kojiki*, Shinto shrine customs, and *waka* and haiku poetry too, all contributed to the formation of my foundation. For example, in Book XVIII: poems 4094–7 of the *Man'yōshū*, the following appears:

Umi yukaba mizuku kabane / yama yukaba kusa musu kabane[10]

At sea be my body water-soaked, / On land be it with grass overgrown. (Keene & Nihon Gakujutsu Shinkōkai, 1965: 51)

I liked both the words and music of the song composed by Nobutoki Kiyoshi (1887–1965) based on these ancient verses when I first heard them, and I still like them now.[11] I found it impossible to devote myself

---

10 *Umi yukaba* (海行かば) is part of a longer poem about an imperial edict regarding the discovery of gold in Michinoku province (modern Tōhoku). The song was particularly popular among the Imperial Japanese Navy, and Nobutoki Kiyoshi's 1937 composition was particularly popular during and after World War II.
11 Nobutoki was a Japanese composer, musicologist and cellist whose major works also include *Kaidō tōsei* (海道東征, a 1940 cantata celebrating the 2600th anniversary of the imperial era) and *Sara* (沙羅, a collection of songs). He was awarded the Order of the Rising Sun in 1964, the year before his death.

to the war's cause, and I maintain my position now that it was not a justifiable war. Even so, when I hear this song in a scene of some historical film, it always moves me, in the same way that a fixed-sash window remains intact in a dilapidated house.

Neither has the lack of factuality and scientific grounding ever made me feel any sort of disdain for the following metaphor in 'Kimigayo', the Japanese national anthem:

> *sazare-ishi no iwao to narite / koke no musu made*
>
> ... till what are pebbles now / By age united to mighty rocks shall grow.[12]

While I am completely against the anthem being forced on children at school events, this is because I oppose the idea of making the glorification of the nation-state compulsory through school ceremonies. Having said that, the animism in these lyrics touches my heart. And, to return to our subject, these feelings comprise the foundation of my appreciation for Ame no Uzume's dance as the sun's power wanes in winter and she tries to awaken her own energy and the energy of Heaven and Earth.

§

During the war, I came across *Dai nihon josei jinmei jisho* (A Biographical Dictionary of Japanese Women, 1936) edited by Takamure Itsue (1894–1964).[13] As I browsed through it, I was deeply impressed by

---

12 The lyrics to 'Kimigayo' (君が代) are based on a *waka* poem written in the Heian period (794–1185). Though the title can be understood to mean 'His Imperial Majesty's Reign', the original subject of the lyrics might not have been the emperor, as *kimi* has been historically used to refer to one's lord. The song served as Japan's *de facto* anthem from 1880, and continued to be sung, even after Japan's defeat in World War II and the demotion of the emperor to a symbolic position. The 1999 Act on the National Flag and Anthem made 'Kimigayo' Japan's official national anthem, asserting that the lyrics did not necessarily refer to the long reign of the emperor, but rather to the continued peace and prosperity of Japan. The use of the anthem, together with the *hinomaru* (literally, 'circle of the sun') flag, continues to generate controversy, particularly in the field of education. While there is no official English translation of the anthem nor its title, this version is by the British translator Basil Hall Chamberlain (1850–1935).

13 Takamure was a Japanese writer, activist, anarchist, feminist, ethnologist and historian. She pioneered research into Japanese women's history, publishing on a range of topics, including matrilineage in ancient Japanese society, ancient marital institutions and property ownership by women.

Chapter 12

the entry for Kaneko Fumiko (1903–1926).[14] What I found truly moving was that even though the editor Takamure had left the anarchist movement by then, she still fearlessly included her contemporary Kaneko in this dictionary even in the midst of all-out war. Kaneko was accused of plotting to assassinate the emperor—an accusation that remains unsupported by any available facts and which was in all probability untrue—and then sentenced to death. Later on, upon receiving a letter of pardon, she tore it into pieces and killed herself. The entry moved me intensely at the time, but now I realise there was another intention at work in the process of editing this dictionary.

According to Kōno Nobuko's (b. 1927) book, *Takamure Itsue* (1990), the dictionary was co-written by Takamure's husband, Hashimoto Kenzō. Apparently Hashimoto told Kōno that since he wrote the majority of the book, he was hesitant to include it in Takamure's collected works (Kōno 1990: 7–8).[15] While working as an editor for Heibonsha, Hashimoto had great success with the modern popular literature series *Gendai taishū bungaku zenshū* (1927–1932, sixty volumes), and his views seem to have had a significant impact upon the choice of which figures, from ancient to modern times, would be featured in the dictionary.

> The ideas of the "two" [Takamure and Hashimoto] up until that time were condensed into their first "collaborative book", *Dai nihon josei jinmei jisho*, which did not overlook "popular publications" and included "names of mythological characters". The "popular publications" present the authors' observations and analyses of "mass consciousness", whereas the "mythologies" contain the shared illusions of the nation as well as the stories of compromise and antagonism towards the authorities of the time. If we were to throw these genres away, the existence of women would be reduced to what Ivan Illich called "economic sex".[16] Given that the "two" had

---

14 Kaneko is discussed in Chapter 9 as one of the subjects of Setouchi Harumi's biographical novels. See footnote 18 in that chapter.
15 The collected works refer to the ten-volume collection titled *Takamure Itsue zenshū* (Complete Works of Takamure Itsue), edited by Hashimoto and published by Rironsha in 1966–1967.
16 According to the Austrian philosopher Ivan Illich (1926–2002), the 20th century saw the notion of sexual equality usurp the traditional complementarity of gender. He argued that gender underpinned cultures' distinct ways of living, dying and suffering, and that 'economic sex' turned men and women into neutered economic agents, stripping their interactions of complementary synergy.

no institutional affiliation, they had no interest in pseudo-academic reductionism. (Kōno 1990: 8–9)

Dai nihon josei jinmei jisho is in fact a grand catalogue of figures that includes categories such as Imperial ancestors, loyalists, prostitutes, beauties, eccentrics and even *dofuku* ('poisonous women').[17] In the field of dance, the legendary figure who follows Ame no Uzume is Izumo no O-Kuni.[18]

The earliest mention of O-Kuni is in the diary of Tamon'in Eishun (1518–1598), who saw her performance in Nara on the eighteenth day of the fifth month of the tenth year of the Tenshō era (1582).[19] The entry in *Tamon'in nikki* reads:

> At the prayer hall of Wakamiya Shrine [in the precincts of the Kasuga Taisha Shrine] a ceremonial Buddhist song performance called *yayako odori* [literally, 'child dance', see Chapter 11] was offered by two girl dancers, the eight-year-old Kaga and eleven-year-old Kuni. [...] People swarmed around each performer, saying how adorable and riveting [the performances were].[20]

On the ninth day of the ninth month of the previous year, Tenshō 9 (1582), the *Oyudono no ue no nikki* (The Official Diary of the Court Ladies) records that a *yayako odori* performance took place before the lion dance at the Chrysanthemum Festival held at the court's Hall for State Ceremonies.[21] According to the diary, the two dancers were

---

17 *Dokufu* (毒婦) is a slanderous term for women thought to be malicious, cunning and deceitful. It originated in the early Meiji era (1868–1912).
18 See Chapter 11, footnote 8.
19 Eishun was a Buddhist monk of the Sengoku period (1467–1615), and was one of three contributors to the *Tamon'in nikki* (多聞院日記, Tamon'in Diary), a diary that recorded the lives of people at Tamon'in, a sub-temple of Nara's Kōfukuji temple, over 140 years (1478–1618).
20 We are grateful to Dr Sachi Schmidt-Hori of Dartmouth College for her assistance with the translation of this quotation and other matters concerning mediaeval and early modern Japanese literature and culture.
21 The diaries, which were originally kept secret, record events at the imperial court over the course of approximately 350 years, from the late 15th century onwards. In addition to describing the activities of the emperor, the entries also describe ceremonial rituals, court politics and cultural events and practices. The Chrysanthemum Festival is one of five seasonal Japanese festivals, and is held on 9 September, an auspicious date due to the doubling of the highest-value single-digit number.

presented with fans. Ogasawara Kyōko's book *Izumo no O-Kuni* (1984) regards these two dancers as the same ones that feature in *Tamon'in nikki*. As *Tamon'in* records the age of the dancers as eight and eleven, we can assume that in the previous year Kaga was seven and Kuni ten. O-Kuni went on to perform in various places including Kitano Shrine (Kyoto), Sado Island, the bank of the Kamo River and Edo, and it has long been accepted that it was Izumo no O-Kuni who founded kabuki. Naturally, there is a lot of interest in a woman who established an art form, and there are numerous novels and plays that feature O-Kuni as the protagonist. The lack of historical documents leaves much room for imagination; therefore, each work represents its author's thoughts on the ideal woman.

One such production was Hanada Kiyoteru's (1909–1974) play, *Mono mina uta de owaru* (All Ends With a Song), which was performed at Nissei Gekijō (Nissay Theatre) from 20 to 25 November 1963.[22] Surprisingly, the play received terrible reviews in the press. It was directed by Senda Koreya (1904–1994), with stage sets by Itō Kisaku (1899–1967), music by Hayashi Hikaru (1931–2012), *kyōgen* direction by Nomura Mannojō IV (b. 1930) and *yōkyoku* direction by Kanze Hideo (1927–2007).[23] The cast included Mizutani Yaeko, Nakadai Tatsuya, Sasaki Takamaru, Sugiura Naoki, Tatara Jun, Tomotake Masanori, Chiaki Minoru, Minami Michirō, Ichihara Etsuko, Yamaoka Hisano, Namino Kuriko and Mitsumoto Sachiko. The script was published in the January 1964 issue of *Shin Nihon bungaku* (The new Japanese literature).

The second production took place ten years later, on 20 and 23–25 November 1973, and 8–17 February 1974, at the Haiyūza Theatre

---

22 Hanada was a prominent Japanese writer, essayist and literary critic, and a leading figure in the post-war avant-garde art movement.

23 Senda was a Japanese stage director, translator, actor and leading figure in the modern theatre movement in Japan who founded the Haiyūza Theatre Company. One of Senda's older brothers, Itō, was an art director and prominent cinematic set designer in post-WWII Japan. Hayashi was a Japanese composer, pianist and conductor, who composed over 30 Japanese language operas and numerous innovative film scores. Nomura (who later became Nomura Manzō VII and then Nomura Man) is a noh performer who specialises in *kyōgen* (狂言, 'wild speech', a form of traditional Japanese comic theatre). Kanze was a Japanese actor and director who specialised in noh. *Yōkyoku* (謡曲) is the vocal component of music associated with classical noh drama.

in Roppongi, Tokyo. It featured young actors from a group called Kirokukai and was produced by Hasegawa Shirō and directed by Senda Koreya, with stage sets by Hirano Kōga and music by Okada Kazuo. This production was a great success.

In this play, Izumo no O-Kuni tries to establish the art of kabuki with the master of the spear (*yari no meijin*) Nagoya Sanza, but before achieving this goal, he is killed by an enemy whom he tried to save. At that moment, O-Kuni decides to become two people. Buried deep inside her, Sanza supports her, and she manages to dance as a woman in male guise in a natural manner. O-Kuni in the guise of Sanza and another actress who plays the role of O-Kuni, sing a duet:

Arishi mukashi no hitofushi o (a tune from the past)

utaite iza ya kabukan (let us sing and play kabuki)

This is Hanada's 'study of the birth of kabuki'.

In another work, Ariyoshi Sawako (1931–1984) serialised her novel *Izumo no O-Kuni* in the magazine *Fujin kōron* (Women's review) from January 1967 to December 1969, prior to publishing it in book format in July 1970.[24] That same month, it was adapted into a play by Hiraiwa Yumie (1932–2023) and staged at the Kabukiza Theatre. The cast included Mizutani Yaeko I, Morita Kan'ya XIV, Nakamura Kanzaburō XVII and Ichikawa Ebizō X.[25] Ariyoshi viewed the matinee on 2 July, the day it opened, but was reportedly not happy with it.

The work was adapted for theatre again from 1972 to 1973, with a script by Tsugami Tadashi (1924–2014) for the Zenshinza Theatre. The

---

24 Ariyoshi was a prolific Japanese writer whose works also include *Ki no kawa* (*The River Ki*, 1959, trans. Mildred Tahara), *Hanaoka Seishū no tsuma* (*The Doctor's Wife*, 1966, trans. Wakako Hironaka and Ann Siller Konstant) and *Kōkotsu no hito* (*The Twilight Years*, 1972, trans. Mildred Tahara). Many of Ariyoshi's works deal with social or environmental issues, and several, including the above and *Izumo no O-Kuni* (translated as *Kabuki Dancer* by James R. Brandon), have been translated into English.

25 Hiraiwa was a Naoki Award-winning author whose works span historical and contemporary novels and mystery novels, as well as scripts for the stage and television. Morita (1907–1975) was a kabuki actor famous for playing *tachiyaku* (young adult male roles). Nakamura (1909–1988) appeared in over 800 roles and was famous for his portrayal of both *tachiyaku* and *onnagata* (female roles). Ichikawa (1946–2013) was a kabuki actor famous for his physicality and strong stage presence. For more on Mizutani, see Chapter 9, footnote 27.

Chapter 12

cast included Imamura Izumi, Arashi Yoshisaburō and Arashi Yoshio.[26]

Ariyoshi's work was adapted yet again into a television series and broadcast from 1 January 1973 in sixteen episodes. The script was written by Ōyabu Ikuko and it was directed by Yatsuhashi Takashi. The cast included Sakuma Yoshiko, Hisatomi Koreharu, Ogata Ken, Hayashi Yoichi, Shindō Eitarō and Zaitsu Ichirō.[27]

In 1990, the Bungakuza theatre company[28] staged the work from 10 August to 6 September at the Mitsukoshi Theatre.[29] The script was by Ishikawa Kōji and it was directed by Inui Ichirō. The cast included Taichi Kiwako (playing O-Kuni), Sugō Takayuki (Sankurō), Shimizu Mikio (Densuke) and Kotō Yoshiharu (Nagoya Sanza).[30] I went to see this production. The scene that left a lasting impression on me was when O-Kuni, pregnant with a child of the master player of the *tsuzumi*

---

26 Tsurumi writes Tsumura, but it is likely that he meant to cite Tsugami Tadashi, a Japanese playwright, director and impresario. The Zenshinza theatre company was founded in 1931 and is one of Japan's oldest theatre troupes. Its repertoire ranges from traditional kabuki to historical dramas. Tsugami's script has been performed by the Zenshinza theatre company on a number of occasions, including in 1976 (https://www.enpaku-jdta.jp/detail/00328-01-1976-02) and 2009 (http://www.zenshinza.com/stage_guide/okuni/2009okuni_staff.htm). Imamura (b. 1933) is a stage and film actress and the current director of the Zenshinza theatre training school. Arashi Yoshisaburō V (1907–1977) was a kabuki actor noted for acting in female roles, and for playing old men in his later years. His son, Arashi Yoshio (1935–1996), became Arashi Yoshisaburō VI.

27 Ōyabu (b. 1929) is a Japanese screenwriter for television and film. Yatsuhashi (1927–2013) was a television and stage director, who worked for Nippon Educational Television (the current TV Asahi) until 1959, before becoming a freelance director. Sakuma (b. 1939) is a film, television and stage actress whose career spans over six decades. Hisatomi (1935–2015) was a TV and film actor who also appeared as a voice actor in radio dramas and dubbed foreign films. Ogata (1937–2008) was an actor who appeared in numerous films and television productions from 1958 until his death in 2008. Hayashi (b. 1942) is a former kabuki actor who also appeared in numerous television *jidaigeki* (period dramas). Shindō (1899–1977) was a prolific film actor who appeared in over 300 movies throughout his career. Zaitsu (b. 1934) is a retired actor, comedian and singer.

28 The Bungakuza theatre company was founded in 1937, and is one of three major *shingeki* (新劇, new drama) theatre troupes, together with the Mingei theatre company and the Haiyūza theatre company.

29 The Mitsukoshi Theatre was built in 1927, on the sixth floor of the Nihonbashi Mitsukoshi Main Store, a department store with a history dating back to 1673, which was heavily damaged by the Great Kantō Earthquake.

30 Inui (1916–2010) was a radio and stage director, and former president of the Bungakuza theatre company. Taichi (1943–1992) was a television, film and stage actress whose career spanned over 30 years from 1960 until her death in 1992. Sugō (b. 1952) is a television and voice actor, particularly known for playing mentors in various audio productions. Shimizu (b. 1943) is a film, television, stage and radio actor.

hand-drum,[31] Sankurō, is on her way to see Osaka Castle, which was built to celebrate the pregnancy of Yodogimi (1569–1615).[32] Sankurō, fearing the intentions of his lord Hideyoshi, would not accompany O-Kuni.[33] In his place, a servant called Densuke goes with her. Although they manage to see the castle off in the distance, due to the cold and their hunger, O-Kuni has a miscarriage on the snowy road. The servant Densuke lifts O-Kuni up into his arms and looks out in the direction of the castle.

According to the Biblical narrative, Mary's husband Joseph also looked after her and continued their difficult journey when she was pregnant with a child that was not his. Densuke's tenderness reminded me of Joseph's. The play gives us a glimpse of the way that a man can be as resilient and gentle as a woman. In a manner that differs completely from Hanada Kiyoteru's portrayal of Izumo no O-Kuni, a man assumes a woman's role. In Ariyoshi's original novel, too, Densuke plays a female role, *itoyori*, appearing on stage dressed as a woman, acting like a woman, and mediating a fight between a man and a woman.[34] Behind the scenes (within the narrative), Densuke continues to support O-Kuni, keeping her troupe together. In contrast to Sankurō, whose attempt to approach the ruler Hideyoshi ruins his relationship with O-Kuni, or to Nagoya Sanza, whose desire to have his own castle makes him leave O-Kuni, Densuke quietly and consistently devotes himself to her.

The difference between Joseph and Densuke is that the latter eventually marries another woman. In the scene where he holds O-Kuni in the snow, we are reminded of the play *Kutsukake Tokijirō*

---

31 The *tsuzumi* (鼓) is a Japanese hand-drum that comprises an hourglass-shaped wooden body wrapped with cords that can be adjusted to change the tension of the drumheads, allowing the player to alter the drum's pitch while playing.

32 Yodogimi was a concubine and second wife of Toyotomi Hideyoshi (see footnote 33), as well as the mother of Hideyoshi's successor, Hideyori. She became a Buddhist nun after Hideyoshi's death and founded Yōgen-in Temple in Kyoto.

33 Toyotomi Hideyoshi (1537–1598) was a Japanese feudal lord who, together with Oda Nobunaga (1534–1582) and Tokugawa Ieyasu (1543–1616), is credited with unifying Japan during the Sengoku period (1467–1615). He achieved this through military means and a number of strict edicts, including the banning of Christian missionaries and the confiscation of swords from commoners.

34 *Itoyori* comes from the name of an actor, Itoyori Gonzaburō, who was active in the mid-17th century, and is thought to have begun the tradition of men playing female roles in kabuki.

Chapter 12

(1928) by Hasegawa Shin (1884–1963).[35] While working as a construction labourer, Hasegawa actually met another labourer who was with a woman pregnant with someone else's child. Based on his impressions of this man, Hasegawa later created the character of the lone yakuza named Kutsukake Tokijirō. The character of the lone yakuza is apparently a completely different type of persona from the boss of a group like Shimizu no Jirochō.[36] This was the theme of Satō Tadao's essay, 'Ninkyō ni tsuite' (Yakuza films, 1954), which marked the beginning of his long career as a film critic. In short, *Kutsukake Tokijirō* is a deeply moving play that has been adapted into numerous films, and the story is familiar to millions of Japanese. It is not a story of the past, but no doubt it will be relevant to Japanese society in the near future by making Japanese think about the meaning of love between partners amidst an ageing society with an increased number of divorces and re-marriages involving step-children.

§

I think that everyone makes their own personal catalogue of Japanese traditions as they go about their lives. I am writing this chapter as a reminder of that. I think it is also true that our minds are kept alive by the traditions that have entered us, even without any sort of calculated strategy. As I get older and more forgetful, my mental state will eventually decline. When this happens, I wonder what sort of person Ame no Uzume will become for me.

It is also possible to consider this question from a wider perspective. Harumi Befu (1930–2022) in his *Ideorogii to shite no nihon bunka ron* (Japanese Cultural Discourses as Ideologies, 1987, revised edition 1990) analyses Japanese cultural theory through mass consumer

---

35 Hasegawa was a Japanese novelist, essayist and playwright whose works also include *Mabuta no haha* (1936) and *Ippongatana dohyōiri* (1931). The eponymous hero of *Kutsukake Tokijirō* is an honourable gangster who takes the pregnant widow of his dead enemy under his protection. The two fall in love, but the play ends with the tragic death of the widow and the title character renouncing his life as a gangster.

36 Shimizu no Jirochō (1820–1893) was a notable yakuza boss in the Tōkaidō region, and is something of a Robin Hood-like folk hero in Japan today. In his later years, he was increasingly involved in business and philanthropy, overseeing land reclamation projects, building Shinto shrines, and even establishing English-language schools.

products of the time.[37] Focusing on the post-war era, Aoki Tamotsu (b. 1938) in his *'Nihon bunkaron' no hen'yō* (Changes in the Discourse of Japanese Culture, 1990) identifies four distinct periods:[38]

1. Cognition of negative uniqueness (1945–1954)

2. Cognition of historical relativism (1955–1963)

3. Cognition of positive uniqueness (1964–1984)

4. From unique to universal (1984–)

Aoki concludes that discussions of Japanese culture have not necessarily progressed with time, and that the present discourse is by no means the most demonstrative, scientific or reliable. Jonathan Swift (1667–1745) and Montesquieu (1689–1755) wrote books to 'bewilder and trouble people rather than comfort them' regarding the largely established views about eighteenth-century European civilisation.[39] Aoki focuses on the fact that Ruth Benedict (1887–1948) perplexed the Americans and the Japanese around 1945 with *The Chrysanthemum and the Sword* in a similar fashion.[40]

---

37 Befu was born to Japanese parents in Los Angeles and spent World War II in Japan before returning to the United States in 1947. He taught anthropology at Stanford University from 1965 until his retirement in 1996 and played an instrumental role both in establishing Japanese studies at Stanford and exposing stereotypes about Japanese people and culture.

38 Aoki is a cultural anthropologist who has taught at Osaka University, the University of Tokyo and the National Graduate Institute for Policy Studies, and has been a visiting scholar at universities in the United States, France and Germany. His research focuses on cultural anthropology and cultural politics in Asia, as well as Europe and the United States.

39 The quotation from Jonathan Swift is part of a 1725 letter to Alexander Pope (1688–1744): 'The chief end I propose to myself in all my labours is to vex the world, rather than divert [entertain] it.' The comparison of Ruth Benedict's work to those of Swift and Montesquieu is found in Geertz (1988: 127–128). See Aoki (1990: 154).

40 Benedict was an American anthropologist and folklorist. In *Patterns of Culture* (1934), she argued that personality, art, language and culture are interrelated and that no individual trait exists self-sufficiently or in isolation. *The Chrysanthemum and the Sword*, published in 1945, aimed at understanding Japanese culture and explaining it to Americans. Benedict played an important role in developing American understanding of the importance of the emperor to Japanese culture, but while her material was thought to be generally accurate, she was also critiqued for what some saw as her 'moralistic' approach to Japanese culture.

Chapter 12

Now that discourses of "Japanese culture" have gone too far to "console" the Japanese, I strongly believe that a Benedict-style *Gulliver's Travels*, as described by anthropologist Clifford Geertz [1926–2006], is what is needed for future Japanese cultural discourse.[41] (Aoki 1990: 155, in reference to Geertz 1988: 127–128)

The Japanese cultural discourse that I was involved in before school age, that is, the glorification of the Japanese in the first Sino-Japanese and Russo-Japanese Wars, occurred before the post-war discourses summarised by Aoki. As far as my generation is concerned, such idealised notions of Japan, which were far removed from reality, produced a false belief in the power of the Japanese military beyond its actual strength, and led to the second Sino-Japanese War (1937–1945), the Nomonhan Incident (1939) and the 'Greater East Asia War'.[42] After this came the discourse of Japanese culture based on what Aoki called the 'cognition of negative uniqueness'.

This lineage presents the ideal types for Japanese men before, during and after the war; had we focused on the attitudes of women dealing on a practical level with their own everyday lives, it seems to me that we might have seen a slightly different pattern from what emerged from the observations of men. As I approach the end of this book, I admit that I have been writing about one form of the ideal that men seek in women. Women who look after the everyday view the nation-state in a somewhat different way from the ways things are discussed when working outside the home and speaking in the *tatemae* style (public stance; official position) within male-dominated groups.[43]

---

41 Geertz was an American anthropologist who strongly supported symbolic anthropology, which promotes the study and use of cultural symbols as a means of better understanding a society. Geertz also championed thick description, an anthropological explanatory method that draws upon detailed descriptions both of human actions and their context.

42 The second Sino-Japanese War was fought primarily between the Republic of China and the Empire of Japan and began with the 7 July 1937 Marco Polo Bridge Incident. It formed part of the broader Pacific conflict in World War II. The Nomonhan Incident was the most decisive of a series of battles fought near the Khalkhin Gol River, along the Soviet-Japanese border. It resulted in the defeat of the Japanese Sixth Army by Soviet forces. For 'Greater East Asia War', see Chapter 2, footnote 13.

43 *Tatemae* contrasts with the term *honne*, which is used to refer to a person's true feelings, often concealed except with one's closest friends and family.

The difference is evident in the following *tanka*[44] by Toki Zenmaro (1885–1980),[45] which records a wife's words to her husband who is disheartened by the defeat:

> Anata wa katsu mono to omotte imashita ka to oitaru tsuma
> no sabishige ni iu
>
> ('Did you really believe that we would win?' my ageing
> wife says sadly)

Aoki Tamotsu cites 'Nihon bunka no sekaishiteki jikken' (Japanese cultural experimentations on world history), the essay (in Yamazaki 1987) by Yamazaki Masakazu (1934–2020),[46] as an example of post-1984 discourse on Japanese culture that is free from the pre-war pattern of viewing Japanese culture as unique (a position which, ironically, shares the same logic as the present Western theories on Japanese culture that are used as a basis for attacking Japan), instead proposing a future direction for Japanese culture away from previous fixed ideas and with a capacity for flexibility. Yamazaki points out that although it is axiomatic that the Japanese language underpins the foundations of Japanese relationships, the same cannot be said in the international community. He then urges Japanese companies and other organisations to correct their characteristically Japanese attitudes in approaching human relationships, advocating the importance of 1) linguistic diversity within each organisation and 2) adjustments to human relations in order to follow methods accepted as 'international' by the international community (Yamazaki 1987).

The fact that Japan continues to boast about its position as an economic power to this day, however, encourages the further

---

44 Here, Tsurumi uses the term *waka*, a type of poetry in classical Japanese literature. As Toki is a modern (naturalist) poet, this has been changed to *tanka*.

45 Toki was a Japanese poet and reporter. His first anthology, *Nakiwarai*, was published in 1910 while Toki was working for the *Yomiuri shinbun*. During World War II, he shifted to writing scholarly works in response to the militarist crackdown on left-wing literature. Toki's liberal stance during the war saw his career flourish in the post-war era.

46 Yamazaki was a Japanese playwright, literary critic, teacher and philosopher, whose accolades included the 1963 Kishida Prize for Drama for the play *Zeami*, the 1984 Yomiuri Prize for *Oedipus shōten*, and recognition as a Person of Cultural Merit in 2006. As a critic, he was an advocate for a new form of individualism grounded in corporate philanthropy and volunteerism and described himself as a cultural conservative.

Chapter 12

spread of the 'cognition of positive uniqueness' that sustained the success of the Japanese economy. In the Afterword of *Uchi naru kabe: Gaikokujin no nihonjin zō, Nihonjin no gaikokujin zō* (The Wall Inside: Foreigners' Images of Japanese, Japanese Images of Foreigners) edited by Hirakawa Sukehiro and Tsuruta Kin'ya, Tsuruta recounts his own experience:

> Within the University of British Columbia, there is an English Language Institute. It is the type of English language school that all major universities have for their overseas students. Two young Japanese students who seemed to be studying there were talking loudly on a bus. Their topic of discussion was which foreigner they would like to marry. After listing negative stereotypes associated with their Chinese, Mexican and Arab classmates, one of them said:
>
> "You know, occasionally you meet a white girl, born and raised in Japan, who speaks Japanese and no other languages. I wanna marry that type."
>
> Some readers may think that I made up this story, because it perfectly fits my context, but I assure you, I actually heard this discussion on the bus.

§

Standing at the parting of Heaven and Earth, and before the odd-looking stranger, the ancient goddess Ame no Uzume sought equality rather than exclusivity. This is precisely the sort of attitude I want to seek today. She presents a model for interceding between Japan and foreign lands, and Heaven and Earth. She disrupts the pursuit of the rigid ideologies pursued by the authorities. Or perhaps it is better that I follow the example of Sarutahiko, and prepare myself to deal with Ame no Uzume when she arrives from the other world.

Afterword

Twenty years ago, when the Heibonsha editors Igarashi Kenkichi and Shibata Michiko first suggested that I write some books for their publishing house, I said that I had three subjects I would like to write about. I have now written all three of the books I had in mind: *Yanagi Muneyoshi*, *Tayū Saizō den*, and *Ame no Uzume den*.[1] I am extremely grateful to both editors. After our initial discussions, Mr Igarashi retired, so Ms Shibata became my editor. Her meticulous care on each project enabled me to complete all three books as planned.

This book is not an attempt to reconstruct the past through the storytelling device of Japanese mythology. Rather, it attempts to traverse the long and narrow road that extends from that mythology to my present place. I spoke about this topic for the first time in the autumn of 1989 at the Shijō Extension Centre at Bukkyō University, Kyoto, at the invitation of the centre's director, Mr Satō Masataka. I am grateful to him for this opportunity, as the talk enabled me to start writing on what was then a difficult topic. From February 1990 to January 1991, these essays were serialised in Heibonsha's magazine *Gekkan hyakka* (Monthly encyclopaedia).

After completing the book, I went to see the Onda Festival at Asukani Imasu Jinja[2] on 3 March this year with Katō Norihiro and Kurokawa Sō.[3] We had a wonderful time.

I dedicate this book to my partner Yokoyama Sadako,[4] who has given me a universe of liberty.

1 April 1991
Tsurumi Shunsuke

---

1 All three books were published in the Heibonsha sensho series, which was initiated by Igarashi Kenkichi. *Yanagi Muneyoshi* was published in 1976, followed by *Tayū Saizō den* in 1979, and *Ame no Uzume den* in 1991. Yanagi Muneyoshi (a.k.a. Sōetsu, 1889–1961) was an art critic and thinker. *Tayū* and *saizō* are the names of the roles in the traditional comic performance genre of *manzai*. For more on *manzai*, see Chapter 4, footnote 21.

2 This festival is held on the first Sunday of February at this Shinto shrine in Nara. It is famous for its comic performance which mimics a sexual act between a *tengu* (a long-nosed goblin) and an *okame* (a woman with a funny face). For more on *okame*, see Chapter 3, footnote 2. Within the shrine grounds, there are numerous stone statues and carvings in the shape of phalli.

3 Katō (1948–2019) was a Japanese literary critic and intellectual whose publications dealt with topics that included contemporary literature, politics and the history of ideas. Kurokawa (b. 1961) is a Japanese literary critic and novelist. Both were involved in editing *Shisō no kagaku* (Science of thought), a magazine edited by Tsurumi and affiliated with Shisō no Kagaku Kenkyūkai (The Institute for the Science of Thought), a think tank founded by Tsurumi in 1946.

4 Yokoyama Sadako (b. 1931) is a scholar and translator of English literature by Isak Dinesen, Flannery O'Connor, Joan Lingard and others, and former professor at Kyoto Seika University. Tsurumi uses some of her translated works in this book.

Bibliography

Alcock, Rutherford (1863), *The Capital of the Tycoon: A Narrative of a Three Years' Residence in Japan*, London: Longman and Co.

Aoki, Tamotsu (1990), *'Nihon bunka ron' no hen'yō* (Changes in the discourse of Japanese culture), Tokyo: Chūō Kōronsha.

Aoyama, Tomoko (2012), 'The aging Ame no Uzume: Gender and humor in Sano Yōko's writing', *PAJLS (Proceedings of the Association for Japanese Literary Studies)*, 13 (Summer 2012): 210–224.

―――― (2019), 'Ame no Uzume crosses boundaries', in Laura Miller and Rebecca Copeland (eds.), *Diva Nation*, Berkeley: University of California Press, pp. 34–50.

―――― (2020), 'Youthful first impressions: Tsurumi Kazuko and Shunsuke in Australia, 1937', in David Chapman and Carol Hayes (eds.), *Japan in Australia*, London & New York: Routledge, pp. 25–43.

Ariyoshi, Sawako (1969–1972), *Izumo no O-Kuni*, 3 vols., Tokyo: Chūō Kōronsha.

Bakhtin, Mikhail M. (1984), *Rabelais and His World*, trans. Hélène Iswolsky, Bloomington: Indiana University Press.

Befu, Harumi (1990), *Zōho ideorogii to shite no Nihon bunka ron* (Japanese cultural discourse as an ideology, revised edition), Tokyo: Shisō no Kagakusha.

Burke, Kenneth ([1937] 1959), *Attitudes toward History*, Los Altos: Hermes Publications.

Calder-Marshall, A. (1959), *Havelock Ellis: A Biography*, London: R. Hart-Davis.

Demetrakopoulos, Stephanie (1983), *Listening to Our Bodies: The Rebirth of Feminine Wisdom*, Boston: Beacon Press. (Trans. Yokoyama, Sadako [1987], *Karada no koe ni mimi o sumasu to*, Tokyo: Shisō no Kagakusha.)

Dorman, Benjamin (2012), *Celebrity Gods: New Religions, Media and Authority in Occupied Japan*, Honolulu: University of Hawaii Press.

Ellis, Havelock (2007), *Impressions and Comments*, Charleston: BiblioBazaar.

Ellis, Havelock, Mrs (1918), *James Hinton*, London: Stanley Paul & Co.

Erikson, Erik H. (1969), *Gandhi's Truth: On the Origins of Militant Nonviolence*, New York: Norton.

Fujioka, Yoshinaru (1989), 'Minkan ryōhō o kangaeru' (Some thoughts about folk remedies), *Shisō no kagaku* (Science of thought), 121: 4–13.

Furuya, Mitsutoshi (2017), *Ganso Dame Oyaji* (The original No-good Dad), Tokyo: Shōgakukan.

Geertz, Clifford (1988), *Works and Lives: The Anthropologist as Author*, Redwood City: Stanford University Press.

Gendai Shisō (2015), *Tsurumi Shunsuke*, *Gendai shisō* (Modern thought), 43(15).

Gorai, Shigeru (1998), *Odori nenbutsu* (Dancing prayer), Tokyo: Heibonsha, Heibonsha Library.

Hanada, Kiyoteru (2021), *Mono mina uta de owaru, Bakuretsudan ki* (All ends with a song), Tokyo: Kōdansha.

Hashimoto, Mineo (1977), 'Furo no shisō' (The ideology of the bath), in Gendai Fūzoku Kenkyūkai (ed.), *Gendai fūzoku '77*.

Hasegawa, Shin ([1928] 2019), *Kutsukake Tokijirō*, Aozora Bunko, https://www. aozora.gr.jp/cards/001726/files/56083_68254.html

Hidaka, Rokuro (1984), *The Price of Affluence: Dilemma of Contemporary Japan*, Melbourne: Penguin.

Hirakawa, Sukehiro and Tsuruta, Kin'ya (eds.) (1990), *Uchi naru kabe: Gaikokujin no nihonjin zō, Nihonjin no gaikokujin zō* (The wall inside: The image of Japanese by foreigners, the image of foreigners by Japanese), Tokyo: TBS Britannica.

Hotta, Katsuhiko (1988), *Obatarian*, vol. 1, Tokyo: Take Shobō.

_____ (1989), *Obatarian*, vol. 3, Tokyo: Take Shobō.

Ichimura, Hiromasa (1987), *Nazuke no seishinshi* (The spiritual history of naming), Tokyo: Misuzu Shobō.

Idemitsu Museum of Arts (2015), *Botsugo 50-nen Kosugi Hōan: 'Tōyō" e no ai* (*Commemorating the 50th Year of the Death of the Artist Kosugi Hōan—Love for the 'East'*), Tokyo: Idemitsu Bijutsukan.

Illich, Ivan (1982), *Gender*, New York: Pantheon Books.

Inoue, Mitsusada ([1965] 1973), *Shinwa kara rekishi e* (From myth to religion), *Nihon no rekishi*, vol. 1, Tokyo: Chūō Kōronsha.

Ishikawa, Sanshirō (1978), *Ishikawa Sanshirō chosakushū* (Collected works of Ishikawa Sanshiro), vol. 1, Tokyo: Seidosha.

Iwaki, Hiroyuki (1984), 'Sonna jōku wa gokanben' (Spare me from that sort of joke, please!), in Katsura Beichō (ed.), *Warai* (Laughter), Tokyo: Sakuhinsha.

Katō, Norihiro (2007), 'Tsurumi Shunsuke san no koto' (On Mr Tsurumi Shunsuke), *Gendaishi techō* (Modern poetry notebook), 50(5): 18–20.

Keene, Donald and Nihon Gakujutsu Shinkōkai. Dai 17 Shō (Nihon Koten Hon'yaku) Iinkai (1965), *The Manyōshū: The Nippon Gakujutsu Shinkōkai Translation of One Thousand Poems, with the Texts in Romaji*, New York: Columbia University Press.

Komada, Shinji (1976), 'Dai nikai kōhan chōsho' (A record of the second trial), *Kikan geinō tōzai* (Performing arts East and West quarterly), January issue.

Kōno, Fumiyo (2012), *Bōrupen Kojiki* (The *Kojiki* drawn with a ballpoint pen), 3 vols., Tokyo: Heibonsha.

Kōno, Nobuko (1990), *Takamure Itsue*, Tokyo: Ribropōto (Libroport).

Kuratsuka, Akiko (1986), 'Ame no Uzume no Mikoto', in Ōsumi Kazuo et al. (eds.), *Nihon kakū denshō jinmei jiten* (A dictionary of fictional names in Japanese folklore), Tokyo: Heibonsha.

Kuratsuka, Taira (1990), *Yūtopia to sei* (Utopia and sex), Tokyo: Chūō Kōronsha.

Langer, Susanne K. (1957), *Problems of Art: Ten Philosophical Lectures*, London: Routledge & Kegan Paul.

MacKeller, Jean Scott (1975), *Rape: The Bait and the Trap: A Balanced, Humane, Up-To-Date Analysis of Its Causes and Control*, New York: Crown Publishing.

Mano, Sayo et al. (1982), 'Hahaoya ni tsuite nanmon, gumon ni okotae shimasu' (We'll answer all sorts of difficult and stupid questions about mothers), *Shisō no kagaku* (Science of thought), 24: 6–25.

Margulis, Lynn, Sagan, Dorion and Thomas, Lewis (1986), *Microcosmos: Four Billion Years of Microbial Evolution*, Berkeley: University of California Press.

Marumoto, Yoshio (1990), *Chihōshoku* (Local colour), Tokyo: Bungei Shunjū.

Mori, Hideto (1975), *Uji no kojiki yo me o samase* (Wake up, maggot beggars!), Tokyo: Daiwa Shuppan Hanbai.

Nagase, Kiyoko (1981), *Kaku atta* (Thus we met), Osaka: Henshū Kōbō Noa.

Nakamura, Shōji (1989), *Kaori no sekai o saguru* (Searching the world of perfume), Tokyo: Asahi Shinbunsha.

Nakano, Shigeharu (1967), 'Sakka to shite bungaku kyōiku ni nozomu' (What I hope for literature education as a writer), in Nakano Shigeharu (1978), *Nakano Shigeharu zenshū*, vol. 22, Tokyo: Chikuma Shobō.

Nakano, Takashi (ed.) (1989), *Chūgakusei no mita Shōwa 10-nendai* (The second decade of the Showa period as viewed by middle school students), Tokyo: Shin'yōsha.

Nakazawa, Atsushi (1988), *Ishi ni yadoru mono* (What dwells in stones), Tokyo: Heibonsha.

Nishizawa, Taku (2006), *Ishikawa Sanshirō no yūtopia kōsō* (Ishikawa Sanshiro's Utopian construct), Tokyo: Tōji Shobō.

Nomura, Masaichi (1983), *Shigusa no sekai: Shintai hyōgen no minzokugaku* (The world of gestures: The anthropology of body language), Tokyo: NHK Books.

Ō no Yasumaro, trans. Heldt, Gustav (2014), *The Kojiki: An Account of Ancient Matters*, New York: Columbia University Press.

Ochiai, Keiko (1982), *Za reipu* (The rape), Tokyo: Kōdansha.

Ogasawara, Kyōko (1984), *Izumo no O-Kuni*, Tokyo: Chūō Kōronsha.

Ōhira, Ken (1990), *Yutakasa no seishin byōri* (The psychopathology of affluence), Tokyo: Iwanami Shoten.

Okkotsu, Yoshiko (1978), *Aikotoba wa tebukuro no katappo* (The password is one glove), Tokyo: Iwanami Shoten.

_____ (1980), *Piramiddo bōshi yo, sayōnara* (Good-bye, pyramid hat), Tokyo: Rironsha.

Olson, Lawrence (1992), *Ambivalent Moderns: Portraits of Japanese Cultural Identity*, Savage: Rowman & Littlefield Publishers.

Ono, Nobuyuki (1977), 'Ichijō Sayuri', in *Gendai jinbutsu jiten* (A dictionary of contemporary names), Tokyo: Asahi Shinbunsha.

Orwell, George (1949), 'Reflections on Gandhi', *Partisan Review*, 16(1): 85–92.

Ozawa, Shōichi (ed.) (1977a), 'Sutorippu daitokushū' (Grand feature on stripping), *Kikan geinō tōzai* (Performing arts East and West quarterly), July issue.

_____ (1977b), 'Maido.... Nihon no hōrōgei: Ichijō Sayuri, Kiri Kaoru no sekai' (As always... itinerant arts in Japan: the world of Ichijo Sayuri and Kiri Kaoru), audio record, Nihon Victor.

Philippi, Donald L. (1968), *Kojiki*, Princeton and Tokyo: Princeton University Press and University of Tokyo Press.

Bibliography.

Pulvers, Roger (1982), 'The top scholar who failed at school', *The Age* (Melbourne), 11 February, p. 11.

Rexroth, Kenneth (1974), *Communalism: From Its Origins to the Twentieth Century*, New York: Seabury Press.

Satō, Tadao ([1954] 1962), 'Ninkyō ni tsuite', *Shisō no kagaku*, 5(2): 60–66.

Setouchi, Harumi (1971), *Odayakana heya* (A calm room), Tokyo: Kawade Shobō Shinsha.

Setouchi, Harumi and Jakuchō (1990), *Waga sei to sei* (My life and my sex life), Tokyo: Shinchōsha.

Shinmura, Izuru (ed.) (2018), *Kōjien* (Dictionary), Tokyo: Iwanami Shoten.

Shishi, Bunroku (1967), *Tajima Tarōji den* (The life of Tajima Tarōji), Tokyo: Shinchōsha.

Shisō no Kagaku Kenkyū-kai (ed.) (1959, 1960 and 1962), *Kyōdō kenkyū: Tenkō* (Collaborative research: Conversion), 3 vols., Tokyo: Heibonsha.

Sorel, Georges, and Jeremy Jennings (ed.) (1999), *Reflections on Violence*, Cambridge University Press.

Sugimoto, Yoshio (2007), 'Shunsuke Tsurumi: Voice of the voiceless', *Overland*, 187: 58–60.

_____ (2021), *An Introduction to Japanese Society*, 5th ed., Cambridge: Cambridge University Press.

Süskind, Patrick and Ikeuchi, Osamu (1988), *Kōsui* (Perfume), Tokyo: Bungei Shunjūsha.

Süskind, Patrick and Woods, John E. (2003), *Perfume: The Story of a Murderer*, Penguin Books.

Takahashi, Kazumi (1966), *Jashūmon* (The heretic faith), 2 vols., Tokyo: Kawade Shobō Shinsha.

Takamure, Itsue (ed.) (1936), *Dai nihon josei jinmei jisho* (A bibliographical dictionary of Japanese women), Tokyo: Kōseikaku.

_____ (1966–1967), *Takamure Itsue zenshū* (Collected works of Takamure Itsue), Hashimoto Kenzō (ed.), 10 vols., Tokyo: Rironsha.

Takeda, Taijun and Tsurumi, Shunsuke (November 1968), 'Kokka to seiji shi' (The nation and the death of politics), *Gendai no me* (Contemporary eye), 9(11): 96–109.

Tanabe, Seiko (1977), *O-Sei-san no horoyoi taidan* (O-Sei-san's tipsy dialogues), Tokyo: Kōdansha.

_____ ([1978] 2000), *Ibu no okurege II* (Eve's stray locks II), Tokyo: Bungei Shunjū, Bunshun web bunko.

_____ (1980), *Iutara nan ya kedo* (Sorry to say this but), Tokyo: Kadokawa Shoten, Kadokawa bunko.

_____ (1983), *Dansu to kūsō* (Dance and fantasy), Tokyo: Bungei Shunjū.

_____ ([1989] 2008), *Busu guchi roku* (A record of grumblings about ugly women), Tokyo: Bungei Shunjū, Bunshun web bunko.

Tanizaki, Jun'ichirō and Hibbett, Howard (2000), *Diary of a Mad Old Man*, London: Vintage.

Tenshō Kōtai Jingūkyō Honbu (ed.) (1951), *Seisho* (The book of life), Tabuse, Yamaguchi: Tenshō Kōtai Jingūkyō.

____ (1966), *Kami no kuni* (The divine country), Tabuse, Yamaguchi: Tenshō Kōtai Jingūkyō.

Tsurumi, Shunsuke (1967), *Genkai geijutsu-ron* (On marginal art), Tokyo: Keisō Shobō (paperback edition published in 1999 by Chikuma Shobō).

____ (1987), *A Cultural History of Postwar Japan 1945–1980*, London, New York: KPI.

____ (1991–1992), *Tsurumi Shunsuke shū* (Collected works of Tsurumi Shunsuke), 12 vols., Tokyo: Chikuma Shobō.

____ (1996), *Tsurumi Shunsuke zadan* (Tsurumi Shunsuke discussions), 10 vols., Tokyo: Shōbunsha.

____ (1997), *Kitai to kaisō* (Expectations and recollections), 2 vols., Tokyo: Shōbunsha.

____ (2000–2001), *Tsurumi Shunsuke shū, zoku* (Collected works of Tsurumi Shunsuke, second series), 5 vols., Tokyo: Chikuma Shobō.

____ (2002), *Mirai ni okitai mono wa: Tsurumi Shunsuke taidanshū* (What we wish to place in our future: A collection of Tsurumi Shunsuke's dialogues), Tokyo: Shōbunsha.

____ (2010), *An Intellectual History of Wartime Japan*, London: Routledge.

____ (2015), *Shōwa o kataru: Tsurumi Shunsuke zadan* (Talking about Showa: Tsurumi Shunsuke discussions), Tokyo: Shōbunsha.

Tsurumi, Shunsuke, Ueno, Chizuko and Oguma, Eiji (2004), *Sensō ga nokoshita mono: Tsurumi Shunsuke ni sengo sedai ga kiku* (What the war has left behind: Tsurumi Shunsuke interviewed by the post-war generation), Tokyo: Shin'yōsha.

Watanabe, Masuo (1983), *Tokushima rajio-shō-goroshi jiken* (The Tokushima radio merchant murder case), Tokyo: Mokuba Shokan.

Wood, Nancy (1974), *Many Winters: Prose and Poetry of the Pueblos*, New York: Doubleday & Company.

Yamazaki, Masakazu (1987), *Bunka kaikoku e no chōsen* (Challenges for opening up culture), Tokyo: Chūō Kōronsha.

Yanagita, Kunio (1929), *Yukiguni no haru* (Spring in the snow country), Tokyo: Kadokawa Sophia bunko.

Yasuda, Naomichi and Akimoto, Yoshinori (eds.) (1976), *Kogo shūi* (Gleanings from ancient stories), Tokyo: Gendai Shichōsha.

Yoshida, Atsuhiko (1989), *Nihon shinwa no tokushoku* (The characteristics of Japanese mythology), Tokyo: Seidosha.

Yūgentei, Tamasuke (1986), *Taikomochi Tamasuke ichidai* (My life as a jester), Tokyo: Sōshisha.

Zahan, Dominique and Grieco, Allen G. (1975), 'Colors and body painting in Black Africa: the problem of the "Half-Man"', *Diogenes*, 23(90): 100–119.

Zahan, Dominique, trans. Yokoyama, Sadako (1980), 'Kokujin Afurika ni okeru shikisai to shintai saishoku: "Hannin" no mondai' (Colours and body painting in Black Africa: the problem of the 'half-man'), *Diogenesu*, 11: 92–107.

Index

A
Aboriginal mythology xv
abstraction 31
ageing 128, 172, 175
Aikotoba wa tebukuro no katappo (The password is one glove, Okkotsu Yoshiko) 54
Alcock, J. R. 98–99
Ama no Hohi no Mikoto 12–14, 23
Amaterasu Ōmikami 13, 18, 20, 25, 57, 61
Ame no Koyane no Mikoto 12–13, 61
Ame no Osume 51
Ame no Sagume 12, 24
Ame no Tajikarao no Mikoto 12, 19
Ame no Uzume vii, ix, 2–3, 6–10, 12–13, 17–27, 29–30, 33–39, 41, 44, 47, 49–52, 54–59, 61, 65, 67, 93, 96–97, 103, 114, 117, 131, 133–134, 143, 147, 160–161, 165, 167, 172, 176
Ame no Wakahiko 12, 14, 23–24
anarchist xiv, 8, 62, 69, 117, 123, 165–166,
animism 164–165
Aoki, Tamotsu 173–175
Ariyoshi, Sawako 8, 169–171
Asaka, Mitsuyo 80
Attitudes toward History (Kenneth Burke) 84
Awa odori 130, 156

B
Bakhtin, Mikhail 59–60
bath, bathing 67, 69–71, 96, 98–100, 102
beautiful woman 42
beauty 37, 41–42, 44, 47, 68, 77, 123, 134, 141
Befu, Harumi 172–173
Beheiren (Citizens' League for Peace in Vietnam) vii, xiv, 68, 70
Benedict, Ruth 173–174
Bible, The 107
Black Musical Theatre 82
bon odori (Bon Festival dance) 151, 154–158, 160
Buddhism 91, 99, 120, 124, 130, 152–153, 157–158, 160
burlesque 5–7, 79, 84–86
'Busu guchiroku' (A record of grumblings about ugly women, Tanabe Seiko) 134
butō 151

C
Cantor, Eddie 64
Capital of the Tycoon, The (Alcock Rutherford) 98
Captain Whitfield 76
carnival 59–60
Charybdis 58–59
Chihōshoku (The local colour, Marumoto Yoshio) 76
Chōhachi of Izu 21
Chrysanthemum and the Sword, The (Ruth Benedict) 173
comedy 3, 8, 45, 65, 79, 85
Communalism: From Its Origins to the Twentieth Century (Kenneth Rexroth) 100
Coomaraswamy, Ananda K. 160

D
Dai nihon josei jinmei jisho (A biographical dictionary of Japanese women, Takamure Itsue) 165–167
Daikokuya, Kōdayū 74
Dame Oyaji (No-good Dad, Furuya Mitsutoshi) 45–46
Dance of Life, The (Havelock Ellis) 150
dancing religion 8, 22, 103, 111–112, 114
Dansu to kūsō (Dance and fantasy, Tanabe Seiko) 140
'Darakuron' (Discourse on decadence, Sakaguchi Ango) 104
death 4, 54–56, 62, 76–77, 82, 87, 93–94, 98, 111, 118, 120–122, 129, 141, 151, 162, 164, 166, 170–172
Declaration of the Rights of Man 85
Demetrakopoulos, Stephanie 95–96
demilitarisation 103
democracy, democratic xi, xiii, 6, 17–18, 27, 114, 119–120, 143
deserter xiv, 2, 70

The Stripper Goddess of Japan

dirty story 52
dōsojin 39

E
Ebizaka, Takeshi 1
election xii, 27, 143
Ellis, Havelock 4, 147–148, 150–151
emperor 14, 36, 50, 53, 55, 57–58, 61–62, 70, 74, 79, 84–85, 103, 106, 109–110, 120, 138, 144, 165–167, 173
Emperor, Meiji (Mutsuhito) 62, 119
Emperor, Shōwa (Hirohito) 62–63
emperor system 79, 84–85, 119–120

F
face 2, 5, 7, 25, 34, 37, 38, 42, 44, 47, 51, 63–64, 72, 126, 141, 151, 154, 156
female swordplay (*onna kengeki*) 80
Foul and the Fragrant: Odor and the French Social Imagination, The (Alain Corbin) 159
Friends of MacDonald Society 74–75
frottage 4–6
FTA Show 68
Fuji, Shigeko 118–119
Fujioka, Yoshinaru 113
Fuku-warai ('the lucky laugh of Otakufu') 44
Funny Face 8, 41, 47–49, 177
Fūten rōjin nikki (Diary of a mad old man, Tanizaki Jun'ichirō) 129
Futodama no Mikoto 12–13, 61

G
Gandhi 8, 96–97
genitals 7, 19, 26, 34, 42
Genkai geijutsu-ron (On marginal art) xii
Ghost Story of Yotsuya 45
Gilbert and Sullivan 79, 82–83
Gorai, Shigeru 152–157
gossip 24, 41, 47–49
Guinness World Records 2
Gurning contest 37

H
Hachigatsu no taiyō o (The sun in August, Okkotsu Yoshiko) 54
hadaka (naked) 67, 72–73, 75

hadaka ikkan (having no capital except one's own body) 73, 75
hadakamushi (featherless insects) 73, 77
Haiyūza Theatre 168
Haiyūza theatre company 168, 170
Haji no Muraji 23
'Hakuchi' (The idiot, Sakaguchi Ango) 104
Hamada, Hikozō 74
hannya (female demon) 45
Hasegawa, Shin 172
Hashimoto, Kenzō 166
Hashimoto, Mineo 99
Hata, Toyokichi 80
Heavenly Cave (Ama no Iwato) 2, 17, 34, 57, 67, 110
Heian period 57, 65, 138, 156, 163, 165
Heiminsha (Commoners' Association) 120
Heisei period 158
Herzen, Alexander Ivanovich 62
Hidaka, Rokurō (Hidaka Affair) xiv, xv
Hinton, James 150
Hiraizumi, Kiyoshi 31
Hirose, Takeo (Commander) 162–163
hōkan (jester) 85
Holmes, Oliver Wendell (Jr.) 49, 102
Honmokutei xv
Hot Mikado, The (Mike Dodd [dir.]) 79, 82–85
humour 8, 12, 53
Hyottoko 41–42

I
Ichijō, Sayuri 4–7, 79, 87–91
Ichikawa, Utaemon 42–43, 163
Idaka, Hiroaki 36
ideological, ideology xii, 10, 26–27, 31, 70, 94, 104, 108, 121, 160
Ideorogii to shite no nihon bunka ron (Japanese cultural discourses as ideologies, Harumi Befu) 172
Iida, Yoshikuni 60
Ikeuchi, Osamu 159
illusion 7–8, 35, 38, 166
imperial family 17, 23, 36, 57, 105–106, 123, 163
Imperial Japanese Navy xi, 162, 164
Inoue, Mitsusada 57–58, 61

Inoue, Yoritoshi   30
Ippen   22, 153
Ishikawa, Sanshirō   8, 69–70
Itō, Hirobumi   63
Iwaki, Hiroyuki   64–65
Izanagi   13, 35, 55–56, 62
Izanami   13, 35, 55–56, 62
Izumo no O-Kuni (historical figure)   8, 161, 167–169, 171
Izumo no O-Kuni (Ogasawara Kyōko)   151, 168
Izumo no O-Kuni (Ariyoshi Sawako)   169

J
Jack the Ripper   93, 98
James Hinton (Edith Ellis)   150
Japanese Communist Party   31, 53, 121, 143
Japanese Constitution   x
Japanese mythology   6, 18–20, 23, 55–56, 62–63, 79, 110, 163, 177
Japanese Red Army   xiv
Japan's defeat   22, 94, 147, 165
Jashūmon (The heretic faith, Takahashi Kazumi)   111
joke   52, 62–65, 133, 139
Joseph   74, 171
Jūsansai no natsu (The summer of a thirteen-year-old, Okkotsu Yoshiko)   54

K
kabuki   8, 42, 45, 85, 129, 140–141, 151, 154–156, 158, 161, 163, 168–171
Kabukiza Theatre   169
kagura, okagura (sacred Shinto music and dancing)   21, 41, 44, 50, 57, 155
Kami no kuni (The Divine Country)   114
Kami, ningen, jiyū (God, human beings, freedom, Okada Torajirō)   120
Kamoka no Otchan (Uncle I'll-bite-you)   133, 138, 142, 144
Kaneko, Fumiko   123, 124, 166
Kaori no sekai o saguru (Searching the world of perfume, Nakamura Shōji)   159
Katō, Norihiro   2, 177
katsujinga (*tableau vivant*, living pictures)   80–81
Kawakami, Hajime   121

Kawano, Kenji   27
Kawasaki, Hiroko   42–43
kengeki (swordplay)   80
Kido, Takayoshi   63
'Kimigayo'   165
Kinoshita, Naoe   120–121
Kitamura, Sayo   8, 22, 103–105, 107–108, 110–112, 114–115
Kobayashi, Tomi   xiii
Kobe   4, 99, 140–142, 148
Kodama (Echo)   53
kōdō (imperial way)   xi
Koenaki Koe no Kai (Voiceless Voice Group)   xiii, xiv
Kogo shūi (Gleanings from Ancient Stories)   50
Kojiki (Records of Ancient Matters)   2, 4, 8, 17–18, 23, 25, 30, 35, 49–50, 55–56, 61, 147, 149, 164
kokutai (national polity)   xi
Kōkonki (A twilight record, Mano Sayo)   26
Koma Theatre   48
Komada, Shinji   88–89
Kon, Shunchō (Tōkō)   124–125
Konjiki yasha (The golden demon, Ozaki Kōyō)   32
Konohanasakuya-hime   13, 36
Kosugi, Hōan   ix, 17, 21, 56
Kotoamatsukami   13, 15, 153
Kropotkin, Pyotr Alexeyevich   62
Kuratsuka, Akiko   34, 102
Kuroda, Seiki   80
Kurokawa, Sō   177
Kutsukake Tokijirō (Hasegawa Shin)   171–172
Kūya   147, 152–153
Kyoto   vii, ix–x, xv, 2, 27, 30, 65, 68, 79, 86, 106, 117, 121–123, 136, 141–142, 151–152, 154, 156, 168, 171, 177

L
laughter   6, 8–10, 26–27, 44, 55–57, 59–60, 63–65, 67, 77
Li, Hongzhang   161
Liberal Democratic Party   xiii, 27
Little Big Man (Arthur Penn [dir.])   77

185

M

MacDonald, Ranald   73–76
Maggot Festival   109
mai   147, 151–152
Man'yōshū   36, 157, 164
manga   xii, 45, 138
manzai   2, 65, 79, 86, 177
marginal art   xii–xiii, xv, 1, 6, 9
Marxism   xii, 59
Mary   156, 171
Masamune, Hakuchō   viii, 29
Matsu no ha (Pine needles)   155
Matsukawa derailment incident   53
Matsumura, Takeo   61
Meiji period   98, 119–120, 151, 154
Microcosmos: Four Billion Years of Evolution from Our Microbial Ancestors (Lynn Margulis)   113
Mikado, The (D'Oyly Carte Opera Company)   79, 82–85
miko   34, 151–153, 155
mikoshi   109
militarism   xii, 105, 114
Mitsukoshi Theatre   170
Miyazawa, Kenji   xii
Mizutani, Yaeko   129, 168–169
Mono mina uta de owaru (All ends with a song, Hanada Kiyoteru)   168
Moore, Henry   60
moralist   49, 173
Muratani, Sōhei   52–54
My Confessional (Havelock Ellis)   150

N

Nagase, Kiyoko   8, 29–30, 34
Nagoya, Sanza (also Sanzaburō)   154, 169–171
Naka, Yoshikatsu   90
Nakahama, Manjirō   75
Nakano, Shigeharu   31
Nakano, Takashi   30
Nakazawa, Atsushi   38–39
'Nakijōgo no tennyo' (The sentimental drinker angel, Tanabe Seiko)   134
naming, name-giving   29, 31–33
Nanashi Kigishi (Nameless Pheasant)   13, 23
Nazis   69

New Spirit, The (Havelock Ellis)   4, 148, 150
nickname   xiii, 29–31, 33–36, 64, 111, 138
'Nihon bunka no sekaishiteki jikken' (Japanese cultural experimentations on world history, Yamazaki Masakazu)   175
'Nihon bunka shikan' (A personal view of Japanese culture, Sakaguchi Ango)   104
'Nihon bunkaron' no hen'yō (Changes in the discourse of Japanese culture, Aoki Tamotsu)   173
Nihon shinwa no tokushoku (The characteristics of Japanese mythology, Yoshida Atsuhiko)   56
Nihon shoki (Chronicles of Japan)   12, 17, 20, 23, 25, 61
Nihon-teki (Japanese-like)   xi
Ninigi no Mikoto   13–14, 23–25, 33, 61
'Ninkyō ni tsuite' (Yakuza films, Satō Tadao)   172
Nissay Theatre   168
Nomura, Masaichi   43
Noyes, John Humphrey   101–102
Nuba, Die (Helene Bertha Amalie 'Leni' Riefenstahl)   68

O

Obatarian (Hotta Katsuhiko)   41, 45–49
obscenity   7, 37, 61, 63, 79, 87, 89
Ochiai, Keiko   8, 94
odori (dance)   147, 151–152
odori nenbutsu (dancing prayer)   147, 152–156
Odori nenbutsu (Dancing prayer to Amitābha, Gorai Shigeru)   152
Ogita, Seinosuke   35–36
Okada, Torajirō   100, 120
Okame   21, 41–42, 44–45, 177
Okkotsu, Yoshiko   8, 53, 54
O-Kuni   *see* Izumo no O-Kuni
Ōkuninushi no Mikoto (aka Ōanamuchi)   14, 23
Omoikane no Kami   14, 20
Ōmori, Shōzō   164
onbe warai (burning of talismans and laughing)   58
Onda Festival   177

Bibliography.

Oneida Community 93, 101–102
Ono, Nobuyuki 4, 87
Orikuchi, Shinobu 57
Orwell, George 96
Ōsobi no Mikuma no Ushi (aka Takemikuma no Ushi) 12–14, 23
Otafuku 44–45
Ototachibana-hime 14–15, 30, 163
Ozawa, Shōichi 81, 87, 90

P
Pacific War xi
pacifism 102
papal infallibility 62
Perfume: The Story of a Murderer (Patrick Süskind) 159
Phallus stones 39
Piichaashan (Beacon Hill, Okkotsu Yoshiko) 54
Piramiddo bōshi yo, sayōnara (Good-bye, pyramid hat, Okkotsu Yoshiko) 54
Plato, platonic 128, 159
political activism xiii, 9, 53, 97, 100, 117, 119
politics 8, 15, 24, 35, 55, 57, 60, 63, 69, 71–72, 98, 120–121, 142, 145, 167, 173, 177
polyhedral, polyhedron 1, 2, 6, 9
Posada, José Guadalupe 71–72
Problems of Art (Susanne K. Langer) 38
public bath 69–70, 99–100, 102

R
Rabelais and Folk Culture of the Middle Ages and Renaissance (Mikhail Bakhtin) 59
rape 4, 93–96, 100
Rape, The (Ochiai Keiko) 94–95
Rape: The Bait and the Trap: A Balanced, Humane, Up-To-Date Analysis of Its Causes and Control (Jean MacKellar) 95
'Reflections on Gandhi' (George Orwell) 96
Reflections on Violence (Georges Sorel) 58–59
revolving stage 55
rumour 49
Russo-Japanese War 120, 161–162, 174

S
sarume 20, 44, 50
Sarume no Kimi 12, 25, 50, 57, 61
Sarutahiko no Ōkami 12, 14, 17, 25
Satō, Kenji 10
Satō, Tadao 172
Satsuma, Jirohachi 130
Sawanobori, Toshio 90
Scylla 58–59
sea slug 50
'Seikōkan aishi' (The tragic history of the Seikokan Inn, Yanagita Kunio) 157
Seki, Hirono 149
Sensō ga nokoshita mono: Tsurumi Shunsuke ni sengo sedai ga kiku (What the war has left behind: Tsurumi Shunsuke interviewed by the post-war generation, Tsurumi Shunsuke, Ueno Chizuko and Oguma Eiji) 3
Setouchi, Harumi (also, Setouchi Jakuchō) 8, 117–119, 121–128, 131, 137, 166
sexual intercourse 20, 81, 101–102, 130, 155
sexual love 127, 128
Shakers, The 93, 100–102
shaman 34, 155
shikome (ugly woman) 45
Shimizu, Jirochō 172
shinobi odori 154–155, 157
Shinto 18, 20–21, 25, 34, 41, 57, 106–107, 109, 121, 153, 155, 158, 164, 172, 177
Shisō no kagaku (Science of thought) vii, xi, xiii, 2, 69, 177
Shitaderu-hime (Princess Shitaderu) 14, 23–24
Shiva 147, 160
Shōwa period 22, 43, 119, 121, 158
Sino-Japanese War 161, 174
smell 71, 97, 147–148, 159
Social Democratic Party 120
Sorel, Georges 58–59
Stalin, Joseph 56, 59
strip show 79–81, 86, 90
striptease 5, 7, 12, 18, 20, 33, 80–81, 84, 87, 97

187

Studies in the Psychology of Sex (Havelock Ellis)   4, 150
Susano'o no Mikoto   12–14, 18
Swing Mikado, The   82–83
'Symbiosis in Cell Revolution' (Lynn Margulis)   113

T
Tachibana, Shūta (Lieutenant Colonel)   162–163
taikomochi   85
Taishō period   41, 69, 100, 158
Tajima Tarōji den (The life of Tajima Tarōji, Shishi Bunroku)   130
Takamagahara   13–14, 19, 33, 110, 153
Takamimusubi no Kami   15, 24
Takamure Itsue (Kōno Nobuko)   166
Takarazuka Revue   163
Takeda, Taijun   71
Tamon'in, Eishun   167, 168
Tanabe, Seiko   8–9, 133–142, 144–145
Tanaka Shōzō, 120
Teinengo (After retirement, Okada Seizō)   126
Teitoza Theatre   79–80
Tekisuiroku (A record of waterdrops, Sōma Kokkō)   121
Tenshō Kōtai Jingūkyō   22, 105, 107–112, 114
Toki, Zenmaro   175
Tokushima Radio Merchant Murder Case   118
tokushutsu (also, *tokudashi*, special performance)   87
Tomita, Masakatsu   74–75
Toyohirume   15, 57–58

U
Uchi naru kabe: Gaikokujin no nihonjin zō, Nihonjin no gaikokujin zō ō (The wall inside: Foreigners' images of Japanese, Japanese images of foreigners, Hirakawa Sukehiro and Tsuruta Kin'ya [eds.])   176
Uchiyama, Gudō   119
Uji no kojiki yo me o samase (Wake up, maggot beggars!, Mori Hideto)   112
Umashi Ashikabi Hikoji no Kami   15, 149
United Nations Decade for Women   117
Utau tanuki goten (Singing Racoon Palace, Kimura Keigo [dir.])   163–164
uzume   34, 37

V
vagina stones   6, 38–39
Vietnam War   xiv, 68, 70–71
violence   59, 93, 96, 98–99, 102
vision   22, 31

W
Waga sei to sei (My life and my sex life, Setouchi Harumi)   119
wartime ultranationalism   95
Watanabe, Kazuko   117
Whitman, Walt   147–148
winter solstice   34, 57–58
Wirgman, Charles   98
World War II   x, 1, 54, 62, 65, 130, 164–165, 173–175

Y
Yamagishi, Miyozō   104, 115
Yamatotakeru   14–15, 163
Yamazaki, Masakazu   175
Yanagi, Muneyoshi   xii, 2, 177
Yanagita, Kunio   xii, 157
Yokoyama, Sadako   96, 177
Yomi no kuni (the Underworld)   56, 110
Yutakasa no seishin byōri (The psychopathology of affluence, Ōhira Ken)   114

Z
Zahan, Dominique   125–126